CLEAR
USE
OF
POWER

A SLICE OF
WYOMING'S
POLITICAL HISTORY
1864 – 2000

By Matilda Hansen

[handwritten inscription:] this account of how, Wyoming's legislature does — and does not — get laws passed

[handwritten signature:] Matilda Hansen

[handwritten:] December of 002

Commentary Press of Wyoming
Laramie, Wyoming
Copyright © September 2002

Other Publications by Matilda Hansen:

To Help Adults Learn
New Horizons in Coping Skills
Let's Play Together
Ratmalana, Ceylon: A Developing Central Place
A Quaker Perspective on Ethics and Politics

Clear use of Power: A Slice of Wyoming's Political History was written during the first three years of the 21st century in response to the counsel and encouragement of Dr. Phil Roberts of the History Department at the University of Wyoming, Laramie.

This journey into the past to explain the present has been an adventure of the first order.

Table of Contents

Foreword

Long-time Wyoming State Representative Matilda Hansen will surprise and delight readers by doing the impossible; she has written a fascinating book on the reapportionment of the State legislature!

As a former chief elections office of the State, I believe her research and conclusions are bound to influence future histories of Wyoming.

With the insights of an insider, she has chronicled the long and sometimes bitter struggle to achieve a population-based apportionment of the Wyoming Legislature. It's a tale unfamiliar to almost all of us.

She makes it clear that rural interests were over-represented in the State Legislature from the very beginning and explains how a minority within the Republican Party fought until the bitter end to resist reapportionment.

In her account, the politics of apportionment not only divided Wyoming into rural voters and urban voters, but also into three regions vying for influence and power: Northern Wyoming, Central Wyoming and the Union Pacific Line.

She helps readers understand how the mal-apportionment of the Legislature has shaped the politics of the State for more than a century.

Ultimately, though, her book may be most valuable as perhaps the first history of the Wyoming Legislature, enlivened by insider anecdotes and verbatim accounts of historic debates.

Her fast-paced and personal account makes

Clear Use Of Power

an easy and enjoyable journey through Wyoming's political history.

And, I recommend it highly.

—Kathy Karpan
July 16, 2002
Cheyenne, Wyoming

Preface

This slice of Wyoming's political history began as the story of reapportionment in 1991 and 1992 that brought Wyoming into compliance with the United States Supreme Court's one-person, one-vote ruling. Then came the realization that the tensions at the end of the 20th century went back to the beginning of the 20th century—even back before Wyoming became a Territory.

Voters in Territorial Wyoming experienced the confusion of non-congruent Council and House seats as the burgeoning population forced biennial reapportionment.

With statehood, conflict soon surfaced over the Preamble to the Constitution's requirement of equality and Article III, Section 3 guarantee of at least one Senate and one House seat for each county.

By the 1920's political power ebbed and flowed among three distinct regions: the southern along the Union Pacific Mainline, the central band of counties in the middle of the state and the northern, more sparsely settled, counties.

For the first three-fourths of the century political power see-sawed between the Democrats and Republicans. Then the "glue" of Republican political power came because of an unwritten alliance between mineral/royalty ranch/legislators and the mineral extractive resource industry lobbyists. Between them, they created a mutually beneficial economy keeping wages low, taxes low and relatively few jobs in Wyoming. Minerals were King.

Challenges to reapportionment began in 1908 in *State ex rel Sullivan v. Schnitger*, followed by *Schaefer v. Thomson, Thompson v. Thomson, Brown v.Thomson* and *Gorin v. Karpan*.

This account includes the explanation of why Rory Cross did not get his bills passed after switching political parties and how Velma Linford gained Senate approval for Federal education funds.

There are stories about Mike Sullivan and Rick Miller, Joe Meyer and Charlie Scott, Patti MacMillan and June Boyle, Carol Watson and Cynthia Lummis, Eli Bebout and Don Sullivan. There is the story of Della Herbst's wash and Scott Farris "bearding the lion's den."

The reader is invited to find a cozy place with good light. Then join the storyteller's walk through more than a century of Wyoming history.

1

It All Began a Long Time Ago

Nearly 30 years ago 49 states conscientiously began work to achieve equal legislative representation in compliance with the rulings of the United States Supreme Court. The 50th state, Wyoming, exempted itself from these rulings. But the story began 100 years before.

In 1864, Wyoming was just Laramie County, a part of Dakota Territory. It was entitled to one representative. The voters in Cheyenne elected attorney James R. Whitehead—one of the nine "first settlers of Cheyenne." But he did not get to Yankton until 10 days before the end of the 40-day session.

Who did make a timely appearance was South Pass City miner Archie J. Turner. Turner was in Yankton as a lobbyist—asking for mining laws and the creation of Carter County. The Dakota Legislature seated Turner. When Whitehead arrived he was denied Laramie County's seat.[1]

Thus the political schisms began early, based on antagonisms and antipathy between those who lived along the Union Pacific Mainline and those who lived "away from the railroad." During Territorial and early Statehood time these animosities "jelled" as advocates emerged championing three regions: southern, central and northern.

The Organic Act of Admissions, signed on July 25, 1868 established a Council and a House of Representatives. In 1869 President Grant appointed John A. Campbell as Wyoming's first

---

[1] This account is from T.A.Larson's *History of Wyoming,* University of Nebraska Press, Lincoln, Nebraska, 1965, p. 42 and 51.

Territorial Governor. By proclamation, he set up Council and House seats for Wyoming Territory.

The Assembly had both multi-member and single-member election districts defined by the boundaries of the counties as shown in Table 1.[2] Only District 1 had Council and House districts with the same boundaries—they were "nested." The rest of the counties had "unnested" districts with various combinations of the electorate represented by their respective Councilmen and Representatives.

TABLE 1
Council and House Seats of the First Assembly

District	County	Number of Council Seats	Number of House Seats
1	Laramie	3	4
2	Albany and Carbon	3	
	Albany		3
	Carbon		1
3	Carter & Rest of State	3	
4	Carter		1
5	Rest of State		1
6	Member At Large		1
Total		9	11

Only Democrats were elected to the First Assembly. The southern boundary of Laramie, Albany, Carbon and Carter counties was the Colorado line. The northern boundary was the Montana line. One of the actions of the First Assembly was to replace Carter with Sweetwater and to create Uinta along Wyoming's western border with Utah and Idaho.[3]

---

[2] From the *Wyoming Blue Book Volume I, Reprint of Part One,* by Marie H. Erwin, edited from the 1946 edition by Virginia Cole Trenholm. Wyoming State Archives and Historical Department, 1974. Pioneer Printing, Cheyenne, Wyoming.

[3] Uinta County was most of the land "confiscated" by Congress from Utah Territory and Idaho Territory to square-off Wyoming's boundaries when Wyoming Territory was established. Appendix A shows the 13 counties created by the Assembly and the remaining 10 created by the Legislature.

Population concentrations shifted from one Assembly session to the next as the economy changed from building a railroad to establishing state institutions, from mining gold near South Pass City to mining coal along the Union Pacific, from buffalo roaming the open prairies to cowboys and herders working cattle and sheep.

In 1870 the Federal Census found 9,118 people. As the Organic Act required biennial meetings of the Assembly, every other year from 1871 through 1879, the Governor issued a proclamation restructuring the election districts to reflect new counties and the expanding population. The Democrats were the dominant political party during Territorial Wyoming.

In 1880 the Federal Census found 20,789 people. Of these 70.4% were rural residents. Under the authority of a June 3, 1880 Act of Congress, Wyoming's Assemblymen took control of reapportionment.

The Council President, House Speaker and the Governor were designated the Board of Reapportionment. Before each Assembly adjourned *Sine Die*,[4] they were charged with reapportioning the Council and House seats for the next Assembly.

When it was time for the Governor and the 8th Assembly to reapportion for the 9th Assembly, Republican Territorial Governor Francis E. Warren and the Democrats, who were controlling the Council and House,[5] did not agree. This was the first time the reapportionment process failed. The U.S.Congress came to the rescue. They passed a law to legitimize the 9th Assembly elected under the apportionment rules for the 8th Assembly.

Territorial elections proved to be confusing to the voters. Combinations of nested and unnested, and single- and multi-member districts changed every time a new county was created. There were small clusters of voters—some here and some there—in most parts of Wyoming.

By 1889 there were 169 United States Post Offices in Wyoming. Clusters of people received mail in places such as

---

[4] Sine Die means without any time set for further consideration of legislation. This motion is made when a legislative body has finished its business and intends not to again convene.

[5] The Democrats controlled the Council leadership with eight seats. The Republicans had five seats. The Democrats controlled the House with 13 seats. The Republicans had 9 seats. There was one Populist.

Little Horse Creek in Laramie County, Sherman in Albany, Leo in Carbon, Almond in Sweetwater, Dry Piney in Uinta, Miner's Delight in Fremont, Oil City in Natrona, Hat Creek in Converse, Inya Kara in Crook and Ohlman in Sheridan.

The 1890 Federal Census found 62,555 people, of which 56.7% were rural residents. In the Special Election on November 5, 1889 to ratify the Constitution 6,272 people voted "aye" and 1,923 voted "no."[6]

Supporters of statehood wanted easily understood election districts defined by county boundaries. They wanted the Council replaced by a Senate. The Assembly became the Legislature.

The new constitution gave each county at least one seat each in the House and Senate.[7] Reapportioning was to be done twice in a decade—once using the Federal Census and once using the (to be created) State Census.

STATEHOOD—1890

An unwritten "rule" emerged with the first Legislative session.

No future Speaker of the House or President of the Senate was allowed to succeed himself in those positions.

A person held the Presidency or Speakership for just one Session—for two years.[8] The reasons for this limitation centered on egos and turf building by the men-in-waiting impatient to wield the "Power Of The Chair." The effect of this limitation made entrenched political power difficult for one man to achieve.

When the first legislators met, they were confronted with the 1890 Federal Census' finding of a 25% decrease in the rural population. This unanticipated change caused a serious imbalance in House seats assigned to two southern-region

---

[6] Women voted from 1869 until Wyoming was accepted as a state in 1891. In order for Congress to accept Wyoming as a State, the Assembly gave up women's right to vote, hold office and serve on juries. They did not give up a woman's right to legally hold real and personal property in her own name.

[7] Wyoming Constitution, Article III, Section 3.

[8] This practice continued for the balance of the 19th and for all of the 20th century.

6

counties: Carbon and Uinta. In the apportionment for the first legislature, in Article III, Section 50, Carbon's 6,897 people got five seats and Uinta's 7,881 people got three seats.

There was another serious problem: the Constitution assigned no seats to Natrona and Weston. These two central-region counties were created in 1888 and 1890 but they were not organized soon enough to be included in the new apportionment.

Therefore, in 1893 the 2nd Legislature reapportioned under the Senate leadership of Republican President Frank W. Mondell of Weston and Populist Speaker L.C. Tidball of Sheridan. In addition to sorting out the seats for Carbon and Uinta and giving seats to Natrona and Weston, Speaker Tidball took the opportunity to corral another House seat for Sheridan thus adding to the voting strength of the northern region.

The more populated southern region along the Union Pacific Mainline was predominately Democratic turf. But during the first decade of statehood, this region provided the Republican Senate leadership. The Republican House leadership came from all three regions. Table 2 identifies the three regions.[9]

TABLE 2
Regions of Political Influence

Southern Region	Central Region	Northern Region
Goshen	Weston	Crook
Platte	Niobrara	Campbell
Laramie	Converse	Johnson
Albany	Natrona	Sheridan
Carbon	Fremont	Big Horn
Sweetwater	Sublette	Park
Uinta	Lincoln	Hot Springs
		Washakie
		Teton[10]

[9] This table specifies the land area of the regions using the names of the 23 counties even though all counties were not created until the 1920's.

[10] Teton really does not fit neatly into either the northern or central region. An arbitrary decision was made placing it in the northern region in recognition of its geographic location in the northwest corner of the state and its tourism economy that matches Park's tourism.

The 1900 Federal Census found 92,531 people, a 47.9% increase, scattered over 97,548 square miles—less than one person per square mile. The rural population increased to 71.2% of the statewide population. Southern-region Republicans were "in charge" of the 1901 reapportionment.

Senate President Edward W. Stone of Laramie County and Speaker Jerome Atherly[11] of Albany created 13 new House seats—for a 50 seat House. They used eight of the seats to increase the voting strength along the Union Pacific: three to Laramie County, one to Albany, one to Carbon, one to Sweetwater and two to Uinta (all the old Utah/Idaho territory).[12]

Big Horn got its first three legislators—thus increasing northern-region voting strength. The central region got the remaining two seats—one each for Fremont and Weston. In the Senate, Stone and Atherly took the 1893 seat given to Sheridan (northern region) and gave it to Laramie County (southern region). They added another Senate seat and gave it to Uinta.[13]

TABLE 3

Legislative Voting Strength and Statewide Population
1900 Census

	Southern Region		Central Region		Northern Region	
Voting Strength	Senate 65%	House 62%	Senate 17%	House 18%	Senate 17%	House 20%
Statewide Population	69%		15%		16%	

---

[11] Both were Republicans. Fourteen years later, in 1915, Stone was again President of the Senate.

[12] At this time Uinta County encompassed land from the Colorado border north to Yellowstone, east to the Continental Divide and west to the border between Wyoming and Utah/Idaho. Thus using Uinta in 1901 as part of the southern region is "fraught with peril" because of the difficulty to campaign and to represent the huge area. All population for pre-Lincoln-County Uinta is here attributed to the southern region because it was easier to settle close to the railroad rather than trekking north into prairie, desert and mountain country. However, there were post offices in Kemmerer and in the Star Valley serving people living there.

[13] Session Laws 1901, Original Senate File 41.

Table 3 shows the relative voting strength of the regions after the 1901 reapportionment. Using counties as election districts did not succeed in achieving Wyoming's constitutional requirement of equal representation among all districts. Stone and Atherly did succeed in strengthening the voting power of the southern region—at the expense of the northern region.

THE TALE OF THE STATE CENSUS

The Constitution required a mid-decade reapportionment based on a State Census. The 1903 legislature authorized the county assessors to take the census in 1905 for reapportioning in 1907. The census was to be "under the direction of and published by the Secretary of State."[14]

But when Secretary of State Fenimore Chatterton got the data from the county assessors, he found wide discrepancies in how much of what was counted. Some assessors did not miss this opportunity to promote their communities. Chatterton decided this first state census was both inadequate and incomplete.[15] Table 4 contains a comparison of the 1900 Federal, 1905 State and 1910 Federal censuses.

Chatterton was selective in what he published in the *Census of Wyoming, 1905, Taken by Authority of Law.*[16] He explained his reasons for omitting material from the county assessors:

> The returns of the census enumerators ... if fully and correctly given would have been of much value, [but they] are so meager and so evidently incomplete and inaccurate that it has been thought inadvisable to publish it. Therefore, only those portions ... evidently nearly correct ... are here given.

---

[14] Chapter 79, 1903 Session Laws.

[15] The assessors who took the census for reapportionment were the same persons who did the assessments for property taxes. The Legislature provided no funds to pay for the extra work required of the assessors.

[16] *1905 State Census of Wyoming*, S.A. Bristol Company Printers and Bookbinders, Cheyenne, Wyoming, 1905. American Heritage Center, University of Wyoming, Laramie, Hebard Collection HA-721.504. 1905.

9

TABLE 4
Comparison of Censuses for 1900, 1905, 1910

County	1900 Federal Census	1905 State Census	1910 Federal Census[17]
Albany	13,084	9,992	11,574
Big Horn	4,328	8,942	8,886
Carbon	9,589	10,313	11,282
Converse	3,337	4,168	6,294
Crook	3,137	3,831	6,492
Fremont	5,357	5,363	11,822
Johnson	2,361	3,027	3,453
Laramie	20,181	18,514	26,127
Natrona	1,785	2,442	4,766
Park	With Big Horn	With Big Horn	4,909
Sheridan	5,122	9,965	16,324
Sweetwater	8,455	7,163	11,575
Uinta	12,223	14,492	16,982
Weston	3,203	3,604	4,960
	92,172	101,816	145,446

Besides people, the assessors tallied wheat at 30 bushels per acre, barley at 25,[18] rye at 20, timothy and oats at 50, corn at 20, average tons per acre of alfalfa (2 ½), other tame grasses (2), native hay and other hay (1 ½). The assessors counted 201 bushels of potatoes, 45 tons of onions, 30 tons of parsnips, 25 tons of beets, 22 tons of sugar beets, 40 tons of turnips, 190 bushels of tomatoes, 133 bushels of cucumbers, 50 bushels of peas and 22 bushels of beans.

Assessors counted the number of plants per acre: pumpkins (950), squash (1,769), watermelons (1,115), muskmelons (1,112) cabbages (2,719) and 4,000 cauliflowers. The assessors looked into kitchen cupboards and found 952 quarts of raspberries, 6,920 quarts of strawberries, 4,356 quarts of cherries, 9,506 lbs of blackberries, 21,000 lbs of currants and 29,000 lbs of gooseberries.

---

[17] Yellowstone's population was 519 but they were not allowed to vote in Wyoming's elections.

[18] Unless otherwise stated, the numbers indicate bushels per acre.

As proud as growers may have been about the "fruits of their labor," the information was not only useless for reapportioning but the inconsistency and incompleteness of the work put into question the accuracy of the people-count. Chatterton declined to "certify as accurate" the head count in the 1905 State Census.

The uncertified 1905 census did not stop the 1907 Republican leadership in both Chambers from reapportioning. The Senate President was O.H. Brown of Uinta. The Vice President was J.L. Baird of Weston. The Speaker was Scott K. Snively of Sheridan. The Speaker Pro Tem was Charles E. Hayden of Big Horn.

The House leadership consisted of northern-region men who used the uncertified State Census to further their political agenda. Speaker Pro Tem Hayden of Big Horn got another Senate seat and three House seats for his county. Speaker Snively got two Senate seats and two House seats for Sheridan.

Northern-region Crook got another House seat, as did central-region Weston. The losers were southern-region Albany (one seat) and central region Converse (one seat). Table 5 shows the relative voting strength of the regions after the 1907 reapportionment.

TABLE 5
Legislative Voting Strength and Statewide Population
1905 Census

	Southern Region		Central Region		Northern Region	
Voting Strength	Senate 59%	House 57%	Senate 15%	House 16%	Senate 26%	House 27%
Statewide Population	59%		15%		25%	

The northern region gained in voting strength, the southern region lost. With the uncertified state census, the 1907 leadership grabbed the opportunity to flex their political muscle to enhance their political power. Wyoming's slide down the slippery slope of unequal reapportionment continued to disregard fairness in representation in the legislature.

But not everyone was happy with the results of the Snively-Hayden political agenda. Republican legislators John Williams of Converse and Patrick Sullivan of Natrona went to State Court challenging the use of the 1905 State Census in the 1907 reapportionment on the grounds it allowed "...at least one and possibly two [counties] to receive a larger representation than they would otherwise be entitled."[19]   They asked the Court to "... order legislative districts to be based on the original, strictly county-based plan as specified by the Wyoming Constitution and to repeal all changes made in 1907."[20]

The plaintiffs lost on technical grounds relating to juris-diction.[21]   The Court refused to address the substance of the challenge.

WINDS OF CHANGE

House Democrats were as "scarce as hen's teeth" during the first decade of the 20th century. There were two in both the 1901 and 1903 sessions, three in 1905 and seven in 1909.

Although Williams and Sullivan lost in the Court of Law, they won in the "Court of Public Opinion." Their challenge to the northern-region Republican leaders did not go unnoticed by the voters in 1910.   They "threw the rascals out"—45 Republicans did not return in 1911.

Only four incumbent Republicans survived this "cleaning of the House."[22]   With the votes counted, 29 Republicans and 28 Democrats were seated—most of them first-year legislators.

Senate Republicans escaped the voter's wrath when the 11th Session convened in 1911.   There were 21 Republicans and 6 Democrats ready to reapportion.   They used the 1910 Federal Census of 145,965 people—a 58% increase over the 1900 Federal Census and a 48% increase over the 1905 State Census.

---

[19] *State ex rel Sullivan v. Schnitger,* 16 Wyo. 479, 95 Pad. 698 (1908). Williams and Sullivan did not approve of the seats given to Sheridan and Big Horn by Snively and Hayden.

[20] Ibid.

[21] Their standing as legislators to use a Writ of Mandamus as a vehicle for remedy is discussed in Chapter 3. See Ross Merlin Beyer in *Notes, Wyoming Law Journal,* Vol. 11, no. 2, p. 136 (1957).

[22] The four were R.A. Baldwin of Big Horn, H.J. Cassell of Crook, Andrew Hamilton of Sweetwater and S.A. Young of Weston. From *Wyoming Historical Blue Book-A Legal and Political History of Wyoming, 1868-1943*, by Marie H. Erwin, Bradford-Robinson Printing Company, Denver, Colorado, 1946.

The rural population dropped 0.8% to 70.4% of the statewide population.

Northern-region men were in charge in 1911. The Senate President was Jacob M. Schwoob of Big Horn. The Speaker was L.R. Davis of Crook. New Park County got two House seats and one Senate seat. A "legislative musical chairs" redistributed the Senate and House seats to reflect changes in population. When the "dust settled," the voting strength among the regions still fell short of equal representation as required by the Constitution (Table 6).[23]

TABLE 6
Legislative Voting Strength and Statewide Population
1910 Census

	Southern Region		Central Region		Northern Region	
Voting Strength	Senate 52%	House 51%	Senate 19%	House 19%	Senate 30%	House 30%
Statewide Population	53%		19%		27%	

In 1911 Wyoming had 14 counties. Essential transportation consisted of a few railroads, horse n' buggy, freight wagons, saddle horses and people's feet. The vast, lonesome spaces of Wyoming remained incredibly open. There were a few automobiles. Roads—gravel surfaced at best—existed, but a long journey on any one of them was "an event."

For practical purposes water transportation was nonexistent. The North Platte River was too thin to plow and too thick to drink. The Powder River was here-again, gone-again—depending on the time of year. The Green River flowed into empty western Colorado. The Little Bear cut across the southwest corner of the state on its way to Utah. The Snake River cascaded over river boulders in its rapid descent into Idaho. The Wind River was so confused it got lost in the Big Horn River. Then the Big Horn meandered its way among ranches and irrigated fields to Montana. None of these rivers went anywhere to commercially affect economic development based on water transit.

---

[23] Chapter 77, Session Laws of 1911.

13

But people wanted easier access to their Court Houses. As "times were good" and tax revenues were deemed sufficient, the 11th Legislature in 1911 created seven new counties. Lincoln was split off from Uinta, Campbell from Crook and Weston. Big Horn and Johnson lost their southern and western lands to Hot Springs and Washakie. Laramie lost its northern lands to Goshen, Platte and Niobrara.

In the election of 1912 Republicans in the nation argued over Teddy Roosevelt and the Bull Moose Party (with Democrat Woodrow Wilson elected President).

In Wyoming the voters sent a new mix of 29 Republicans and 28 Democrats to the House. The House Democrats were strong enough to get their man, W.J. Wood, elected Speaker Pro Tem. There were 19 Republicans and eight Democrats in the Senate.

In 1915 another State Census was authorized. April 15th was designated "Census Day."[24] Again the county assessors did the counting. Again they counted people, wheat and hay, onions and cabbages, strawberries and gooseberries. Again, the Secretary of State, this time Frank L. Houx, refused to certify the census. He called it a "harvest report" and issued a scathing critique.

> [N]o officer had authority to supervise … the enumerators …. [I]nformation…was meager … incomplete and inaccurate…. It was unfortunate … the work … was added …to the duties of the county assessors. …The census [was taken] just two months … after the tax assessments were done … [and] … much of the territory had to be covered twice. No provision [was] made for safeguarding information … no authority given … to compel … answers … to questions…. The assessor-enumerators [were] paid a fixed amount [no matter who or what]…. The enumerators were given nearly three months to [do] … their work.

Again, the uncertified State Census did not deter mid-decade reapportioning led by the Republicans.[25] With seven new counties, Senate President Joseph W. Todd of Johnson and Speaker W.K. Jones of Laramie-Platte-Goshen set about cutting the size of government.[26] They eliminated two Senate seats and

---

[24] Chapter 43, Session Laws of 1915.

[25] The 1915 State Census found 141,705 people.

[26] For the 1917 Session the Senate had 16 Republicans and 11 Democrats. The House had 32 Republicans and 25 Democrats.

three House seats. With 25 Senate seats, four counties each got two seats: Laramie, Lincoln, Sheridan and Sweetwater. The other counties each got one seat. [27]

Again, legislative musical chairs rearranged the occupants of the furniture in the Senate and House Chambers. Leadership wrote the law to further their political agenda—a clear use of power.

Equal representation continued to be elusive as the northern region consolidated its ability to control the legislative agenda at the expense of the more heavily populated southern region. Table 7 shows the shifting of political power to the more sparsely populated northern region.

TABLE 7
Legislative Voting Strength and Statewide Population
1915 Census

	Southern Region		Central Region		Northern Region	
	Senate	House	Senate	House	Senate	House
Voting Strength	36%	41%	28%	28%	36%	31%
Statewide Population	40%		28%		30%	

THE 1920'S

Oil was discovered and the mineral extractive industry began to bring new jobs to sparsely settled lands. Discoveries, recovery, supply and transport of oil and gas needed many workers. By 1917, Casper and Greybull each had two oil refineries. Other communities with one refinery each were: Cowley, Lovell, Thermopolis, Riverton, Lander, Thornton, Lusk, Laramie and Glenrock. Oil fields operated in 13 of Wyoming's 23 counties: Park, Big Horn, Hot Springs, Fremont, Natrona, Converse, Weston, Niobrara, Albany, Carbon, Sweetwater, Uinta and Sublette. [28]

---

[27] Chapter 104, Session Laws of 1917.

[28] Robert H. Brown, *Wyoming*. Westview Press, Boulder, Colorado, 1980, p. 252.

Coal was mined in Sheridan, Hot Springs, Sweetwater, Lincoln and Carbon.[29] Railroads were major users of coal. By the mid 1920's the Union Pacific had 537 miles of track in southern Wyoming. The Chicago/Burlington & Quincy began track building 20 years after the Union Pacific. In 1887 it got to Newcastle, 1890–92 to Gillette, 1894 to Sheridan on the east side of the Big Horn mountains on its way to Billings, Montana. By the mid 1920's the C/B & Q had 686 miles of track in northern Wyoming.[30]

Central Wyoming began getting railroads in the 1890's when another C/B&Q line came from the east—from Scottsbluff, Nebraska, and eventually to Casper by 1914. The Chicago and Northwestern entered Wyoming in Niobrara County and got to Casper in 1905, then to Riverton in 1906.

Between 1901 and 1907 the CB&Q built on the west side of the Big Horn Mountains to Cody, Powell, Lovell, Greybull, Worland and Thermopolis. They cut through the Wind River Canyon in 1910–11, connecting to Casper and Riverton, thus giving central Wyoming a railroad outlet north into Montana.[31]

By the mid 1920's Wyoming's agriculture was more than cattle, sheep, horses and hay. Sugar beets were raised on irrigated lands in northern and eastern Wyoming to supply the sugar mills in Worland, Sheridan, Lovell and Torrington.[32]

Transportation gradually improved with more cars and trucks moving on upgraded roads. Construction work on the State Highway System began in 1917. By 1926 the state system reached 59 of Wyoming's 73 incorporated towns.[33] Many amenities such as fresh oysters from the East and oranges from the West were available to the state's residents—for a price.

Others, besides legislators, exercised political "muscle." The "old pros" at Capitol lobbying were the Union Pacific Railroad, the Wyoming Stock Growers and the Wyoming Sheep Growers. With wells, refineries and oil service businesses, the Wyoming Petroleum Association became "a presence" among Capitol lobbyists.

---

[29] Ibid, p. 66.

[30] Encyclopaedia Britannica, Fourteenth Edition (1929), *"Wyoming"* p. 830.

[31] Brown, op. cit., p. 283.

[32] Ibid., p. 154.

[33] Ibid., p. 66.

Other interests doing lobbying were the highway contractors, coal miners, farmers on irrigated or dry acres, dairymen, banking, insurance, commercial and retail businesses, municipalities, county governments and those communities with a state institution. Alliances were made—and broken—from session to session, from issue to issue.

"Times were good" when the 16th Legislature convened in January 1921 and carved up Lincoln County to create Teton and Sublette—the final two Wyoming counties.[34]

The Republicans controlled both Chambers. W.W. Daley of Carbon was President of the Senate. L.R. Ewart of Park was Speaker of the House. There were three Democrats in the Senate, one in the House. Thurman Arnold of Albany held his House caucus "in a phone booth."

The 1920 Federal Census found 194,402 people, a 33% increase over the 1910 census. The rural/urban mix remained essentially the same at 70.6% rural. Reapportionment was on the agenda—this time using the new Federal Census.

Northern and central Wyoming experienced significant population expansion during the decade between 1910 and 1920. The changes in population by regions are shown in Table 8.

The aggregate increase in both the northern and central regions was many times greater than the aggregate decrease in the southern region. Therefore, the regional increases were only partially due to the creation of seven new counties.

The new phrase "major fraction thereof" was included in the statutorially-designated ratio stipulating the number of residents per senator or representative. This phrase allowed another seat to be assigned to an election district (county) when its population exceeded by at least one person one-half of the designated ratio number.[35]

With the additional "wiggle-room" of "major fraction thereof" and with huge percentage increases in population, the Republicans rearranged the occupants of the furniture in both Chambers to solidify the political power of the northern region, at the expense of the southern region.

---

[34] A 1929 law placed limits on more counties. Chapter 69 of the 1929 Session Laws stated: "...no new county [will be created] unless [there was] a population of 3,000 and property value of at least $7 million" and leaving the remaining county with "...5,000 people with an assessed valuation of $9 million."

[35] In 1921 the Senate ratio was 9,000:1 and the House ratio 3,250:1.

TABLE 8
Changes in Population by Region—1910 to 1920

Southern Region	1910 Federal Census	1920 Federal Census	Percent of Change
Albany	11,574	9,283	-20%
Carbon	11,282	9,575	-15%
Goshen	With Laramie	8,064	
Laramie	26,127	20,699	-21%
Platte	With Laramie	7,421	
Sweetwater	11,575	13,640	+18%
Uinta	16,982	6,611	-61%

Central Region			
Converse	6,294	7,871	+25%
Fremont	11,822	11,820	- 2 people
Lincoln	With Uinta	12,487	
Natrona	4,766	14,635	+207%
Niobrara	With Laramie	6,321	
Weston	4,960	4,631	-7%

Northern Region			
Big Horn	8,886	12,105	+36%
Campbell	With Crook	5,233	
Crook	6,492	5,524	-15%
Hot Springs	With Big Horn	5,164	
Johnson	3,453	4,617	+34%
Park	4,909	7,298	+49%
Sheridan	16,324	18,182	+11%
Washakie	With Big Horn	3,106	

But this time, too, reapportionment fell short of the constitutional requirement for equal representation.[36] Equality remained elusive as shown in Table 9.

By 1924 Wyoming was first in the nation in wool production. In 1926 it was 5th in oil production.[37] During the

---

[36] Chapter 9, 1921 Session Laws of Wyoming.

[37] Encylopaedia Britannica, 14th Edition, "Wyoming" p. 830.

decade of the 1920's royalties from mineral production became a significant source of income to thousands of landowners. Mineral royalties on state-owned lands and property taxes on oil production contributed millions to K-12 education and to the General Fund.

TABLE 9
Legislative Voting Strength and Statewide Population
1920 Census

	Southern Region		Central Region		Northern Region	
Voting Strength	Senate 36%	House 40%	Senate 28%	House 27%	Senate 36%	House 33%
Statewide Population	37%		30%		31%	

The state income from mineral extraction meant lower taxes for individuals, commercial and retail businesses. It also began the state's dependence on a single industry for tax revenues—a dependence that dominated the state's tax structure into the 21st century.[38]

In 1925, the 18th Legislature authorized another State Census—this time requiring accountability from the assessor-enumerators and instructing them to

> ...personally visit each dwelling house in his County and each family therein ... [asking] color, sex, age, nativity, citizenship, occupation, literacy or illiteracy of every person in each school district and incorporated city or town.[39]

This was not to be a "harvest report." The Secretary of State was given the authority to set rules, procedures and provide the census forms—then publish the results by the first Monday in September. The county commissioners were directed to pay the assessors $100 from county funds. The census was published.[40]

---

[38] Joan Barron said in the *Casper Star-Tribune*: "The biggest chunk of the state's tax base—60.3 percent—continued to be minerals with an assessed value of $6.7 billion...." July 13, 2002, Section B, p.1.

[39] Chapter 3, Session Laws of 1925, Section 1-5.

[40] A copy is in the American Heritage Center, Rare Books Division, University of Wyoming, Laramie.

It was never used for reapportioning. The 1925 Census was the last State Census.

The boom in Wyoming's oil patch provided jobs and markets for ranch and farm products. The farm depression in the rest of the nation did not significantly touch Wyoming. But this cushion from economic hard times did not last into the 1930's.

THE 1930'S

The 1930 Federal Census found 225,565 people—a 16% increase over the 1920 Census. Rural residents were 68.9% of the statewide population. Republicans ignored reapportionment in 1931. Senate President Clarence Gardner of Lincoln and Speaker Charles B. Mann of Big Horn missed the opportunity to keep the status quo Republican hold on political power for another decade.

The Depression and Franklin Delano Roosevelt changed the economy and politics of the state. The 1932 election returned Democrats to power—both in Wyoming and in Washington D.C. Wyoming Democrats put reapportionment on the legislative agenda.

They won control of the House.[41] The Speaker was William (Scotty) Jack of Natrona. The House distributed seats "according to the arithmetic" of populations within county election districts. They decreased the size of the House by four seats.

The Republicans retained control of the Senate—but only with a three-seat margin. Senate President was Roy H. Cameron of Crook. The Senate "did as they saw fit," maintained two seats each for Laramie, Natrona, Sheridan and Sweetwater, gave the rest of the counties one seat each—including recently organized Sublette and Teton.

Their work kept the political power in the Senate in the control of northern- and central-region legislators—at the expense of the southern-region electors.

The voting strength in the House nearly reflected the distribution of the statewide population. With the disparity in

---

[41] The Senate had 15 Republicans and 12 Democrats. There were 42 Democrats and 16 Republicans in the House.

the Senate, the 1933 reapportionment also failed to achieve equity in representation—even on a regional basis (Table 10).[42]

TABLE 10
Legislative Voting Strength and Statewide Population
1930 Census

	Southern Region		Central Region		Northern Region	
Voting Strength	Senate 33%	House 41%	Senate 30%	House 30%	Senate 37%	House 29%
Statewide Population	43%		28%		29%	

SPECIAL SESSION—1933

After Wyoming's legislators adjourned the 22nd Session *Sine Die*, Franklin Roosevelt was sworn in as President of the United States. Acts of Congress were passed and Executive Orders were issued as the snow was melting in Wyoming. Many of Roosevelt's programs needed either state participation or state authorization. Democratic Governor Leslie A. Miller called a Special Session, to begin December 4, 1933, to consider Roosevelt's banking laws and emergency relief programs.

Senate President and Crook County Republican, Roy H. Cameron, addressed the Senate.[43]

> Probably at no other time in history have a large share of the population ... been given the franchise without being required to contribute towards the support of the government which gave them that franchise.... Now ... we have representation without taxation....
> When citizens of the state receiving [25%] of the income pay all the taxes in the state and the citizens receiving the other [75%] of the income ... pay no taxes at all, a condition is created which will in time wreck the governmental structure..."

---

[42] Yellowstone's 201 people were counted in the statewide population but they were not represented in the Wyoming legislature.

[43] Senate Journal, Special Session, 1933, p. 6.

His solution was to shift the tax burden from the mineral industry to the citizens in the form of an income tax—an unpopular concept the House refused, for 12 years, to consider.[44]

But he also quoted from the most recent report of the Board of Equalization:

[O]ne-fifth of the real estate in the state was bid in by the counties for delinquent taxes at the tax sale last July [1933], and after the tax sale this coming July [1934] the counties will, in all probability, be owners of at least one-third of the real estate in the state.

Taxable private property in Wyoming included mineral extraction operations, farms and ranches, commercial and retail enterprises and residential property. With nearly 47% of Wyoming's land in private hands, this eroding of the tax base was indeed serious.

That December the Republican Senate and the Democratic House passed finance laws on:

Conservator of Banks,
Security for Deposit of Public Funds,
Banks and Banking—Preferred Stock,
Temporary Federal Deposit Insurance Fund,
Borrowing Money in Liquidation of Insolvent Banks,
Refunding Bonds of Drainage Districts,
Refunding of Bonds of Irrigation Districts,
Power District Bonds,
Homeowner's Loan Corporation,
Reinstatement of Defunct Corporations,
Amending the Investment of Permanent State Funds,
The State Relief Act[45]

Even those with the "pull-yourself-up-by-your-bootstraps" attitude wanted the legislature to authorize the relief act.

[T]he widespread unemployment resulting in existing or threatened deprivation of ... the necessities of life ... for a considerable number of families and individuals [and] ... the power [of the County Commissioners] to raise funds by taxation ... are inadequate to meet present conditions.

---

[44] Governor Miller's message also called for an income tax. However, the only tax passed during the Special Session was 4 cents on gasoline.
[45] Senate Journal, Special Session, 1933, p. 6.

The Legislature enacted a State Industrial Recovery Act[46] designed to dovetail with the National Industrial Recovery Act of June 16, 1933. They enacted a law on Public Works Financing to mesh with the Federal Emergency Administration of Public Works. There was a DUI law and one to implement the sale of booze because prohibition was no more.

Problems in the oil patch were addressed by prohibiting unfair discrimination in production, manufacture and distribution of petroleum and petroleum products.[47] The penalty included putting a corporation in prison!

A large volume of very complex legislation was passed in the 22nd Special Session. It was well done and handled expeditiously. The Session adjourned on December 23—barely in time for the legislators to get home for Christmas.[48]

The timely legislation passed in 1933's Special Session helped Wyoming through the Depression. During the last years of the decade, war clouds darkened Europe as Hitler's war machine began to roll.

Reapportionment again was imminent in 1941—or maybe in 1943.

---

[46] Chapter 16, Wyoming Session Laws, Special Session 1933.

[47] Chapter 42, Wyoming Session Laws, Special Session 1933.

[48] In the 1935 and 1937 Sessions, the Democrats controlled both Chambers. The Republicans regained full control for the 1939 Session.

2

None—For 30 Years

No Senate Files and House Bills on reapportionment were debated during the 1940's. The Depression ended and the world was fully engaged in World War II. The 1940's were a time of heartache, rationing, dislocations, separations, disappointments, new experiences, workforce shifts, military service, military bases and the Japanese-American Relocation Center in Wyoming.

More than 12,000 citizens of Japanese-American heritage were interned in tarpaper shacks on the wind-swept steppe prairie of Park County. Before these accomplished gardeners were allowed back to the West Coast, they transformed many arid acres into productive cropland.

While their living conditions were extreme, given the heat of summer east of the Big Horn Mountains and Wyoming's cold winters, their compound was the third largest city in the state. Only Casper and Cheyenne had more people. The legislative leadership ignored reapportionment for, in the patriotic climate of those days, it was unthinkable to recognize them as the citizens they were.

Another reason reapportionment was ignored was the absence of many Wyoming men and women in the Armed Forces or working in defense industries in other states.

Demographers characterized the 1930's as a decade of little growth in the nation's population. It was no different in Wyoming. The statewide population increased by 11% from 1930 to 1940—up to 250,472 people. Rural residency decreased by 6.2%, down to 62.7%.

Less than 1,000 people were added to seven counties, ranging from Crook's 130 net gain to Sublette's 834.[49] There was a net loss in five counties, ranging from Natrona's loss of 414 to Hot Springs' loss of 869.[50] Platte County lost the most people: 1,682.

There were six counties with a net gain of between 1,000 and 2,000 people.[51] Sheridan gained 2,380 people and Park gained 2,769 people. However, 49% of the population increase was in two counties: Fremont and Laramie.[52] Except in these two counties, the population changes were not enough to make a significant difference.

The record shows the leadership was unwilling to request a Special Session when the final 1940 Federal Census was available. They were unwilling to increase the number of seats in either the House or the Senate. They were unwilling to change the ratio of citizens to legislators. They were unwilling to have more legislators elected by the Democratic voters in Laramie County, and, they didn't want the swing voters in Fremont County to elect Democrats.

In 1941 control of the House was a shared proposition. There were 28 Democrats and 28 Republicans. Democrat Carl Robinson of Lincoln County was Speaker. Republican Walter W. Hudson of Goshen was Speaker Pro Tempore.

The Republicans had 16 Senate seats. The Democrats had 11. Earl Wright of Sweetwater County was President of the Senate. William H. Cross of Converse was Vice President.

They were unwilling to reapportion. Each political party had the votes to stop any action of the other party. Therefore, the demographics of population distribution and the static allocation of Senate and House seats meant the inequality in regional voting strength in the Senate and House continued (Table 11).[53]

---

[49] These counties were Crook-130, Johnson-165, Weston 285, Goshen-453, Teton-540, Uinta-651 and Sublette 834, for a total gain of 3,058.

[50] These counties were Natrona-414, Converse-514, Lincoln-608, Campbell-672 and Hot Springs- 869, for a net loss of 3,077.

[51] These counties were Sweetwater-1,242, Carbon-1,253, Niobrara-1,265, Big Horn-1,689, Washakie 1,749, and Albany 1,905.

[52] Laramie County gained 6,806 and Fremont gained 5,605.

[53] The Federal Census counted the persons living in Yellowstone National Park as part of Wyoming's statewide population. In 1930 Yellowstone had 201 people; in 1940 it had 416.

TABLE 11
Legislative Voting Strength and Statewide Population
1940 Census

	Southern Region		Central Region		Northern Region	
Voting Strength	Senate 33%	House 41%	Senate 30%	House 30%	Senate 37%	House 29%
% Of State Population	43%		28%		29%	

There was no reapportionment in 1943. The electorate chose a Republican majority: 17 to the Democrats' 10. R.H. Nichols of Natrona was President of the Senate. George A. Cross of Fremont was Vice President. The Republicans held the House majority: 39 to 17. Richard J. Luman of Sublette was Speaker. [54] For the remainder of the decade, succeeding legislative leaders never allowed reapportionment to be debated.

THE 1950'S

The next war was the Cold War. That war of deterrence came to the grasslands of Laramie County in the silos for nuclear missiles: the Atlas, the Minutemen and eventually the MX. The old historic D.A. Russell Army Base, an air force training facility in World War II, became the F.E. Warren Air Force Base. It was the command quarters for "wings" of missiles in their launch silos in Laramie, Goshen and Platte as well as silos in western Nebraska.

These silos held the thrust and re-entry vehicles—the nuclear bombs. Air Force personnel were welcome participants in the economy of the region. One of the requirements imposed before F.E. Warren was designated "home base" for the missile operational center was the closing of the brothels in the city of Laramie. The basis for this requirement was the Air Force's

---

[54] *Wyoming Blue Book*, *Reprint of Part* One, by Marie H. Erwin, edited by Virginia Cole Trenholdm from the 1946 edition. Wyoming State Archives and Historical Department, 1974.

experience during World War II. The City of Laramie complied.[55]

The 1950 Federal Census found 291,529 people, a 15.9% increase over 1940. There was a significant increase in the number of urban residents, now at 49.8% of Wyoming's statewide population. The wide-open spaces and the long, long miles empty of human habitation meant Wyoming had 2.98 people per square mile. With the population clustered in cities and towns, it was becoming an urban state!

Again, the population changes were not evenly distributed. The smallest net gains were in four counties in the northern region: Teton, Big Horn, Hot Springs and Sheridan.[56] The biggest gains in the northern region were in Park and Washakie.[57] The net gain in the northern counties was 4,612 or 11% of the increased statewide population.

By 1950 the population increased in Natrona, Fremont and Weston in the central region.[58] Natrona's county seat, Casper, was becoming a significant service center for the petroleum industry. Central-region counties that lost population were Niobrara, Converse, Sublette and Lincoln.[59] The net gain for the central-region counties was 9,294 or 23% of the increased statewide population.

All the Union Pacific Mainline counties gained in population: Laramie, Albany, Carbon, Sweetwater and Uinta. Goshen also gained, while Platte lost population.[60] The southern region had the largest net gain: 24,975 people, or 61% of the increased statewide population.

------

[55] The author, as Director of Albany County School District's Adult Basic Education program during the Johnson Administration was a member of the CAMP (Coordinated Action Manpower Planning) group charged with the responsibility, as part of Johnson's Great Society, to address the educational, employment, health and welfare needs of the "needy" in Albany County. Two of the madams were on the client list—they became "needy" due to Air Force rules.

[56] Northern region counties that gained population: Teton-50, Big Horn-265, Hot Springs-643 and Sheridan-30.

[57] Park gained 4,206 people and Washakie gained 1,394 people.

[58] Natrona gained 7,579 people. Fremont gained 3,485 and Weston gained 1,775 people.

[59] Niobrara lost 1,287, Converse 698, Sublette 297 and Lincoln 1,263.

[60] The gains were: Laramie 14,011, Albany 5,109, Carbon 3,098, Sweetwater 2,610, Uinta 108 and Goshen 427. Platte lost 388 people.

During the 1950's there was no reapportioning. The legislative voting strength among the regions as a percent of the statewide population became more skewed. The southern region was seriously under-represented (Table 12).[61]

TABLE 12
1951 Legislative Voting Strength and Statewide Population

	Southern Region		Central Region		Northern Region	
Voting Strength	Senate 33%	House 41%	Senate 30%	House 30%	Senate 37%	House 29%
% Of State Population	45.4%		27.4%		26.7%	

In 1951 the President of the Senate was Robert J. Rymill of Goshen. Frank C. Mockler of Fremont was Speaker of the House. The Republicans controlled both chambers.

In 1952, when Eisenhower was elected President, 81,047 people voted in Wyoming. In 1953 with the final census in hand, there was no will to reapportion. Floyd W. Bartling of Converse was President of the Senate and R.L. Greene of Johnson was Vice President. Population decreased in both their counties. Legislation was prepared but none came to the floor for debate.

In the 32nd Session, in 1953, the Senate had 21 Republicans and six Democrats. The Democrats were Rudy Anselmi and Louis Boschetto of Sweetwater, David Hitchcock of Albany, Allen Hunter of Campbell, Pratt Wilson of Lincoln and Orvel Bridgmon of Platte. No new Democrats were elected to the Senate in 1952.

In the House David Foote, Sr. of Natrona was Speaker. The Republicans controlled with 45 seats. The Democrats held 11 seats representing people from five counties: Albany, Carbon, Sweetwater, Uinta and Washakie.

By not reapportioning, the leaders in the 32nd Legislature made sure no more seats were distributed to counties in the Democratic southern region. The Republican leadership similarly refused to reapportion in the 33rd and 34th sessions in 1955 and 1957.

---

[61] Yellowstone National Park, with 353 people, still was not included for legislative representation.

For these four consecutive years in the 1950's the Senate President and the House Speaker were from Johnson County. Men from Converse and Washakie counties served with them, representing agricultural/mineral communities. They held enough political clout to continue to deny equal representation to residents in urban communities—a clear misuse of power.

In the elections of 1958 restless voters elected Democrats to the state's highest offices. Democrat Gale McGee of Albany was elected to the United States Senate—unseating Republican incumbent Frank Barratt. J.J. (Joe) Hickey of Cheyenne was elected Governor, Jack Gage of Sheridan as Secretary of State and Velma Linford of Albany as Superintendent of Public Instruction. Thus the voters placed Democrats in four of the top seven elected positions.

Governor Hickey's solution to the state's dependence on minerals was to diversify the economy—bringing more jobs into the state and broadening the tax base.

When the 35th Legislature convened in January 1959, the Senate Republicans held 16 seats, the Democrats 11. Norman Barlow of Sublette was Senate President. In the House the Democrats held the majority with 30 seats, the Republicans had 26. The Speaker was Jay R. House of Carbon.

The southern region sent 19 Democrats. This constituted 63% of the House Democrats and 34% of House members. The voters sent Democrats from the other regions as well: 16% from the central region and 20% from the northern region.

Technically it was legal for the House Democrats to reapportion in 1959 using the 1950 Federal Census. Politically this was a bad idea so soon before the next census.

However, much as some Democrats may have wanted to get representation that reflected their population, they had to reckon with Senate President Norman Barlow. He represented central-region Sublette County's agricultural/mineral interests. He upheld the sanctity of the 1933 distribution of seats. He had the political power to prevent Senate consideration of any House reapportionment bill.

For Senator Barlow and his colleagues their political power was closely tied to the land—not just to cows or corn, sheep or sugar beets, but to the mineral rights that brought royalty payments for the extraction of oil (mostly) from deep under their pastures and fields. The rural legislators clearly understood the connection: To keep royalty money flowing, take good care of us—the mineral industry.

The minerals men nurtured a viable symbiotic relationship between themselves, the rural legislators and each new "crop" of rural candidates for the legislature. Government services depended on tax dollars from the extractive industries.

The ag-men "carried the water" for this industry by proclaiming: "no" to taxes, "no" to government regulations on safety and the environment, "no" to property taxes committed to retire bonds for local schools, municipal services or hospitals, "no" to bringing in new industry and new jobs because more people demanded highways, fire protection and public safety. They wanted no changes in the allocation of legislative seats. They did not want any reapportioning.

And so the decade of the 1950's closed.

3

The Entrenchment Of Power

The rural legislators were not fools. They knew if they recognized any increases in urban populations more seats were needed in the Senate and House. Or, any redistribution of the existing 27 Senate and 56 House seats meant dilution of their political power.

Because the constitution guaranteed each county one senator and one representative, the perception prevailed that political power was closely tied to the land.[62] For many "the land" meant royalty payments.

Whether the mineral was oil or gas, coal or iron ore, uranium or bentonite, trona or phosphate, gold or gypsum, the extractors operated in every county except Teton. They paid royalties to thousands of Wyoming voters.

Those associated with resource extraction wanted to keep political power away from Democrats from the denser populated southern region. They held the perception that Governor Hickey wanted to raise taxes for local or state purposes.[63]

The rural legislators liked the mineral industry tax base and their consequent low property taxes that enhanced their own

---

[62] Article III, Section 3 of the Constitution of Wyoming.

[63] For the 1959 legislative session Governor J.J. (Joe) Hickey—a Democrat—advocated expansion of the tax base through attraction of more diversified businesses and/or industries as the best long-term solution to Wyoming's extreme dependence on taxes from the mineral industry for government services. In his view, the state's dependence on property taxes for public services was not good. His proposal fell on deaf ears. Source: Conversation with Win Hickey.

31

political power. They gladly made "common interest" with the people engaged in extracting non-renewable resources. This association extended beyond royalty income to all who participated in the discovery, recovery and transportation of minerals—extracted for export beyond Wyoming's borders.

During Hickey's time as Governor, little value was added to what was produced in the state. Thus most of the jobs were elsewhere. Wyoming was a "resource exporting state" much like third world countries. As the decade of the 1960's began, the minerals-men were happy and the rural legislators enjoyed their political power.

No reapportionment during the 1950's made unequal representation even more unequal by the 1960's. The 1960 Federal Census found a 13% population increase.

Because final census numbers were not available for the 1961 Session, Senate President Albert C. Harding of Crook and Speaker Joseph L. Budd of Sublette—both Republicans—found it easy not to touch reapportioning, thus maintaining the status quo in the Senate. Each county had one seat, except Sheridan, Sweetwater, Natrona and Laramie, which had two seats each.

But the pressure was on. The Final Census found more urban residents than rural residents: 56.8% to 43.2%. The statewide population was 330,066. Now Wyoming was an urban state.

Table 13 shows the population shift from rural to urban from 1930 to 1960.

TABLE 13
1930 to 1960 Population Shift from Rural to Urban

Federal Census	Rural Population	Urban Population	Statewide Population
1930	68.9%	31.1%	225,565
1940	62.7%	37.3%	250,742
1950	50.2%	49.8%	291,529
1960	43.2%	56.8%	330,066

Huge individual population gains were experienced in Albany (from 12,041 to 21,290), in Fremont (from 10,490 to 26,168), in Laramie (from 26,845 to 60,149) and in Natrona (from 24,272 to 49,623).

The aggregate population change among the regions clearly indicated the shift from rural to urban. The southern region (with 42,553 more people) and the central region (with 42,029 more people) were dominated by urban dwellers. The northern region (with only 13,441 more people) remained predominately rural. Table 14 shows the change in population.

TABLE 14
Change in Population 1930–1960

	1930 Federal Census	1960 Federal Census	% of Increase	% of Decrease
Albany	12,041	21,290	77%	
Big Horn	11,222	11,898	6%	
Campbell	6,720	5,861		13%
Carbon	11,391	14,937	31%	
Converse	7,145	6,366		11%
Crook	5,333	4,691		12%
Fremont	10,490	26,168	149%	
Goshen	11,754	11,941	2%	
Hot Spgs	5,476	6,365	16%	
Johnson	4,815	5,475	14%	
Laramie	26,845	60,149	124%	
Lincoln	10,894	9,018		17%
Natrona	24,272	49,623	104%	
Niobrara	4,723	3,750		21%
Park	8,207	16,874	106%	
Platte	9,695	7,195		26%
Sheridan	16,875	18,989	13%	
Sublette	1,944	3,778	94%	
Sweetwater	18,165	17,920		1%
Teton	2,003	3,062	53%	
Uinta	6,572	7,484	14%	
Washakie	4,109	8,883	116%	
Weston	4,673	7,929	70%	
Total	225,364[64]	329,646	46%	

---

[64] The census showed Yellowstone had 201 people in 1930 and 420 in 1960.

The northern region kept its hold on political power by not acknowledging that more people were living in southern and central Wyoming—especially in Albany, Laramie, Fremont and Natrona— and by its continued resistance to mid-century reapportionment. After the 1960 Federal Census the legislative voting strength in the regions continued to tilt toward the northern region and away from the southern region where the population was greatest (Table 15).

TABLE 15
Legislative Voting Strength and Statewide Population
1960 Census

	Southern Region		Central Region		Northern Region	
Voting Strength	Senate 33%	House 41%	Senate 30%	House 30%	Senate 37%	House 29%
% Of State Population	42%		32%		25%	

Albany County's political activist Sarah Gorin identified this serious imbalance of political power in her Master's thesis.[65]

The population per senator ranged from 3,000:1 in Teton County to 30,000:1 in Laramie County. And, counties containing 24.2% of the population elected a majority of the Senators.

Predictably, legislative leaders from the predominately rural counties liked the power they wielded.

Prior to the 1960's no political will existed that acknowledged the increasingly urban character of Wyoming's electorate. The intransigence of those resisting change prevented any shift of political power to urban legislators.

Wyoming's Constitution[66] gave the legislature the power to reapportion. Legislature after legislature refused to do its constitutional duty.

---

[65] Sarah Augusta Gorin, *A History and Analysis of Wyoming Legislative Reapportionment Cases 1963-1991*. MA Thesis, Political Science Department, University of Wyoming, 1992, p. 25.
[66] Article 1, Sections 1 and 3.

WHO CAN FORCE REAPPORTIONMENT?

Thoughtful members of the electorate were troubled by the audacity and arrogance of those legislators refusing to recognize shifts in the state's population. If the state's constitution required reapportioning at 10-year intervals and the legislators clung to "land area" not "population" as the essential factor controlling the distribution of Senate and House seats, what was the remedy? Politically savvy citizens asked two questions:

> Who has standing to object if there is no reapportioning?
>
> and
>
> If the legislature does not reapportion, who can?

Wyoming's Constitution provides the answer to the second question: only the Legislature can reapportion.

> [N]o person...charged with the exercise of powers properly belonging to one of these departments shall exercise any powers properly belonging to either of the others....[67]

If the legislature never got around to reapportioning, the executive branch had to remain silent and inactive. The rural legislators with the political power "sat in the cat-bird's seat."

Because reapportionment case law was ill defined the answer to the first question was obscure. But restless and concerned citizens refused to accept continued legislative inaction. Was it possible for them to "force the issue" through citizen action in the Courts?

THE LEGAL REASONING

One of the restless citizens was Ross Merlin Beyer. Writing in the *Wyoming Law Journal*,[68] he sorted through case law

---

[67] Section II, Article 2, Wyoming Constitution. The author found no mention of the use of Initiative as a possible remedy.

[68] Ross Merlin Beyer, "Possible action to force the Wyoming Legislature to Reapportion," "Case Notes" in the *Wyoming Law Journal*, Volume 11, No. 2 (Winter 1957) pp. 136-142. "Case Notes" in this issue were papers written by law students at the conclusion of their first year of Law School at the College of Law, University of Wyoming, Laramie Wyoming. All subsequent references to Beyer are from this work.

seeking answers to the first question. He explored the seriousness of not reapportioning. He considered the impact of inequity in representation in the state legislature.

In the Journals of the Wyoming Legislature[69] he found that,

> [A]pportionment bills have been introduced in almost every session since 1941. The counties which would either lose representatives or lose representation in comparison proportionately with the other counties have apparently been able to muster enough votes to defeat all such bills.

The essential and basic question was whether or not a federal district court had jurisdiction to hear reapportionment issues. Ross Beyer looked at *Dyer* and noted that Hawaii's last apportionment was in accordance with the Hawaiian Organic Act of 1900—55 years earlier. The Court ruled in *Dyer* that by not acting since then, those succeeding legislatures

> ...denied a voter, who became under-represented by reason of population shifts, of his rights to due process and equal protection of the laws granted by the Fifth and Fourteenth Amendments to the United States Constitution. The Court [Federal] held that the Federal Civil Rights Act[70] and its parallel jurisdictional provision give a federal district court the power to grant equitable relief for the deprivation of these fundamental rights by ordering the legislature to reapportion or requiring an at-large election.[71]

In this case, Beyer found precedent that a court could get involved in reapportionment. When the under-representation due to shifts in population among the several election districts became especially grievous, then a citizen's rights to due process and equal protection were violated. Court intervention was

---

[69] The official record of each legislative session is written in a Journal each year the legislature is in session, a single book for the House and a single book for the Senate. Originally these books were in the custody of the Secretary of State. In the 1990's the legislature authorized custody to the State Archives within the Division of Cultural Resources of the Department of Commerce. After each session a digest of the House and Senate Journals is published and distributed to libraries. A Digest is only a summary; it does not contain all the transactions of a legislative session.

[70] Act of April 20, 1871, c.22, 17 Stat. 13, as amended 42 U.S.C. & 1983.

[71] Ross Merlin Beyer, op. cit., p. 137.

possible based on the Fifth and Fourteenth Amendments. The fact that the increasing population was not recognized by the legislature through reapportionment was a denial of due process. In *Dyer*,

> The legislature's failure to obey the fundamental law of Hawaii was equivalent to affirmative electoral legislation which operated to discriminate against a class of persons. The ultimate effect of this failure was intentionally to discriminate against a class, in that a voter in one electoral district was being given a decided preference over a voter in another electoral district, although all were entitled to equal treatment. ... In one district a vote had 6.8 times as much weight as in another. This was held to be a denial of the equal protection of the laws.

Beyer continues:

> The Hawaiian court pointed out that the denial of equal protection of the laws and due process can overlap,[72] and discriminatory legislation may amount to a denial both of due process and of equal protection.[73] ... The Hawaiian legislature arbitrarily discriminated against persons having equal rights by failing to reapportion in accordance with population shifts, thus in effect the legislature pointedly favored one regional class of persons over another regional class. This ... is a denial of due process.

Thus Beyer found precedent on which to base a challenge to no reapportionment in Wyoming since 1933. He also found precedent for the southern "regional class" of persons to challenge the northern "regional class" over the fact of unequal voting strength in the legislature in relation to the populations of the respective regions. Due process provided standing for court action.

For Beyer the next issue was in which court? At issue was the separation of powers. He found a convoluted answer in *Colegrove v. Green*,[74] where seven United States Supreme Court justices gave their opinions. Three said federal jurisdiction did not exist. Three said federal jurisdiction did exist and should be

---

[72] *Bolling v. Sharpe*, 347 U.S. 497, 74 S.Ct.693, 98 L.Ed. 884 (1954).

[73] *Bolling v. Sharpe*, supra note 15; Kiyoshi Hirabayaski v. U.S., 230 U.S. 81, 100, 63 S.Ct. 1376, 87 L.Ed. 1774 (1943).

[74] *Colegrove v. Green* 328 U.S. 549 (1946).

exercised in these cases. One said federal jurisdiction did exist but it should not be exercised. The seventh justice essentially said reapportionment was purely a political question but four justices ruled there was federal jurisdiction.

Prior to 1946 the courts identified reapportionment as a "purely political question" and therefore not subject to federal jurisdiction. *Colegrove v. Green* ended this view. Beyer concluded that jurisdiction was in the Federal Court.

Beyer recommended mandamus to challenge Wyoming's non-reapportionment.

> In a Writ of Mandamus a court order requires the performance of a particular, specified duty and results from the official position of the party to whom the writ of mandamus is directed. In *Fergus v. Marks*[75] the Illinois Supreme Court said that mandamus "will not lie to compel law." But the use of mandamus by federal district court was a slippery slope due to the reality stated in many state constitutions that the legislature had exclusive control over matters pertaining to legislative functions.[76]

But Beyer knew mandamus had been used in 1908 in *Schnitger*,[77] when Patrick Sullivan of Natrona and John Williams of Converse challenged the validity of the 1893, 1901 and 1907 reapportionments. Sullivan and Williams got no ruling on their challenge: the validity of past or existing reapportionments.[78] Instead, the state court said they had no standing (neither as citizens nor as legislators) to bring a Writ of Mandamus because they had no official position that entitled them to mandamus. Beyer hinted that mandamus might work if handled differently.

Beyer concluded his *Notes* with five observations:

> 1. The 1908 Wyoming courts had chided those bringing the case because they could not show a valid apportionment to replace any past or existing laws should they be declared invalid.

---

[75] *Fergus v. Marks*, 321 Ill. 510 N.E. 557, 46 A.I.R. 964 (1926).

[76] *Dyer at* 139 and 140.

[77] *State ex rel Sullivan v. Schnitger,* 16 Wyo. 479, 95 Pac. 698 (1908).

[78] Sullivan and Williams wanted the ruling on the validity of past and existing reapportionments because they perceived the 1905 State Census contained gross inaccuracies and therefore was not a valid census upon which to base legislative representation.

2. The Court did not consider "at-large" elections.

3. Wyoming did not have any laws equivalent to the Federal Civil Rights Act upon which to base any challenge on the grounds of equal protection or due process that would enable a state court to assume jurisdiction.

4. A suit filed in federal district court that relied on the Civil Rights theory would have only the *Dyer* case as precedent for reapportioning as well as having to deal with the reluctance of the courts to take jurisdiction based on *Colegrove v. Green.*

5. Substantive law would definitely favor a Wyoming plaintiff seeking court ordered reapportioning, but the procedural holdings "are definitely against" such a plaintiff.[79]

Some southern-region citizens read Beyer's "Notes," and gave considerable attention to his admonition that a Writ of Mandamus might succeed if it were handled differently.

Despite the 1960 Federal Census and Beyer's learned writing, in 1961 rural legislators led by Senate President Albert C. Harding of Crook and Speaker Joseph L. Budd of Sublette happily let "sleeping dogs lie." They did no reapportioning. But in 1962 Wyoming's southern-region citizens "set the dogs to barking."

IN STATE COURT

On June 18, 1962 plaintiffs Edwin Whitehead, Harry H. Schaefer, Clayton A. Trosper, Rae R. Martin, Louis Leichtweis, Burton Marston, KATI Corporation and Ralph A. Urbigkit filed an action in State District Court—*State v. Gage.*[80] Using a Writ of Mandamus they requested Secretary of State Jack Gage and the Attorney General to reapportion the state. Walter C. Urbigkit of Cheyenne argued the case for the plaintiffs.

The plaintiffs tried to require the Court to act swiftly. Because of the pending 1962 elections, they directed the Secretary of State and the Attorney General to expeditiously reapportion in time to seat a newly configured legislature.

---

[79] Beyer, op. cit., pp. 140-1.

[80] *State v. Gage,* Wyoming 377 P 2d 299.

But just in case the court rejected this action and learning from 1908 *Sullivan v. Schnitger,* the plaintiffs included a provision for another remedy. If the Secretary of State and Attorney General did not act quickly enough, then the 1962 November General Election was to be "at-large" for 56 House seats and the 15 expiring Senate seats. All candidates for the 71 seats were to be voted on by all the electors in the state—a statewide election for the legislature. Thus equal representation was to be achieved because everyone was in one election district.

The case was filed in June just five months before the November General Election. Delay was the "order of the day." The court schedule provided the "cover" for no action as requested by the restless citizens.

The Wyoming Supreme Court ruled on January 7, 1963. The 37th Legislature was already in session—elected under the 1933 law. The Court found that

...members of the 37th Legislature are now elected. This legislature has not yet had opportunity to take such action as is necessary to comply with its duty under the state constitution. We must assume it will perform such duty....

By focusing on the use of the petition for a Writ of Mandamus, the Court avoided the central issue of no reapportioning since 1933. It chose to rule against the plaintiffs on technical grounds.[81]

One: ...a Writ must be effectual....

Two:...a Writ can not be made to serve [the] purpose of [an] ordinary suit...[The Court] will issue [a Writ] only where [the] duty to perform is clear, certain and undisputable..."

Three: ...Mandamus ... [is] not [an] issue ... since proceedings were commenced, a primary and general election [have been held] of new members to the State Legislature on the basis of ratios fixed by prior law.... Neither the secretary of state nor the attorney general had clear duty to assume function which had not been imposed upon them by law."

By declining to consider population changes in each county between 1933 and 1962, the state supreme-court judges didn't just "punt"—they left the playing field.

---

[81] *State v. Gage,* Wyoming 377 P 2d 299, 1963.

The State Supreme Court assumed that the leadership was willing to reapportion in 1963. This reasoning effectively maintained the political power of northern-region legislators. It closed all doors for judicial involvement unless and until a legislature did another reapportionment. It was of no help to citizens wanting equal representation.

The early 1960's were a "quiet time" in Wyoming. The state's economy was "in the doldrums." Not much was happening outside production/services for farming/ranching and for petroleum operations. Modest numbers of tourists kept coming with their welcome dollars. The railroads continued to haul passengers and freight. Coal was taken from mines along the Union Pacific corridor.

There was no income tax, no taxes on corporate activity, few sales taxes, low fuel taxes and some inheritance taxes. Taxes on land/buildings were based on 1935 market value.

Democrat Jack Gage was Acting Governor and Secretary of State. J.J. Hickey resigned to accept appointment to the U.S. Senate following the death of U.S. Senator-elect Keith Thomson.

Most political leaders were content with the languid status quo. The rest of the world was "out there" somewhere, but many citizens didn't care where. Other citizens were vocal in expressing their anti-government opinions. Some northern-region folks thought John Birchers were too far to the political left! Others grudgingly conceded the State was part of the United States. We were "independent cusses" who were disinclined to have anyone "from outside" tell us anything.

ENTER BAKER V. CARR

Outside Wyoming's borders scholarly and media attention was on the abominable apportionment of most of the state legislatures. Mayne Miller[82] and his brother Haynes accepted Tennessee's League of Women Voters as clients and argued *Baker v. Carr*.[83] They claimed the continued use of the 1901 Tennessee statute apportioning their legislature deprived them (Mayne and Haynes) and other voters of equal protection of their

---

[82] Mayne Miller's law practice was in Casper. He was the husband of Casper's grande dame Mariko Miller.
[83] *Baker v. Carr*, 369, U.S. 186. 82 S.Ct. 691, 7 L.Ed.2d 629 (1962).

41

rights accorded them by the Fourteenth Amendment to the United States Constitution.

The United States Supreme Court heard their case, then ruled reapportionment plans enacted by a state legislature "are valid unless shown to be invidiously discriminatory."[84]

On appeal the United States Supreme Court asked three questions:

1. Are there extremes for which there is no rational explanation?
2. Are there subsequent actions that at first appearance seem to be invidious yet may be overcome by a showing of rational or legitimate justifications by a state or local government?
3. May a legislature's decision not be invidious, but nevertheless violate the Constitution?"

Reapportionment was a matter for the Federal Courts because unequal representation was a violation of the Fifth and Fourteenth Amendments to the United States Constitution. Whether or not invidious discrimination existed or appeared to exist became the bedrock question for every reapportioning effort for the rest of the 20th century.

When invidious discrimination was found, the violation was a violation of the Federal Constitution (Fifth and Fourteenth Amendments). It was not a violation of a state constitution or state law. Thus reapportionment was no longer within the jurisdiction of state courts nor was it a "local political issue."

With *Baker v. Carr* the restless and concerned citizens understood the Federal Court had jurisdiction to rule on their quest for fairness. This "law of the land" said people, not land, was to be represented in state legislatures. If a legislature did not get it right, a Federal Court had the authority to provide "appropriate relief" and to retain jurisdiction for as long as necessary to achieve equal representation.

---

[84] The dictionary defines invidious "as tending to rouse ill will or envy or containing or implying a slight."

4

Finally, 1963 and Reapportionment

Reapportionment was forced to the top of the agenda of the 37th Legislature, elected in 1962 according to the 1933 law. Public pressure was increasing as more people became aware of the skewed distribution of Senate and House seats. No longer was the leadership able to let reapportionment "slip through the cracks."

Senate President Charles G. Irwin of Converse and House Speaker Marlin T. Kurtz of Crook led the revision of the distribution of legislative seats based on the 1960 Federal Census. The Republicans controlled both Chambers. Republican Clifford P. Hansen of Teton was Governor.[85]

No one was interested in using the Court's recommendation in *State v. Gage* of "ratio based on previous law." Such a ratio required a Senate of 37 seats and a House of 81 seats. Physically, there just wasn't room in either Chamber.

With a 46% statewide population increase since the last reapportioning in 1933, the 1963 legislators used the traditional allocation of at least one seat in each Chamber for each county—as guaranteed in the Wyoming Constitution.

The Republicans had 59% of the political power in the Senate with 16 Republicans and 11 Democrats. They also held

---

[85] In 1962 just 64,970 people out of 122,494 voted for Hansen for Governor.

66% of the political power in the House with 37 Republicans and 19 Democrats. Edness Kimball Wilkins of Natrona and Victor Garber of Sheridan were the only Democrats who were not from the southern region.[86] The number of senators was decreased by two. Only Laramie and Natrona counties each retained two senate seats. Sheridan and Sweetwater each lost a seat. No county gained a seat.

TABLE 16
1960 Population of Counties with
Fewer Than 10,000 People

County	1960 Federal Census	County	1960 Federal Census
Campbell	5,861	Platte	7,195
Converse	6,366	Sublette	3778
Crook	4,691	Teton	3,062
Hot Springs	6,365	Uinta	7,487
Johnson	5,475	Washakie	8,883
Lincoln	9,018	Weston	7,929
Niobrara	3,750		

The 1917 precedent of only one senator for 21 counties meant the electorate was over-represented in 13 counties where populations were less than 10,000 (See Table 16).

One senator for each county meant this plan, too, ignored the counties with burgeoning populations. The 1933 Senate inequality for Albany, Fremont, Park, Sheridan and Sweetwater became larger.

In 1963 equity in representation was achieved for the House by adding five seats—at least equity within the "major fraction thereof" deviation range. The eight counties with the smallest populations continued to have one representative each. These were Campbell, Crook, Hot Springs, Johnson, Niobrara, Sublette, Teton and Weston counties.

Of the remaining five counties with populations less than 10,000 Converse, Platte and Uinta each lost a seat. Lincoln dropped from three seats to two seats. Washakie got one more seat.

---

[86] In 1963 the Senate ratio of persons per senator was 30,000:1 and the ratio for the House was 5,400:1.

44

The 1960 population in Big Horn, Carbon and Goshen was between 10,000 and 15,000 (Table 17). Each had three representatives in 1933. Carbon kept three seats, the other two each lost a seat.

TABLE 17
1960 Population of Counties with 11,000 to 15,000 People

County	1960 Federal Census	1933 Number of House Seats	1963 Number of House Seats
Big Horn	11,898	3	2
Carbon	14,937	3	3
Goshen	11,941	3	2

Albany, Fremont, Park, Sheridan and Sweetwater—the counties clearly discriminated against in the distribution of Senate seats—fared better in the House (Table 18).

Laramie and Natrona were the two counties with the largest gains in population. In 1963 Laramie county gained five seats. Natrona gained three seats. From 1933 to 1963 Laramie County's population increased by 124% and Natrona increased by 104% (Table 19).

TABLE 18
1960 Population of Counties with 16,000 to 30,000 People

County	1960 Federal Census	1933 Number of House Seats	1963 Number of House Seats
Albany	21,290	3	4
Fremont	26,168	3	5
Park	16,874	2	3
Sheridan	18,989	4	4
Sweetwater	17,920	4	4

The legislators of the 37th Session nearly achieved equal representation in both the Senate and the House for the central region, as shown in Table 19. Equity in representation was within "shouting distance" in the House. The Senate continued to be seriously skewed in favor of the northern region.

The policy of one senator for each county was basic to the disparity. Fremont's 26,168 people were seriously under-represented.   Teton's 3,062 people were seriously over-represented. The resulting "weight" or the magnitude of influence of the vote of the senator from Teton was nearly 12 times greater than the vote of the senator from Fremont.

TABLE 19
1960 Population of Counties with 31,000 to 62,000 People

County	1960 Federal Census	1933 Number of House Seats	1963 Number of House Seats
Laramie	60,149	6	11
Natrona	49,623	6	9

The "weight" of the vote was skewed even for the two largest counties: Laramie and Natrona. Each kept their two senate seats and 16% of the voting strength in that Chamber. However, these two counties had 109,772 people or 32% of the state's population.

TABLE 20
1963 Voting Strength and 1960 Statewide Population

	Southern Region		Central Region		Northern Region	
	Senate	House	Senate	House	Senate	House
Voting Strength	32%	41%	32%	33%	36%	26%
% Of State Population	43%		32%		25%	

Behind the decision of a senate ratio of 30,000:1 was pure politics: the "opportunity" to deny Sweetwater (and Sheridan) their second senate seats.   Sweetwater Democrat Rudy Anselmi's senate seat was the target or "victim" of this Republican strategy.

The loss of these senate seats eviscerated the weight of the electorate's vote.   This diminution of power focused on Sweetwater—a Democratic county—and on Sheridan—a sometimes-Democratic county—was an especially sweet and clever move by the Republicans. It was a clear use of political power.

The loss of two seats in the 5th and 6th most populous counties, justified as "just applying the ratio," was symptomatic of the endemic inequality deeply buried in Wyoming's historic rendering of equal representation. In 1963 the Republicans deliberately contrived to negate any challenge to the political power base of northern regional interests, with the intent to solidify for another decade the power of Wyoming's Republican Party.

This 1963 reapportionment was the product of careful manipulation within a limited definition of legal acceptability. It was yet another example of the hallowed Republican caucus tradition of passing just enough law to placate possible objectors. By reapportioning, the leadership gained the approbation of Wyoming's Supreme Court while retaining their stance of "not too much law." With nearly equal representation in the House they hoped to satisfy and/or muzzle the "restless and fuss making citizens" of 1962 who forced the legislature to appear before the court in *State v. Gage.*

The holders of political power claimed success and misled the electorate into thinking equity in representation had been achieved. No further challenge was expected. Case closed.

BUT NOT SO FAST

Article 1, Section 34 of Wyoming's Constitution states: "...all laws of a general nature shall have a uniform operation..." There was precious little "uniform" about county boundaries used to define election districts.

When the "restless fuss-making citizens" read the 1963 law, they found that nine—or 36%—of the senate seats were allocated to seven counties with a total of 211,643 people—or 64% of the population. These seven under-represented counties were Albany, Fremont, Laramie, Natrona, Park, Sheridan and Sweetwater. They were seven solidly or "swing" Democratic counties.

Then the restless fuss-making citizens found the seven counties with the fewest people—32,982 or 10% of the population—controlled seven or 28% of the senate seats. These low-population, senate-powerful, over-represented counties were Campbell, Crook, Hot Springs, Johnson, Niobrara, Sublette and Teton. They were all Republican counties.

But many of Wyoming's citizens saw nothing wrong with weighting the legislative voting strength in favor of the counties with the smallest populations. Representation in the Senate of the United States favored smaller states. Therefore Wyoming's legislature should favor smaller counties.

But others were troubled by the 37th Legislature's success in keeping Republican, northern, rural, mineral special interests effectively exercising larger political power. These powerful legislators "turned a deaf ear" to meaningful equity in representation, especially in the Senate. No Republican legislator took notice of case law being built by other states—rulings that might just as well have been on another planet.

When Governor Clifford Hansen signed the Enrolled Act,[87] the "restless fuss-making citizens" howled in outrage. They were upset. The under-represented 64% of the population were urban residents, most of them living along the Union Pacific. These southern-region residents had a different view of public policy than the folks in the rural northern region.

One hot issue was the post-World-War-II federal dollars flowing into the states. It all depended on whether the money was "for me or for thee": for public education (important in the southern region) or for support of the sheep industry (important in the northern region). This policy divide was obvious to the late Velma Linford, when she was Superintendent of Public Instruction.

During one legislative session she was trying to get the Senate to accept Wyoming's share of Federal Aid To Education. She saw the federal dollars as a timely opportunity, given the reality of the scarcity of property tax monies then available to support K-12. But the lobbying was going against her advocacy of accepting the money to benefit the children.

She said[88] she "nearly lost her patience" during one northern senator's attack. He claimed accepting federal aid for children's education was the beginning of the "perdition of federal control." After hearing his declaration of how awful federal aid was, she drew upon her considerable dignity and asked,

"Did you get your wool check today?"

She knew her question was timely because she knew the wool checks had arrived in the mail. She secured approval for federal dollars for the children.

---

[87] Enrolled Act means the bill as signed by the President of the Senate and Speaker of the House and sent to the Governor for his signature. A signed Enrolled Act (or allowed to become law without signature) becomes a Session Law when filed with the Secretary of State.

[88] Velma Linford, private communication.

This philosophical divide between Federal affairs and Wyoming affairs, that tended to distinguish southern-region legislators from northern-region legislators, was far from theoretical. For example, Park County's Alan Simpson was first a State Representative, then a United States Senator. In Washington, when he was asked about the impact of federal dollars on Wyoming's social programs, he replied,

"We were doing pretty well until the feds forced us to acknowledge we had social problems."

The many years of unequal representation in the legislature resulted in the tendency to ignore many of the state's emerging educational, social and cultural concerns. The clear retention of political power in the hands of rural northern legislators gave the Senate the ability to undo any egalitarian proclivities emanating from the House. The northern region was acting like the British House of Lords!

SPECIAL SESSION—JULY 1964

With the *Baker v. Carr* ruling in 1963 and *Reynolds v. Sims*[89] in the early summer of 1964, Governor Hansen called a special session of the legislature.[90] In his Call he said: fix a mistake in the tax code made in the 1963 session and "do something" on reapportionment.

Chapter 100 of the 1963 Session Laws removed the phrase "for the purposes of raising revenue" from Wyoming's Tax Law. Because of this omission Hansen claimed, "The cities are presently having difficulty collecting gasoline taxes." But the driving factor behind this interruption of the haying schedules was *Baker v. Carr* and *Reynolds v. Sims*.

In opening the special session Governor Hansen used a quote from Governor A.G. Crane's Special Session Message in 1950:

> If I fail to convene the legislature, I will have shut the
> door to legislative action.... My duty is plain. I must
> set the stage for a fair hearing by the legislature, the
> only agency with the power to act....

---

[89] Both houses in a bicameral legislature had to be districted on a population basis with substantial equality of population among all districts.
[90] Governor's Call in *Legislative Journals*, 1964.

Hansen did not want the albatross of inaction around his neck. The November elections were to follow the "...dictates of that legislation." (the 1963 reapportionment law).

> But in light of the Court decision handed down on June 15 [*Reynolds v. Sims*]... it is apparent that the new Wyoming law is not a valid solution to the problem now before us.... Since both bodies of our legislature must now be elected in proportion to population, it is evident that Section 3 of Article III needs to be changed.

After the *Baker* and *Reynolds* rulings, the Governor asked Attorney General John Raper to convene a committee of seven distinguished Wyoming attorneys to prepare recommendations for the legislature. They were: Elmer Scott of Washakie, William H. Brown of Natrona, David Hitchcock of Albany, Frank Trealease of Albany, A.G. McClintock of Laramie, Edward Halsey of Weston and Robert Sievers of Sublette.[91]

Besides agreeing with the Governor that Article III, Section 3, needed to be changed they made three recommendations:

1. To specify the federal census as the official state census;
2. To provide for altered congressional districts as the state population increased;
3. To authorize the Legislative Council to put together detailed election districts using the doctrine of equal population to be presented for consideration by the 38th legislature.

Hansen said if the Attorney General's recommendations were followed,

> there will be avoided any possibility of attack on the Wyoming Constitution as a violation of any right under the Constitution of the United States....

The Governor's Message included an optimistic revenue report. The General Fund balance on June 30 was $7,096,724.20. Recent revenues to the General Fund were $18,638,614.24. For the first time sales and use tax revenues exceeded $13 million. The balance in the Unemployment Compensation Fund was increasing and funds to pay Workmen's Compensation continued in "good condition."

---

[91] Sarah Augusta Gorin *A History and Analysis of Wyoming Legislative Reapportionment Cases 1963-1991*. Masters Thesis, University of Wyoming, 1991, p. 18.

As he concluded his message, Govrnor Hansen told all the legislators:

> If you fail to agree to a plan, the State will not be excused, nor will the status quo remain. If this legislature fails to reapportion, the task will be taken up by a panel of federal judges. They will be forced to perform what is a legislative responsibility.

Then the legislators began their work in their respective chambers. The House passed the "feed bill."[92] It passed the bill to add back the six revenue tax words. It passed memorials to deceased legislators. It twiddled its thumbs. The action was in the Senate, where the Republican leadership placed the issues raised by *Baker v. Carr* and *Reynolds v. Sims*.

---

[92] The appropriation to pay the expenses of the Special Session.

5

Serious Discussion on the Status Quo

Senate President Earl Christensen of Weston put the senators to work on Senate Joint Resolution 1 (SJR 1): the constitutional amendment to change Article III, Section 3. It authorized combining two contiguous low-population counties to make a senatorial district with one senator, thus cutting in half the voting strength of counties with the smallest populations. President Christensen had a "vested interest" in this proposal because three low population counties—Crook, Campbell and Niobrara—bordered his own low-population county.

The day of the Governor's Message SJR 1 went directly to the Committee of the Whole. One small change was made. Second Reading was July 29th. Third Reading and final vote was July 30th. The vote was 15 ayes, 10 noes, 2 excused. All the Republicans voted aye. All the Democrats voted no. The Resolution failed.[93] Republican Norman Barlow of Sublette County and Democrat Robert J. Murphy of Natrona County were absent.

Now the prime reason for the Special Session was gone. To the rescue came R. L. Greene of Johnson, Senate President in 1955–56. His institutional memory and his knowledge of how to work the system brought new life to SJR 1. He moved to

---

[93] To gain approval, a proposed constitutional amendment needs two-thirds affirmative vote from the legislature and a majority of those voting in the election. Wyoming Constitution, Article XX, Section 1.

recommit it to the Senate Judiciary Committee, chaired by John O. Callahan of Big Horn.

There the process started over. SJR 1 came out of Committee on July 31st essentially gutted except for the title. The Judiciary Committee acknowledged that future election districts had to be based on population but they wanted Wyoming's Constitution to include *other relevant factors* to mitigate the impact of *Reynolds v. Sims* on counties with low populations. SJR 1 now said:

> The Legislature shall in establishing senatorial and representative districts, consider the following factors in the order named, so long as the basic standard of apportionment substantially on a population basis is maintained:
>
> A. Counties or other political subdivisions
> B. Geographical location
> C. Economic interests
> D. Transportation and communication.

Translated, this amendment said legislators can reapportion so long as they recognize counties as election districts, keep cities and towns intact within election districts, recognize mountains, deserts and reservoirs as barriers or division elements between districts, protect the intertwined agricultural/mineral interests and keep election districts navigable and accessible for candidates.

In his message the Governor said, "Our labors together at this time need not be lengthy." As it was July 31st the Senate hurried to meet his standard. The "other relevant factors" amendment passed Committee of the Whole. Second Reading was suspended. Third Reading and Final Vote was taken: 17 ayes, 8 noes, 2 excused.

This time two Democrats, LeRoy Christinck of Campbell and Carl Robinson of Lincoln, joined the Republicans. If Norman Barlow had attended and voted with his brethren SJR 1 would have passed the Senate. But he was gone and the resolution died. None of the recommendations from Governor Hansen's committee of attorneys were considered.

WITH NOTHING TO DO, THE HOUSE TALKS

The House members spoke to those in the Chamber but more important, they spoke for the record.

Edness Kimball Wilkins, a Democrat and respected minority leader from Natrona expressed her sadness at the failure of SJR 1 and her hope that the House would have solved this involved problem. She was confident the House the Representatives could have discussed it in harmony and reached agreement. She was "...deeply grateful that we are all parting as friends...." In her inimitable way Edness poured oil on troubled waters.

William F. Craft of Big Horn was vocal, forceful and intent on keeping those waters churning.[94] His prepared statement was read by the Chief Clerk and seconded by all 37 House Republicans:

> This Legislative session was called by Governor Hansen for the purpose of submitting a proposed amendment to the Constitution of Wyoming so that our Constitution would comply with the requirements of the decision of the Supreme Court of the United States. Though we are opposed to the principles set forth in the decision which we feel constitute unwarranted Federal encroachment upon and usurpation of states rights, nevertheless as the decision is the law of the land, we Republican members of this legislature have made every effort to pass a just and equitable resolution that would conform to the dictates and the opinions of the majority of the United States Supreme Court.

Then he blamed the Democrats for the failure in the Senate.

> In order to place this resolution before the voters of Wyoming, Democrat support in the State Senate was required. This support in the State Senate was not forthcoming in the several efforts to pass same.... It is with profound regret that this Special Session of the Legislature must close without giving the voters of Wyoming an opportunity to accept or reject a valid amendment to their constitution and the sole respon-

---

[94] This is the opinion of Representative June Boyle of Albany County whose desk was in front of his. Subsequent quotations in this section are from the official Journals.

sibility therefore rests upon the Democrat members of our State Senate.

William Craft and his fellow Republicans conveniently ignored the two Democrats who voted with them the second time. They also ignored the absence of Senator Barlow from scarcely populated Sublette. The Republicans, not the Democrats, "controlled the shop."

House Minority Leader Walter Phelan did not let Craft have the last word. Noting that he spoke only for the House Democrats, he recounted how Governor Hansen included the Democrats in the decision to call the Special Session. Senators Rudy Anselmi and W.A. Norris, Edness Kimball Wilkins and himself were asked if a session on reapportionment was needed and whether the date of July 28th was suitable. Each responded in the affirmative. He stressed that at no time had Governor Hansen elicited from any of them a pledge to vote for a particular piece of legislation.

> I speak for all nineteen members of the minority party
> in this body when I state to you that if a measure for
> fair, just and equitable reapportionment of our State by
> constitutional amendment had been presented to this
> House, that we would have voted with possibly two
> exceptions, in mass for that constitutional amendment.

From his status as a leader of the minority party he "exerted influence," not only on Democrats in the House, but Democrats in the Senate who assured him they "...would vote for a reasonable amendment" if no district included more than one county.

Phelan anticipated charges and counter charges about whose fault it was that nothing was done in the special session:

> I believe that the honest statement will be that the
> responsibility lies with all of us. This body...would
> have passed a reasonable constitutional amendment.
> The Senate, whether we call it eight irresponsible
> Democrats or fifteen irresponsible Republicans,
> probably would not have.

The Governor came and said goodbye. He thanked them for four busy summer days. What did not get done was history that did not need rehashing. What was important was "for each of us ... is the job of searching our own conscience to see if we have done the best we can and that's about as far as we can go."

There was no looking back. The government continued. Everyone had a job to do. The session adjourned *Sine Die* at

3:05 pm. With "ruffled feathers" the legislators went home to their hay fields and businesses.

The "fuss-making citizens" watched the special session with interest. They saw no surprises. The entrenchment of the northern and central regional interests prevailed. No changes were made for the upcoming November elections.

Walter Phelan left his law practice to spend long days traveling many miles recruiting and coaching Democratic legislative candidates. As per the 1963 law, at the 1964 general election persons were elected to two fewer senate seats and five more house seats.

INTO COURT IN 1964

The "restless fuss-making citizens" filed suit on November 23, 1964 in United States District Court.[95] Three Federal judges heard the case: Circuit Judge Pickett and District Judges Kerr and Daugherty. The plaintiffs brought action as "citizens and voters" to determine the constitutionality of the reapportionment law passed by the 37th Legislature.

The plaintiffs were Harry H. Schaefer, Adrian W. Reynolds, Burton W. Marston, Patrick H. Meenan, Darlene Elliot, Ralph A. Urbigkit and Edwin H. Whitehead. Attorneys for the plaintiffs were from Cheyenne: A. G. McClintock, Walter C. Urbigkit and Maxwell E. Osborn. Five of the plaintiffs had been plaintiffs in S*tate v. Gage* in 1962: Pat Meenan, as KATI Corporation, Harry Schaefer, Burton Marston, Ed Whitehead and Ralph Urbigkit.

The defendants were members of the State Board of Election Canvassers: Secretary of State Thrya Thomson, Treasurer Everett T. Copenhaver, Auditor Minnie A. Mitchell and Governor Clifford P. Hansen. Defending the state were Attorney General John Raper[96] and his deputy Dean W. Borthwick.

The plaintiffs based their case on *Baker v. Carr, Gray v. Sanders* and *Reynolds v. Sims*. It was in *Gray v. Sanders* that Justice William O. Douglas established the concept that political

---

[95] *Schaefer v. Thomson*, 240 F. Supp 247 (1964).

[96] John Raper and A. G. McClintock served on Governor Hansen's committee that made recommendations on reapportionment to the July 1964 Special Legislative Session. Now they were on opposite sides of the state's third lawsuit on reapportionment.

equality means only one thing: "one person, one vote."[97] *Baker v. Carr* stated that the federal courts had jurisdiction over reapportionment of state legislatures.[98] *Reynolds v. Sims* said that both houses of a bicameral legislature had to be apportioned on the basis of population with substantial equality of population among the several districts.[99]

The plaintiffs were voters in Wyoming's most populous counties—the ones seriously under-represented in the 1963 senate reapportionment. They charged invidious discrimination and claimed protection under the 14th Amendment of the United States Constitution.

In their Opinion, the Court said,[100]

1. If the plaintiffs show invidious discrimination and substantial disparity in representation in the legislature, the federal court has jurisdiction.
2. The equal protection clause of the 14th Amendment to the United States Constitution requires *both* chambers in a bicameral legislature to be based on population.
3. Mathematical exactness of a strict population standard is not required so long as divergences are based on legitimate considerations that fit a rational state policy.
4. The same rules apply for the reapportionment of both the Senate and House.
5. Reapportioning is the job of the legislature.
6. The legislature shall reapportion the Senate.
7. While the court is not to be questioned on policy or wisdom, they are not to bring about "palpable absurdities."
8. In determining constitutionality the fundamental purpose of the court is to give effect to their [the legislature's] purpose and intent.
9. Great weight needs to be given to the intent of the constitutional convention in 1890 that the legislature continues to be of relatively small size.

---

[97] *Gray v. Sanders*, 372 U.S. 368 (1963).
[98] *Baker v. Carr*, 369 U.S. 186 (1962).
[99] *Reynolds v. Sims, 377* U.S. 533 (1964).
[100] *Schaefer v. Thomson*, 240 F. Supp 247 (1964).

10. The 1963 reapportionment of the Senate is invalid because it constitutes invidious discrimination and violates the equal protection clause of the Fourteenth Amendment of the United States Constitution.
11. The 1963 reapportionment of the House is valid.
12. The state constitutional provision that each county is to be represented by one senator was ineffective and was not to be considered when determination was made reapportioning the state senate in accordance with the Fourteenth Amendment of the United States Constitution.

In the first reason Judges Pickett, Kerr and Daugherty applied *Baker v. Carr* to claim federal jurisdiction. Wyoming's Constitution says the state "...is an inseparable part of the federal union..."[101] and "the Constitution of the United States is the supreme law of the land."[102]

In the second reason the Judges used *Reynolds v. Sims*.[103] The 37th Legislature acted on the theory and belief that the apportionment on the basis of population of one house was enough to satisfy constitutional requirements. Pickett, Kerr and Daugherty said they were wrong.

In the third and fourth reasons the judges turned to *Reynolds v. Sims* for clarification and application of mathematical exactness. *Reynolds* required that

...a state make an honest and good faith effort to construct districts, in both houses of its legislature, as nearly of equal population as is practicable and that some deviations from the equal-population principle are constitutionally permissible.

The same criteria had to be applied to every election district and in both the Senate and the House.

While the Court said apportioning was the legislature's job they retained jurisdiction in order to require the state to meet constitutional standards.

Judges Pickett, Kerr and Daugherty told the 37th Legislature[104] to go back and redo the Senate apportioning with the goal to achieve the same degree of equal population per

---

[101] Wyoming Constitution, Article I, Section 37.

[102] Wyoming Constitution, Article 1 Section 21.

[103] *Reynolds v. Sims*, 377,U.S.533 (1964).

[104] *Schaefer v. Thomson*, 240 F. Supp 247 (1964).

Senate election district as they achieved for the House election districts.

Then the Judges said in effect "don't mess with us." They knew the resistance their decision was to generate. But they directed that "neither their policy nor their wisdom" be questioned. Everyone was to look for the true meaning intended by their ruling even if some meanings were not explicitly stated. And the Judges were mindful of historic precedent to keep Wyoming's legislators few in numbers.

The last three statements from the Court were especially significant. The 1963 Senate was invalid. The 1963 House was valid. No more was Article III, Section 3 to be used to justify one senator and one representative per county without regard to the size of the population. No longer were counties to be identified as the sole criteria for election districts.

Thus the Judges agreed with the plaintiffs, found invidious discrimination because 64% of the population got to elect only 36% of the senators in violation of the equal protection clause of the Fourteenth Amendment to the Constitution of the United States.

The "fuss-making citizens" were vindicated. They won. Case law developed in other states did apply to Wyoming. Holders of Wyoming's political power, those who thought their policy on reapportionment was unchallengeable, encountered their first serious comeuppance in *Schaefer v. Thomson*. The Rule of Law, not the tyranny of the majority, governed. Redress was possible for the under-represented citizens.

When the Court handed down its Opinion in *Schaefer v. Thomson*, the general election of 1964 was over. By an avalanche, not a landslide, Lyndon Johnson was the new President of the United States. He won in Wyoming too—the first time since Harry Truman carried Wyoming in 1948. His coattails needed just one more senator for the Democrats to control the Senate. His coattails brought Democratic control of the State House. The Republicans lost both in Federal Court and at the ballot box.

6

The Legislature Tries Again

The House had 31 Democrats and 30 Republicans. Walter Phelan's long hours traveling many miles paid off. He became Speaker of the House. Edness Kimball Wilkins was Speaker Pro Tem. Don Hubbard of Albany was Majority Leader.

Politically entrenched Republican northern-region agriculture/mineral interest's worst nightmare became a reality. Not only were the House Democrats in control, but legislators from the southern region chaired all the committees except two: Edness Kimball Wilkins of Natrona chaired Revenue and Alfred E. (Lefty) Graham of Hot Springs chaired Oil-Gas-Mines-Mining.

Five of the southern-region House chairmen were from Laramie County: George Cox in Ways-Means, Arthur Buck in Education, Barney Cole in Corporations-Public Utilities, Howard Burke in Transportation-Bridges-Highways and Robert "Bob" Adams in Federal Relations-Military Affairs.

Two chairmen were from Carbon County: Elton Trowbridge in Livestock and O.R. "Bud" Daily in Labor. Sweetwater chairs were Al Christian in Game-Fish and Richard Forsgren in Welfare-Buildings-Institutions-Sanitary-Medical Affairs.

Other southern-region chairs were John Sullivan of Albany in City-County Affairs, Carl Otto of Goshen in Agriculture, William Megeath of Uinta in State-Lands-Farm-Loans-Irrigation and Ed Herschler of south Lincoln in Judiciary.

Even the political power of the House Rules Committee, which Speaker Phelan chaired, was controlled by southern-region legislators: Don Hubbard, Ed Herschler and John F. Sullivan and from the central region Edness Kimball Wilkins.

There were 13 Republicans and 12 Democrats in the Senate. No southern-region Republican held leadership political power. Andrew McMaster of Niobrara was Senate President. Pete Madsen of Sheridan was Vice President. The Majority Leader was Earl Christensen of Weston.

Three men from the central region chaired committees: Dick Tobin of Natrona in Judiciary, Charles G. Irwin of Converse in Revenue and Donald W. Jewett of Sublette in Public-Lands-Irrigation-Agriculture.

But the real political power rested in the northern region. Dick Jones of Park chaired Ways and Means. Pete Madsen of Sheridan[105] chaired Education-Health-Welfare and Corporations-Political Subdivisions. Howard Flitner of Big Horn chaired Livestock, Transportation-Highways and Journal. James Brunk of Hot Springs chaired Mines-Minerals and Labor-Manufacturing. Other northern-region chairs were R. L. Greene of Johnson in Elections and Harry C. Barker, Jr. of Teton in Game-Fish. But Jones, Madsen, Flitner and Brunk pretty much "ran the show."

They exerted strong influence over the central-region men, including President Andrew McMaster. Majority Leader Earl Christensen was happy to be part of their cadre. He chaired the Senate Rules Committee. The other Republican members of Rules were R. L. Greene and Dick Jones.

The Democrats on Rules were Elmer D. Kinnaman of Carbon and W.A. Norris, Jr. of Laramie. Kinnaman was the Minority Leader in the Senate.

The power of committee chairmen was considerable because Wyoming allowed the Senate President, Vice President and Majority Leader to serve only one term in each position. Often a senator chaired a committee and served on one, or maybe two, other committees. It was very unusual for so many senators to chair more than one committee. The three who did—Madsen, Flitner and Brunk—were power-wielding, enterprising senators.

---

[105] Madsen was also Vice President of the Senate.

PHELAN AND MCMASTER SPEAK[106]

Upon acceptance of their election as the leaders of their respective chambers both Speaker Phelan and President McMaster followed tradition and addressed their chambers.

Walter Phelan said he intended to step aside and not seek reelection next year. But, being Speaker "...is the greatest honor, and the greatest responsibility, that has ever been given to me. ...Not in 40 years had Laramie County had the honor of the Speakership." Then he talked about the upcoming session.

There are some who predict a controversial session. It will be. But controversy if honest and sincere breeds progress and progress is the father of history. There are those who predict an historical session. They are correct. It will be a session in which the issue of paramount importance will be—is—this legislation for the betterment of Wyoming and its people. Others direly prophesy that narrow and sterile partisanship will be rampant here and that no good will come of our deliberations. They are in error. Differ we will—but quibble we will not. Sincere differences of opinion we will have—but stalemate never.

Our vision is the future. Our history is our guide. Wyoming's good is our dream. We must—we shall— we can succeed. Any great society must start at home. We mean to see it start here in our deliberations. May God grant us the wisdom to see the problems and meet the challenge.

President McMaster recognized the "expert politicians" in his audience. Then he did a bit of reminiscing about the remarkable things he had seen during his tenure as a senator. He remembered the end of World War II and the need to fix the highways that had "gone to pot." He remembered, "...compacts on driver licensing, vehicle equipment safety and the yellow and the white stripe."

Then he came to his favorite subject—the federal government.

It is the state that does the building, the maintaining and the policing. The Federal Government contributes our own money which we have sent to them. ... It might be well to remember that when Uncle Sam plays

---

[106] From the House and Senate Journals of the 1965 Legislature.

Santa Claus it is the taxpayer who holds the bag. I would say that judging from the amount of the public debt now, it is no longer much of a compliment to tell a lady she looks like a million dollars.

The cost of educating the children was another of his "bones of contention." He thought poor, long suffering legislators could never win because of the bumper crop of babies born during World War II.

How this was accomplished has mystified many a commanding officer but the problem ... existed of how to get teachers and schools to put these little darlings into. It was the individual legislatures and the men and women in them that did the job. They reduced the number of school districts, they raised the standards of teachers ... they recognized the need and met it. Now all of this while resisting offers of help from the Federal Government. ... [E]very offer to help had strings attached which would remove local autonomy of school district control. This problem of schools will exist as long as there are children, mothers and legislators with a listed telephone number.

President McMaster didn't like taxes either. "When you make out your income tax correctly you go to the poor house and if you don't you go to jail." He also thought the legislators had done good things for those in the executive branch, like budget agencies, new accounting and auditing practices, but they had not done anything for themselves—like a pension plan for legislators. Then he returned to his favorite litany.

The Federal Government is now and has been taking over many of the functions of our everyday living. These ... were never given to the Federal Government in the Constitution or anywhere else. ... [W]e have just taken an oath to uphold and defend the Constitution of the State of Wyoming. The meanings ... of the Bill of Rights are being used in many ways that were never intended to encroach upon and run the business of the several states of the Union. ... [T]hese encroachments are being done to build a larger and larger base upon which to build a larger and larger bureaucracy which has many larger and larger executive salaries at the top. Reapportionment, states rights, wilderness, the Wind River, federal aid to education, and natural resources, the minerals and the waters of the many states of the Union.

McMaster called upon the senators,

Somewhere there will have to be a stand taken and I am staking my hopes upon the legislator who rises and says in a quiet voice: "Mr. President, I want to be heard upon that subject.

Speeches finished, the Senate and the House turned to the business of the Session.

The House Republicans were not interested in single-member districts. Their three bills—HB 84, 221 and 336—were sponsored by Cliff Davis of Campbell, William. F. Swanton of Natrona, Harry McMillan, Edward Breece and Fremont Miller of Fremont, James Thompson of Niobrara, Lawrence Yonkee of Sheridan, LaVerne Boal of Weston and Nels Smith of Crook.

These legislators were used to wielding the political power of their northern and central regions. But Speaker Phelan consigned their bills to oblivion in Ed Herschler's Judiciary Committee where they "reposed" until the legislature adjourned *Sine Die*.

All 31 Democrats "signed on" to House Bill 50. The sponsors were Democratic heavyweights: Speaker Phelan and John Rooney of Laramie County, Majority Leader Don Hubbard and Judiciary chairman Ed Herschler. John Rooney was the principal author of the bill.

The bill, based on population, combined a few low-population counties. It was simple, easy to administer and followed the directives of the three Federal judges. It was constitutional.[107] HB 50 was introduced in the House on January 14th, and passed the House 36–25 on January 21st. It immediately went to the Senate. On January 22nd the Senate sent it to Elections Committee chaired by veteran Republican senator R. L. Greene of Johnson.

There it stayed until February 18th, the 38th of the 40-day session, when it was reported to the floor for debate. Howard Flitner tried to amend it into a senate file. He did not succeed. HB 50 died on the Senate's General File[108] when the legislature adjourned *Sine Die* on February 20th.

---

[107] More details of HB 50 are in Senate Minority Leader Kinnaman's remarks to the Senate at the conclusion of the 38th Session.

[108] The roster of bills from which the Majority Leader makes daily selections for consideration in Committee of the Whole.

Six House Republicans voted for HB 50. Three were from Natrona: Robert L. Adams,[109] D. Thomas Kidd and Gordon A. Ward. The other three were Bill Nation of Laramie County, Lawrence Yonkee of Sheridan and H. W. Fausset of Washakie.

THE SENATE STRUGGLES

The Senators again worked on the issue they found so difficult. Many Republicans found it hard to be gracious about their one-seat margin of control in the Senate and about losing control of the House. Acrimony against the Democrats remained from the previous summer's special session. Many were the under-currents and counter-currents swirling about the two chambers.

The responsibility to pass court-mandated reapportionment was squarely in the hands of the Republicans. Worse, they had to face the reality of the loss of their own seats.

Between January 14 and January 29 three Senate Files and two Senate Constitutional Amendments were filed. Dick Jones of Park and James Brunk of Hot Springs sponsored SF 95. A very complicated bill; it used the 1960 census tracts to subdivide the state into election districts. The Democrats howled "gerry-mander!" The sponsors replied, "The districts are equal in population and are contiguous." This bill quietly resided in R. L. Greene's Election Committee until adjournment *Sine Die* on February 20th.

The Judiciary Committee referred the first legislation to reach the Senate floor. A Joint Resolution (SJR 6), it called on the Congress to amend the United States Constitution to allow "other factors besides population" to be considered in the reapportionment of state legislatures.

As sometimes happens in Wyoming politics, party affiliation took a back seat to self-interest. Resolution sponsors were eight Republicans and four Democrats. These sponsors were from counties with low populations and were vulnerable to losing their senate seats.

The prime sponsor was Democrat Carl Robinson of Lincoln. Other sponsoring Democrats were Otis Wright of Campbell, John C. Simons of Goshen and J. W. Myers of Uinta. The

---

[109] That Session both Robert "Bob" Adams of Laramie County and Robert L. "Bob" Adams of Natrona County served in the House.

sponsoring Republicans were Howard Flitner of Big Horn, Harry Barker Jr. of Teton, R. L. Greene of Johnson, Earl Christensen of Weston, Pete Madsen of Sheridan, James Brunk of Hot Springs, Don Jewett of Sublette and Charles Irwin of Converse.

The resolution got to the floor on January 19th. It passed the Senate on January 21st by one vote: 17 ayes, 6 noes, 1 excused, 1 absent. Democrats Corbitt, Halseth, Kendig, Kinnaman, Rector and Scully voted no, with Norris excused and Murphy absent.

SJR 6 immediately went to the House where Speaker Phelan started the Resolution on a very circuitous path. First he sent it to Bob Adams' Federal Relations-Military Affairs Committee where it stayed a week. On January 27th Adams re-referred it to Art Buck's Education Committee, which kept it until February 6th. Then Buck re-referred it to Ed Herschler's Judiciary Committee which finally sent it to the General File on February 15th. Majority Leader Don Hubbard called it up for debate in Committee of the Whole on February 20th—the last day of the session.

To begin debate this late in the Session was an insult to the Republicans and deliberately made a shambles of Republican strategy on court-ordered reapportionment. It showed Democratic disdain for amending the Nation's Constitution to further the political power of those fighting against equal representation based on population.

Section 1 of Senate Joint Resolution 6 stated that,

Nothing in this [United States] Constitution shall prohibit any state [that has] bicameral legislature from apportioning the membership of one house of such legislature on factors other than population, provided … plan of such reapportionment shall have been submitted to and approved by the electors of the state.

There was nothing subtle in SJR 6. It was a direct challenge to the use of the Fourteenth Amendment for equal representation in state legislatures. The resolution, designed to legitimize Wyoming's practice of using "other relevant factors" instead of equal representation, was clearly self-serving. Knowledgeable, fair-minded, clear thinking Wyomingites cringed at the thought of SJR 6 actually getting to Congress.

In the 1960's the rising tide of equal rights elsewhere in the nation was creating an unbeatable steamroller for fairness. Thus the House Democrats practice of "passing off" the Senate File from one committee chair to another saved everyone from ridicule.

The sponsors of SJR 6 counted on the disgruntlement of other like-minded state's rights legislators to join them. They thought many people did not want equal representation based on population.

Soon after SJR 6 went onto the House committee merry-go-round, Senate Joint Resolution 11 was introduced, sent to Senator Greene's Elections Committee where it "rested" until February 11th, when it appeared in Committee of the Whole. Sponsored by senators Dick Tobin and Robert Murphy of Natrona, it amended Wyoming's Constitution to allow, "...senatorial districts and representative districts [to be] apportioned substantially on a population basis in such manner as the legislature shall provide...."

The measure passed the Senate on February 15th: 21 ayes, 3 noes, 1 absent. The no votes were from Democrats Edward Kendig, J. W. Myers, and Republican Frank Watson of Washakie. Otis Wright was excused.

When SJR 11 got to the House, Speaker Phelan did not like the "wiggle-room" words "substantially on a population basis as the legislature shall provide."[110] He kept it until February 18th then sent it to the General File. There it stayed until the session adjourned *Sine Die*.

But the Senate had to come up with something on reapportionment. House Bill 50 was reported to General File from Greene's committee on February 18th. But the Senate leadership did not want to deal with HB 50. So, on January 28th Dick Tobin introduced SF 136. Pete Madsen was co-sponsor. This Senate File also went to Greene's Committee where it stayed until it went to General File on February 18th, just two days before the 40-day session ended, with no Standing Committee amendments.

Senate File 136 was a patch-together plan using elements from James Brunk and Dick Jones' SF 95 and from House Bill 221 sponsored by Fremont's Harry McMillan, Edward Breece, Fremont Miller and Natrona's William F. Swanton.

The election districts in SF 95 were the ones the Democrats charged were gerrymandered. But HB 221 was a curious mixture of senate election districts based on voting precincts in

---

[110] Besides Greene the other members of the Elections Committee were Republicans Frank Watson and Leslie W. Hauber of Crook and Democratic leader Elmer Kinnaman of Carbon and William G. Rector of Laramie counties.

Fremont, Natrona and Sheridan counties and of election districts based on census tracts in the remaining 20 counties. Residents of all ages were counted in census tracts, but only adults who voted in the last general election were counted in voting precincts.[111] The crafting of a reapportionment plan that used two different counting methods produced a mishmash that clearly was an invitation to constitutional challenge. But the Senate wasn't finished.

An unidentified Second Reading amendment increased the size of the Senate to 31 giving Laramie five seats and Natrona four seats. This amendment failed.

The final Senate vote was 12 ayes and 13 noes. Voting no were four Republicans: R.L. Greene, Dick Jones, Dick Tobin and Andrew McMaster. Democrats voting no were Elmer Halseth, Ed Kendig, Elmer Kinnaman, Robert Murphy, J.W. Myers, W.A. Norris, Bill Rector, Pat Scully and John D. Simons.

SF 136 failed in the waning hours of the 38th Legislature. The Court was spared consideration of this grievous insult and mockery of equal representation. Since the Legislature failed to reapportion, the Court was ready to do it for them.

But before the motion to indefinitely postpone SF 136 was made, both the Republicans and the Democrats wanted to speak to the people of Wyoming "On the Record" in the Senate and House Journals.[112]

R. L. GREENE FOR THE REPUBLICANS

Claiming his committee had looked carefully at all pro-posals, Greene said they rejected SF 103, HB 84 and HB 336 because election districts were still defined by county—the practice the Court ruled unconstitutional. His committee decided

---

[111] The evident discrimination in HB 221 was especially unfortunate in Fremont County. It was 1965, the middle of the Civil Rights era, when fairness in political representation was front-and-center in the nation's psyche. Children and non-voting adults on and near the Shoshone and Arapaho Wind River Reservation were excluded. But also excluded were all the children and non-voting adults in two of the largest counties in the state.

[112] Not included in the Senate and House Digests. The remarks are in the Journals in the State Archives in the Cultural Resources Division in the Department of State Parks and Cultural Resources.

the constitutionality of HB 50 and HB 221 was "extremely doubtful" based on the variation of population between senate districts.

As evidence he identified HB 50's allocation of one senator to each of the following:

Park County with 16,874 people

Carbon County with 14,937 people

Hot Springs County with 6,365 people

Teton/Sublette Counties with 6,840 people

Plate County with 7,195 people

Uinta County with 7,484 people.

Thus in all five of these smaller counties a voter would have twice the representation of a voter in the two larger counties. The ratio ... between Park County and Hot Springs County was 2.65 to 1.

His next objection to HB 50 was that Weston (with 7,929 people) and Converse (with 6,366 people) were combined with other counties and each "lost" a senator while Platte and Hot Springs—with fewer people than either Weston or Converse—each retained their senators.

His final objection to HB 50 was that the over-represented counties in the House were also over represented in the Senate. Attorneys of both political parties "were of the opinion" that HB 50 was unconstitutional.

HB 221 had the same defects as HB 50, though to a lesser extent. In SF 136 Greene's committee liked the population variance ration of 1.5 to 1. They concluded SF 136 was, "...overall the fairest bill considered, and the one coming closest to the United States Supreme Court's edict of 'one person, one vote'."

Greene reported that they rejected dividing counties as an alternative to floterial districts.[113] In SF 136 only Lincoln was divided because of "little access" between the northern and southern portions of the county. He noted the interests of southern Lincoln were similar to the interests in Uinta and northern Lincoln had more in common with Teton and Sublette.

---

[113] A technique to achieve equivalent representation by adding an at large "floating" member, i.e., one member represents subdistrict A, another member represents subdistrict B and a third member represents both A and B as an at-large member.

Greene's committee decided to keep county boundaries for other senate districts. To do otherwise "would create serious problems."

Greene gave the rationale for two senators in the Platte/ Goshen district. Platte's 7,195 people were not enough to justify a senator of its own. By combining Platte with Goshen's 11,941 people the resulting election district qualified for two senators. He reported they considered putting western Goshen with northern Laramie but they were

> ...unable to make a satisfactory division and in view of the fact the economic interests of Platte and Goshen counties were almost identical... both had irrigated and dry land farming and ranching. [They] adopted ... SF 136.

SF 136 had 31 senators, each representing 11,366 people. By using the multi-member floterial district concept they combined the populations of Sweetwater and Carbon (32,857 people) and gave them three senate seats. Likewise, in the Big Horn Basin they combined those four counties with 44,020 people and gave them four senators. Each of these senators was to run "at large" in their respective multi-member districts comprising two and four counties respectively.

On whether or not to sub-district within a county, Greene identified three questions: Should they subdivide? If yes, to what extent? And, how to subdivide? The smaller counties did not need subdividing because,

> [T]he population of each of the smaller counties was homogenous and a candidate for the legislature was generally known, or had the opportunity to be known, throughout the county.

But Laramie, Natrona and Fremont should be subdivided

> in order that the legislators might be more closely identified with their constituencies and ... to avoid loss or diminution of the voting rights of minority groups....

To illustrate how minority groups were deprived of representation, the Committee looked at Laramie where 43,505 of the county's 60,149 people lived within the city. The rural people were discriminated against because;

> [I]t has been impossible to elect a person from the rural areas to the the legislature for many years ... [and a] substantial number of Spanish-American, Mexicans and Negroes who reside in the south and west areas of

70

the city ... have never been able to attain office in a countywide election. It is not only possible, but probable, that under the sub-districting plan which we propose these groups will be represented.

Greene reported complaints from Laramie county candidates of their inability to personally contact "even a reasonable portion" of the voters. Complaints were heard that limits on campaign spending prohibited the use of newspapers, television and other advertising "to acquaint the voters of their views."

Greene said that "reasonable representation" was possible in larger counties if each senatorial district included two representative districts. If the population called for another representative, that person was to be elected at-large in the entire county. SF 136 sub-districted five counties and did not sub district 18 counties.

Greene said objections to this plan focused on "the necessity of printing an unduly large number of different ballots." He explained the use of both census tracts and voting precincts in SF136:

> HB 221 uses the 1964 election returns and election [voting] districts as a basis of sub-districting. SF 136 sub-districts Natrona and Fremont Counties on the same basis as HB 221. It sub-districts Sheridan County on the basis of election precincts and election districts based on the 1964 election returns but uses a slightly different division plan which results in a more even division between the two districts on a population basis.
>
> SF 136 subdivides Laramie and Albany on the same basis as SF 95. This sub-districting is based on the 1960 census and was performed by a professor of political science at the University of Wyoming at the request of the Governor. This professor belongs to a different political party than the Governor and states that no consideration whatsoever was given to politics in subdividing the counties.[114]
>
> The reason given ... for not using the 1960 census ... and method of subdivision [from] ... SF 95 for Natrona, Sheridan and Fremont counties is that such sub-division would be unduly disruptive of existing

---

[114] The professor was Dr. John Richards. "[He used] city maps from telephone books...." Gorin, op. cit., p. 20.

election districts and did not give the same consideration to racial or economic groups as was given by the use of existing election districts.

Greene maintained that in none of the Republican-sponsored bills was there "any attempt to gerrymander or obtain any political advantage." The bill sponsors attempted to draft legislation "in accordance with the wishes of the residents ... involved. And for this reason adopted the provisions of HB 221 as to certain counties and the provisions of SF 95 as to other counties." He also maintained that "whether election districts or census tracts were used, the populations within the legislative districts were substantially equal."

Then he talked about Laramie, the county with the most people:

> [T]he five districts varied in population from 10,418 to 15,907 but the district having a population of 15,907 included Warren Air Force Base personnel, many of whom did not vote, and its voting population is fairly close to that of the other districts. In addition, the two smallest districts are those in which has occurred the largest population increase since 1960.

Greene noted that SF 136 reapportioned the House as well as the Senate. It kept House seats at 61 and only changed House districts in the sub-districted senate districts in five of the counties. He acknowledged the three Federal Judges found the 1963 House reapportionment constitutional, but "...the issue of whether the failure to sub-district deprives minority groups of representation was not before the Court."

The Republicans, through Greene, expressed their disdain and distress over the elimination of county election districts and their unhappiness over the Court telling them what to do. Greene speech was confusing and difficult to understand—a deliberate obfuscation of the issue.

Wyoming's knowledgeable citizens disputed Greene's claim that SF 136's senate districts contained "equal population" because Greene's "equal population" counted the number of adults voting in a previous election in three counties and the number of people living in census tracts in the remaining 18 counties. Also, it was curious that Greene extolled the merits of SF 136 when earlier 13 senators decided it was flawed, voted no and killed the Senate File.

ELMER KINNAMAN FOR THE DEMOCRATS

Senior Elections Committee Democrat and Senate Minority Leader Elmer Kinnaman of Carbon spoke for the Senate and House Democrats. Kinnaman claimed HB 50 was "far superior" to SF 136 in three major ways: simplicity, practicality and probable constitutionality. He stated

> HB 50 is simple in design, operation and result.... [It] does not disturb the present makeup of the House.... [It] makes a few basic county combinations for Senate reapportionment—nothing more. The county concept as a basis for reapportionment ... is preserved insofar as possible.... It will not be necessary to re-do ... present precinct(s).... It will be unnecessary to split counties or to have the unusual and almost impossible situation whereby one Senator represents two separate counties, each ... being ... represented by their own Senator.[115] A glance at a map [of] the zig-zag district boundaries ... [in] SF 136 ... [and the] overlapping districts ... emphasize the complexity [and] the absurdity of the plan.... [T]he simplicity of the HB 50 plan establishes its superiority.

Kinnaman claimed that the simplicity of HB 50 attested to its practicality. The needed "election machinery" already existed. Those elected knew "the interests they represented." He claimed the quality of candidates running for office will be maintained because multiple candidates can be elected, "even if they lived on the same block" whereas with sub-districts candidates with "perhaps lower quality and ability would be elected from another sub-district."

He claimed HB 50 did not "require reference to complex enumeration district maps reflecting a crazy quilt pattern." He said SF 136 combined more counties than did HB 50 and "SF 136 provided overlapping or dual or floating representation. It requires sub-districting. It affects two houses instead of one. Its comparative impracticality is obvious."

As for probable constitutionality, Kinnaman chided the Republicans saying, "it is never good fashion to attempt to predict court results," but he anticipated it was "reasonable" for

---

[115] Here he is referring to the floterial districts created in SF 136 for Carbon-Sweetwater and counties in the Big Horn Basin.

the Court to be fair and just. He asserted the Court would prefer "simplicity to complexity, practicality to impracticality."

Kinnaman and the Democrats justified the absence of mathematical equality by quoting from *Reynolds v. Sims*.[116]

Mathematical exactness or precision is hardly a workable constitutional requirement. ... What is marginally permissible in one state may be unsatisfactory in another. ... So long as the divergences [that] form a strict population standard are based on legitimate considerations incident to the effectuation of a rational state policy, some deviations from the equal population principle are constitutionally permissible. ... [In] the reapportionment of seats in either or both ... houses of a bicameral state legislature.

The Democrats thought it was hard to see how anyone could consider HB 50 unconstitutional. Granted it did not reach mathematical exactness but the divergences were based on Wyoming's historical concept of county election districts. The Court told them to ignore Wyoming's constitutional requirement of counties as election districts and one senator per county. The Court had been conservative in not specifying county combinations, the splitting of counties or sub-districting. So the Democrats were being conservative too in HB 50 by complying with the Court's directive. But unlike SF 136 "...it does not saddle up and ride off into all directions at the same time."

Kinnaman said the 1965 reapportioning and the court's directives were just the beginning of a new, dynamic process to gain equal representation. They anticipated that "in a few more years" more solid guidelines would be developed on "what can and can not be done."

HB 50 was written to "do what must be done" but time would "dictate how much further to go." They saw SF 136 as a law that committed Wyoming to "a course of action that denies the possibility of a cautious but sure evolution" where Wyoming could benefit from the "mistakes of others and the experience of time."

The Democrats defended the extremes in Park and Hot Springs counties. A ratio of 2.65:1 is a "vast improvement" over 1963's law of 20:1 and was nearly equal to the Court's approved ratio of 2.6:1 between Teton and Weston's House seats.

---

[116] *Reynolds v. Sims*, 377 U.S. 533 (1964).

On the frequency of reapportioning, the Democrats noted that by 1965 the 1960 census was outdated and SF 136 began with old numbers. They asserted if a "big change was going to come" it could wait until after the 1970 census.

Again and again in Kinnaman's statement the Democrats took exception to the Republicans allegation that SF 136 carried the "probability of constitutionality" and HB 50 carried the "probability of unconstitutionality." The Democrats thought it was the other way around.

But what really got the Democrats "lathered-up" was the Republicans denial of gerrymandering in SF 136. They pointed to the map of SF 136 with its

> long and slender … irregular chunks … or protruding, irregular arms and hooks … [with] great areas of [a] city detached from normal city districts and put into districts [with] the rest of the county.

The Democrats took exception to the Republican argument that districting should reflect national origin, calling that argument a fallacy. There was "considerable trouble" elsewhere in the nation where efforts were made to distinguish between "races … national origin … minority groups." They thought this distinction was not needed in Wyoming.

> To paternalistically say to any race or national origin group that we will district so that they will have an "area of their own" is to insult them and is contrary to our American principles and ideals. All barriers, all demarcations, all separations are things long past. Reapportionment is based on the principle of equality. It should not be sullied by an un-American suggestion that it be geared to distinctions based on race, on national origin, or on so-called minority groups. In *Wright v. Rockefeller* the Supreme Court indicated that "legislative contrivance" to segregate on the basis of race or place of origin would make an apportionment unconstitutional.[117]

The last thing the Democrats found wrong with SF 136 was the amendment concerning the relative size of the two chambers. It was in violation of the Wyoming Constitution and in violation of the equal vote decisions of the Supreme Court. In the Democrats view HB 50 was, "fair, just and equitable."

---

[117] *Wright v. Rockefeller*, 376 U.S. 52.

It is simple; it is practical. It is constitutional. In the minds of some, the only real objection to it is that it was sponsored and introduced by Democrats and that it was conceived in and passed by a Democratic House. Partisanship is necessary and often desirable, but to allow it to impede the enactment of a necessary, fair, simple, practical and legal measure, would be a misuse of true partisanship.

Thus Kinnaman proclaimed the constitutionality of HB 50. The absence of the new senate reapportionment demanded by the Court wasn't the fault of Democrats.

The talk ended. The remaining enrolled acts were signed. The Senate leadership retained their seats. The 38th Legislature failed to reapportion the Senate. The Session adjourned *Sine Die* on February 20th, 1965.

And Wyoming's reapportionment problem returned to Federal Court.

7

The Court Reapportions

Because the Court retained jurisdiction to allow injunctive and affirmative relief to plaintiffs if the Wyoming legislature failed to apportion the senate before the 1966 elections, re-apportionment now was the job of Federal Judges Pickett, Kerr, Daughery and their staffs. The pretrial conference was on August 31, 1965.

The same plaintiffs, defendants and their attorneys were in attendance. They were joined by interveners: William H. Harrison, Kenneth Youtz, Wilbur Mead, Lewis F. Hanson and Carl Emerich. Their attorneys were Paul B. Godfrey and Arthur Kline. The plaintiff's attorneys were Democrats. The rest of the attorneys were Republicans.

All parties agreed that, "No additional evidence was necessary," that the Court did find "invidious discrimination" in the legislature's 1963 distribution of Senate seats and did not find "invidious discrimination" in the 1963 distribution of House seats. They also agreed that according to the Court's decree the requirement in Article III, Section 3 of a House and a Senate seat for each county, "...is ineffective and is not to be considered when determination is made of the reapportionment of the Wyoming state senate...."[118]

All parties agreed to keep the senate at 30 seats. This fit nicely within the constitutional mandate for the House never to be less than one twice the size of the Senate.[119] The Court staff

---

[118] *Schaefer v. Thomson,* 251 F. Supp. 450 (1965).

[119] Wyoming Constitution, Article III, Section 3.

divided the 330,066 statewide population by 30, and declared a ratio of senators to residents of 11,500:1.

The Federal Judges found the solution to be simply a matter of mathematics and geography. Just combine contiguous over-represented counties with small populations with their neighboring counties with small populations into senate election districts with one senator each. The Judges were unencumbered by considerations of regional political power.

The Republican leadership of the 38th Legislature had been *very encumbered* with considerations of political power. They found it impossible to agree on any legislation—forget about "satisfactory to the Court"! Too many senate leaders feared their senate seats, like Rudy Anselmi's, were about to evaporate into thin air through a change in the law.

The staff and Judges wrestled with the geography problem in the Old Utah/Idaho Territories where people were scarce. The area encompassed roughly 210 north-south miles—from Colorado to Yellowstone and roughly an equal number of east-west miles from the crest of the Wind River Mountains in Sublette, across all of Lincoln to the Idaho border.

The federal government owned most of this land but there were state-owned lands too. This area included Wyoming's highest mountains and some of its vast desert. There were sagebrush plains and occasional fertile valleys. Private land ownership was confined to a few small towns, the deeded acres of large cattle ranches, dairy farms with irrigated pastures in the Star Valley, coalmines near Kemmerer and the checkerboard along the Union Pacific.[120]

Tourism was dominate in Teton; huge ranches with few deeded but many leased acres were characteristic of Sublette. Lincoln had coalmines and Uinta had the Union Pacific Railway. Dairy cattle, fledgling manufacturing and tourism were typical in the Star Valley in the north end of Lincoln. When the staff for the Court did their counting, there was more livestock in Old Utah/Idaho Territory than people.

So the Court decided to divide Lincoln County into north and south sections at the township line common to Townships 26 and 27 North, 6th Principal Meridian, Wyoming. This existing,

---

[120] The "checkerboard" of the Union Pacific Railroad refers to every other section of land for 20 miles on each side of the right-of-way given to Union Pacific by the Congress when the first transcontinental railway was built.

accepted, uncontested, easily understood survey demarcation avoided all the dire consequences prophesied by opponents of population-based apportionment. The staff created a Teton-Sublette-North Lincoln senate district with a population of 11,234 and a Uinta-South Lincoln senate district with a population of 12,097. It was equal representation cleanly achieved.

The old Utah/Idaho Territory counties lost two senate seats—the question was which two! Was one lost seat to be that of Public-Lands-Irrigation-Agriculture chair Donald Jewett of Sublette or the seat held by Game and Fish chair Harry C. Barker Jr. of Teton? Was the seat of Democrat J.W. Myers of Uinta to be lost or the seat of Democrat Carl Robinson of Lincoln?

In their Opinion of October 8, 1965, the Court wasn't impressed with the Senate's promotion of SF 95 and SF 136. They didn't think either plan was feasible because,

> [The plans] were too complex. ... Defendant's proposed plans do not contain a clear, concise, convenient or equitable method of outlining the districts.[121]

The intervenors, representing rural Laramie County residents, were in Court to argue for sub-districting. But the Court wasn't impressed with their arguments either. They said the intervenors were, "unable to cite any authorities, nor have we been able to find any, directing the federal courts to sub-district the multi-member districts."

The calculations in the Court's plan met the standards in *Reynolds v. Sims*,[122] where the vote of any citizen is approximately equal in weight to that of any other citizen in the State.

The Court's apportioning changed the voting strength ratio from 20:1 down to 2.08:1. Their goal was not to intrude into the affairs of the legislature but to

> formulate a basic pattern of equity in the right of suffrage to guide the state legislature in its future periodic readjustments and revisions as they become necessary to accommodate population shifts and growth.

---

[121] *Schaefer v. Thomson*, 251 F. Supp. 450 (1965) at 453.

[122] *Reynolds v. Sims*, 377 U.S. 533, 579, 84 S, Ct 1362, 1390m 12 L.Ed.2d 506.

TABLE 21
1965 Senate Reapportionment Combined Counties

Election District	Population	Seats in HB 50	Seats in Court Apportionment
Campbell-Johnson	11,336	1	1
Converse-Niobrara	10,116	1	1
Crook-Weston	12,620	1	1
Hot Springs-Fremont	35,533	Not Applicable	3
Sublette-Teton	6,540	1	Not Applicable
Sublette-Teton-North Lincoln	11,245	Not Applicable	1
Uinta-South Lincoln	12,097	Not Applicable	1

The Court's apportionment of the Senate mirrored the combinations in the Democrats HB 50 for six counties—Campbell-Johnson, Converse-Niobrara, Crook-Weston—and nearly so for Teton-Sublette (Table 21).

They combined Fremont and Hot Springs. Hot Springs did not have enough people for a senator. Fremont did not have enough for a third senator. The counties were contiguous. Their shared community of interest centered on the Native American population and on ranching, tourism and irrigated lands. They even shared the river that changed its name during its progress through the canyon: the Wind River when it left Fremont and the Big Horn River when it arrived in Hot Springs. To the Court the Fremont/Hot Springs district looked like a good fit.

Two of the remaining small counties retained their senators—Platte and Washakie. Their populations were near the bottom of the allowed "major fraction thereof" but not far enough down to do major damage to the voting strength ratio. Here the Court's and the Democrat's HB 50 allocation of senate seats were identical. Park County fared better in the Court's reapportionment (two seats) than it did with HB 50 (one seat).

For the remaining eight counties the Court's assignment of seats was identical to the Democrats in HB 50 (Table 22).

The constitutionality of the Democrats HB 50 became evident when it was compared to the apportioning done by the Court. This was a bitter pill to swallow for many Wyoming Republicans. However, Laramie County and Natrona Republicans were happy because each county got additional seats in recognition of its large populations.

TABLE 22
1965 Senate Court Reapportionment Identical to HB 50

Election District	1960 Federal Census	Seats in HB 50	Seats in Court Apportionment
Albany	21,290	2	2
Big Horn	11,898	1	1
Carbon	14,937	1	1
Goshen	11,941	1	1
Laramie	60,149	5	5
Natrona	49,623	4	4
Sheridan	18,989	2	2
Sweetwater	17,920	2	2

With the Court's reapportionment the political power shifted away from the northern and central regions to the southern region (Table 23).

TABLE 23
1965 Court-Ordered Senate Voting Strength
and Statewide Population – 1960 Census

	Southern Region	Central Region	Northern Region
Voting Strength	41%	31%	28%
Statewide Population	43%	32%	25%

Opponents of change worried over how the transition to combined-county senate districts was to be accomplished. Half the senators still had two years to serve in their terms.[123] The Court's solution in 1965 was simple. It copied from the 1891 transition of Territory Council seats to State Senate seats by putting all senate seats on the ballot in 1966.

The Court directed the Senate Chief Clerk, on January 10th, to place slips of paper in a hat with "two years" or "four years" written on each. Then each newly elected senator was to draw from the hat either a "short term" or a "long term."

The Judges knew well to whom they addressed their Findings of Fact and Conclusions of Law. They clearly stated that Article III, Section 3 of Wyoming's Constitution was "invidious discrimination" in its requirement that each county be a senatorial district. They ruled that Chapter 22 of the 1963 Session Laws pertaining to senate reapportionment was unconstitutional and void. They directed that no attempt be made to hold an election in accordance with Chapter 22 and that all future elections were to be conducted in accordance with this Opinion.

They ruled that the intervenors "take nothing by their complaint."

Nothing in the Court's Opinion was to "have retroactive effect" on any laws passed by the 38th Legislature, nor any effect on the terms of any sitting senators. All senate terms were to begin anew in January 1967.

Fremont liked having three senators, while Hot Springs felt abandoned. Fremont's population outnumbered Hot Springs' by a factor of 4:1. In the subsequent elections—1966, 1968, and 1970—all persons chosen for that senate seat were from Fremont. None were from Hot Springs. There was no senator from Hot Springs after the Court's reapportioning when James (Don) Brunk, chairman of two committees in 1965, left the legislature.

Crook's Leslie W. Hauber was gone. Earl Christensen of Weston won the Crook-Weston senate district.

In the Campbell-Johnson district, Democrat Otis Wright of Campbell, appointed to the 38th Session, did not return. R. L. Greene of Johnson, veteran legislator, former Senate President,

---

[123] In 1911, when six new counties were created, it took three election cycles before the necessary adjustments were completed.

1963 Elections Committee chair and Rules Committee member, called it quits.

In Converse-Niobrara, 1963 Revenue Chairman Charles Irwin of Converse County left, as did Senate President Andrew McMaster of Niobrara.

Democrat J. W. Myers of Uinta and Sublette's Don Jewett, the Public-Lands-Irrigation-Agriculture chair, did return. Democrat Carl Robinson of South Lincoln and Teton's Harry C. Barker Jr., chair of Game-Fish did not.

Of the 30 senators seated in January 1967, 11 were returnees (six Republicans and five Democrats), six switched from the House to the Senate and 13 were new legislators.

Under Senate President Dick Jones of Park County the Republicans again controlled the Senate in 1967. But Jones had only Flitner of Big Horn, Madsen of Sheridan, Tobin of Natrona, Jewett of Sublette and Christensen of Weston with senate experience to help him wield political power for the agriculture/mineral interests.

The returning Democrats were: Minority Leader Elmer Kinnaman of Carbon, J. W. Myers of Uinta, Elmer Halseth of Sweetwater, William A. Norris Jr. of Laramie County and Ed Kendig of Platte. The institutional memory of Republicans and Democrats was nearly equal.

In 1965, for the first time, "the restless fuss-making citizens" won.

8

THE 1970'S

It was a "no growth" time—a time of relative quiet. The 1970 Federal Census found only 2,350 more people, or .007%, than were counted in 1960. Some counties gained in population, some lost, some stayed essentially the same. Residents continued to shift from rural to urban—to 60.5% urban in 1970, up 3.7% from 1960. The northern-region representatives and their mineral-lobby friends were pleased with "no growth" and with the way the legislative and executive branches conducted their affairs.

For more than a decade tax revenues were too slim to cover all the requests for funds for highway construction, public schools, higher education (there were now seven community colleges and one university), and the rising demands for state dollars to match federal dollars for social programs. The Legislature was scrambling for money—without raising taxes.

The actual expenditures for state government were relatively small. Due to the way the legislature conducted its business, the public was denied useful information, not only on who voted aye or no on specific items in the budget bills, but the line-items themselves were incomplete and uninformative.

The budget bill adopted in 1969[124] for the first two years of the 1970's was eight pages long and contained 64 sections—from the Governor and the Executive Branch through all the

---

[124] The previous 1967 budget bill had the same format, just different numbers.

State District Courts and the State Supreme Court. The line-item listings were as follows: [125]

Contingent, Secretary of State	$166,765
Contingent, Superintendent of Public Instruction	$700,000
Contingent, Education of Handicapped Children	$45,000
Contingent, Library Services for the Blind	$7,101
Contingent, Future Farmers of America	$4,045
Contingent, Future Homemakers of America	$1,800
Contingent, Vocational Education	$100,000
Contingent, Vocational Rehabilitation	$177,745
Contingent, Services for the Blind	$160,000
Contingent, University of Wyoming	$25,796,987

By 1969 federal funds were part of many different programs, but nowhere in Chapter 201 were federal funds identified as the source of funding. No total of any amount of money appeared anywhere to show what the legislature approved. Nor was there a total number of employees listed in any agency.

Appropriations were the business of the Ways and Means Committee working in "the Hole,"[126] where interested citizens were barred from observing the committee's proceedings. There was no space for a "press table" for the media. No one except committee members heard the agency heads make their presentations or heard the debate of the committee. No one observed the voting. The public and other legislators just had to "trust" the Ways and Means Committee.

When "fuss-making" citizens objected to the secrecy surrounding the spending of taxpayer's money, they were told the 40-day session was not long enough for others to participate. When the legislature was not in session, Governors Hansen and Hathaway, according to tradition, consulted with Ways/Means chairmen about moving money from here to there or there to

---

[125] Chapter 201 Wyoming Session Laws 1969, Section 45, 1970-1971.

[126] The Ways and Means Committee used the Governor's Conference Room during the session. It was called "The Hole" because of cramped quarters for committee members, governor's staff, House and Senate staff, those testifying before the committee. Space was also scarce for everyone's budget books and papers.

here as they might agree. "Adjustments" were made within the total appropriation in the budget bill—however much that was!

The public considered these practices to be "a shell game." The executive branch of government was an octopus with long tentacles and various centers of power. Agency heads were not accountable to the Governor because once Senate confirmation was achieved they had the job unless they committed malfeasance in office. The Governor's only removal power was his ability to "jaw-bone" those he asked to leave. Agency heads could and did decline to resign.

The Wyoming League of Women Voters shared the concerns over the entrenched power of northern and central rancher/ mineral interests. One day in 1971 the Wyoming League of Women Voters appeared to testify before a Senate Committee. The five men on the committee met in the Senate's First Aid room. They sat on wooden chairs haphazardly placed among the wheeled white metal medical stands, the examining table and multiple goose-necked lamps. Committee papers were strewn about. The committee secretary and her papers were packed into a corner.

The League ladies[127] had to wait in the hall until their bill was "up for consideration," that is, placed before the committee chairman. Then they were invited into the First Aid room (adding to the congestion) and gave their testimony. The men listened. The chairman thanked them for coming. Then there was a pause. The chairman waited for the ladies to leave. But, once in the room, the ladies wanted to stay and observe the handling of the remaining bills before the committee. They were politely—but firmly—told to leave. In 1971 Senate Committees were not open to the public.

In 1971 Governor Hathaway began to make changes. He led the creation of the Department of Administration and Fiscal Control designed to bring order and accountability into state affairs. He "beefed up" the computer services division with $2,200,000 new money in addition to their regular budget of $1,073,383. In 1973 he successfully led the creation of the Department of Revenue and Taxation, fashioned from unconnected and leaderless former "offices" charged with collecting

---

[127] Matilda Hansen was one of the "three league ladies." That year she held the "State Government" portfolio for the State League. Jane Maxwell of Cheyenne, another of the "three league ladies" was then State Chair of the Wyoming League of Women voters.

taxes due the state. With the public demanding more accountability, he got the money to implement his proposals.

The Ways and Means Committee responded to the public need for more information. The 1971 budget bill contained 19 pages, with major expenditure categories listed for each agency. The Department of Education had 12 categories, total authorized expenditure of $12,391,984 and 165 employees. The University of Wyoming had 25 categories, total authorized expenditure of $54,414,788 and 3,634 employees.

While the public welcomed these changes, they were not satisfied. If more time was an essential solution to Wyoming's "bad" fiscal practices, they wanted longer, annual, legislative sessions.

Therefore, the 1971 legislature sent the voters a constitutional amendment, to be voted on in November 1972, for annual sessions of 60 legislative working days a biennium. The amendment passed. The vote was close. It needed 75,771 votes to be a "majority of those voting" in that election. There were 76,170 yes votes. The margin of acceptance came from southern-region counties. Annual sessions were "proclaimed in effect" December 12, 1972.[128]

By the mid 1970's legislators began to make long-needed improvements of their own. Too often committee chairmen were capricious on whether their meetings were closed or open and who was welcome and who was not.

For decades law firms or self-proclaimed bill-drafters prepared bills for introduction. In the late 1960's a legislative office was created to assist legislators. It soon became a "hand-maiden" of the Republican leadership. Democrats and rank-and-file Republicans wanted it gone.

In 1971, the non-partisan Legislative Service Office was created. All bill drafting became the responsibility of the new office. Legislators, through the LSO, were paid salary, per diem and mileage for "official" out-of-session meetings. Lawyer Ralph Thomas of Fremont County was the first Director of the LSO.

By 1975, legislative committees were open to the public. The lobbyists for Wyoming's League of Women Voters continued to watch their legislators. One particularly galling experience was during consideration of a utility bill. In the committee room the League ladies had to stand with their backs

---

[128] Wyoming Constitution, Article III, Section 6.

to the wall while lobbyists for Utah Power and Light sat at the table with committee members—taking part in "mark up" of the bill.

The legislature "claimed" the second and third floors of the Capitol as "theirs" and "off-limits" for the Governor or any of his agencies to use—even if rooms were empty when the legislature was not in session. House, Senate and Joint Rules were changed. Harold Hellbaum of Platte and Nels Smith of Crook were instrumental in achieving these and other improvements.[129]

THE POPULATION SHIFTS

Despite "no growth" in statewide population there were significant shifts among the counties (Table 24). The largest population increase, 121%, was in Campbell County. Workers came to scoop up low sulfur coal as the electricity generating plants changed their "mix" of coal to met new clean air standards.

TABLE 24
Population Shifts within the Northern Region
1970 Federal Census

County	1970 Federal Census	Change Since 1960	Percent of Change
Big Horn	10,202	(1,696)	–14%
Campbell	12,957	7,096	+121%
Crook	4,535	(156)	–3%
Hot Springs	952	(1,413)	–22%
Johnson	5,587	112	+2%
Park	17,752	878	+5%
Sheridan	17,852	(1,137)	–6%
Teton	4,823	1,761	+58%
Washakie	7,569	(1,314)	–15%

---

[129]Hellbaum was Speaker 1975-1976 and Smith 1977-1978. In the final remarks at the end of his term as Speaker, each man said he was proudest of the changes made in operations and policies during his career as legislators. At a February 17, 2000 ceremony in the House Chambers in recognition of former legislative leaders, each said again how important those changes had been to bring Wyoming out of its archaic legislative practices.

Teton's 58% increase was tied to tourism, especially the development of ski resorts. People had more discretionary incomes because the economy was better. The "car of choice" was a station wagon and the Interstate highways made travel pleasant. Parents had time for longer vacations. They hauled their baby-boomer school-age children to Yellowstone to see the geysers and to Grand Teton National Park to ski near the magnificent towering Tetons. The other northern-region counties experienced population decreases. The net gain for the region was only 5%.

Changes in the oil patch underlay the population exodus in the central region. "Traveling shoes" took 20% of Weston's population and 22% of Niobrara's. Improvements in the quality of work by the census takers on the Wind River Reservation accounted for some of Fremont's 8% increase (Table 25). The net gain in the central region was 0.5%.

TABLE 25
Population Shifts within the Central Region
1970 Federal Census

County	1970 Federal Census	Change Since 1960	Percent of Change
Converse	5,938	(428)	–4%
Fremont	28,352	2,184	+8%
Lincoln	8,640	(378)	–4%
Natrona	51,264	1,641	+3%
Niobrara	2,924	(826)	–22%
Sublette	3,755	(23)	Insignificant
Weston	6,307	(1,622)	20%

These shifts in population were indicators of stagnant economic activity. Wyoming was in the last days of a "bust" economy. The state was exporting its young non-workers. There were not enough jobs in the resource extractive nor in the fledging manufacturing industries. The number of workers able to be absorbed into public sector employment was limited.

In the southern region, Albany's 24% increase was tied to increasing enrollments and new emphasis on research at the University of Wyoming. Sweetwater gained a few people.

Otherwise, the southern region lost population—a 1.35% decrease (Table 26).

There wasn't enough room in the State for young adults to stay on irrigated acres or to remain as productive participants in ranching. Many left. The wages of those who remained were kept low.

TABLE 26
Population Shifts within the Southern Region
1970 Federal Census

County	1970 Federal Census	Change Since 1960	Percent Of Change
Albany	26,431	5,141	+24%
Carbon	13,354	(1,583)	−10%
Goshen	10,885	(1,056)	−9%
Laramie	56,360	(3,789)	−6%
Platte	6,486	(709)	−10%
Sweetwater	18,391	471	+3%
Uinta	7,100	(384)	−5%

Those who liked the status quo were content. The wind blew the native grasses on the sparsely populated plains. Cattle and wildlife roamed over thousands of mostly unfenced acres. The people who chaffed at the sleepy pace of these doldrums years were frustrated. With the new census in hand and time for another reapportionment, the 41st Legislature speedily "corrected" the flaws identified in the Court's 1965 mandate.

REAPPORTIONMENT—1971 VERSION

Leading the 41st were Pete Madsen of Sheridan as Senate President, Howard Flitner of Big Horn as Vice President, and Dick Tobin of Natrona as Majority Leader. These three men, along with Earl Christensen of Crook-Weston and Dick Jones of Park worked diligently to keep the political power firmly in their hands.[130]

---

[130] Pete Madsen had been Senate Vice President in 1965 and 1967, and Majority Leader in 1969, before becoming President in 1971. Earl Christensen had been Majority Leader in 1965 and 1967, before

They liked the senate ratio given them by the Court: 11,500:1—or major fraction thereof. They kept the number of seats at 30 from 16 senate districts. Then they "fixed" Hot Springs by separating it from Fremont and putting it with Washakie. This action freed up a senate seat badly needed in the Campbell/Johnson district because of Campbell's burgeoning population.

In 1965 the Court gave Platte and Goshen one senator each. In 1971 Goshen and Platte became one district with two senators. But Platte had enough people for a senator of its own under "major fraction thereof" (6,486). Goshen also had enough people for a senator of its own (10,885). An interesting game was being played. In the combined district both senators had to campaign in both counties. The combined number of Republicans in both counties was greater than the combined number of Democrats in both counties. This little maneuver assured no Democrat was ever to win a senate seat in that district.

This was the first Republican move to ensure Republican control of the senate since the Court changed the election districts. Republicans didn't want another Goshen John C. Simons. Especially, they wanted to get rid of Ed Kendig of Platte. Having successfully rid the legislature of Rudy Anselmi of Sweetwater by deleting his senate seat, they got rid of veteran and effective Democrat Ed Kendig of Platte County by diluting the Democratic vote in his senate district.[131] These were the only changes made in 1971 to the Court's 1965 apportionment. No changes were made to the South Lincoln-Uinta district and the North Lincoln-Sublette-Teton district.

The House had 44 Republicans and 17 Democrats. Ward G. Myers of Big Horn was Speaker. C.H. "Cliff" Davis of Campbell was Speaker Pro Tem. William F. Craft of Big Horn was Majority Leader.

The top six House majority leadership positions were held by five Republicans from the northern region and one from the central region (Dick Tobin of Natrona).

---

becoming President in 1969. Carbon County's Democrat, Elmer Kinnaman, was Minority Leader in 1965, 1967, 1969 and 1971.

[131] Ed Kendig's 14 years in the Senate ended January 3, 1977. He ran in 1976, won Platte County with 2,139 votes but lost the combined vote by 560 votes. The Republican strategy worked. For the remainder of the 20th century, no Democrat won a senate seat in the Goshen-Platte senatorial district.

Democratic leaders were Art Buck of Laramie County as Minority Leader and O.R. "Bud" Daily of Carbon as Minority Whip. They were southern-region men.

The last item in Governor Hathaway's Message to the Joint Session on January 13, 1971 was a challenge to his fellow Republicans to, "...reapportion the Legislative Body in a fair and equitable manner with the implementation of sub-districting in counties with more than 20,000 population."

But the legislators declined to respond to his challenge. Because the Court found no "invidious discrimination" in the previous reapportionment of the House, the leadership saw no reason to "march into the thicket" of sub-districting.

They increased the size of the House by one—to 62. The ratio was set at 5,300:1. Sheridan and Washakie each lost a seat; Albany and Campbell each gained a seat. A new seat became Natrona's 10th seat.

The legislative voting strength among the three regions was as equal as it was possible to get it using county election districts and "major fraction thereof" that allowed a possible deviation range of 98%. However, representation in the legislature was not based on regions but on counties. Therefore, the weight of legislator's votes continued to be distorted in relation to the number of residents in their district (Table 27).

TABLE 27
1971 Legislative Voting Strength
and Statewide Population—1970 Census[132]

	Southern Region		Central Region		Northern Region	
	Senate	House	Senate	House	Senate	House
Voting Strength	43%	42%	30%	32%	27%	24%
% Of State Population	43%		32%		24%	

The reapportionment bill was sent to the Governor for his signature on February 15th. It became Chapter 161 of the 1971

---

[132] With South Lincoln added to Uinta, one-half of Lincoln County's population was assigned to the southern region to reflect the population in southern Lincoln. Other senate districts of combined counties were within their respective regions.

92

Session Laws. The Legislature adjourned *Sine Die* on February 20th.

While the legislators may have been satisfied with their work, more "restless fuss-making citizens" were not. The population of Wyoming was not equally represented in the legislature. The parade of plaintiffs to Federal Court continued to challenge reapportionment.

COURT AGAIN

This time central-region legislators were the plaintiffs. The case was *Thompson v. Thomson.*[133] The lead plaintiff was Representative James Thompson of Niobrara. His predecessor, former Speaker Andrew McMaster, joined him, as did their legislator/neighbor Lee Grande Page who ranched in the north part of Platte. They were all Republicans.

The other central-region plaintiffs were five Fremont legislators and one citizen: Roy Peck, Don Lockhart, Percy Davis, Bob Novotny, Fremont Miller and Larry King.[134] Lockhart was a Democrat. The others were Republicans. In the 1971 session Percy Davis held the Fremont-Hot Springs seat that was abolished and transferred to the Campbell-Johnson district.

John Turner of Teton was the only northern-region plaintiff. Harold Meier of Fremont was attorney for the plaintiffs.

Thrya Thomson, as Secretary of State and chief elections officer, was again the lead defendant. The others were State Canvassing Board members: Governor Stan Hathaway, Treasurer Jim Griffith and Auditor Everett Copenhaver. Attorney General Clarence Brimmer defended the state.

Two of the 1965 Judges were on the 1972 Federal Panel: Circuit Judge Pickett and District Judge Kerr. New to the case was District Judge Templar.[135]

The plaintiffs challenged the constitutionality of the 1971 Law on the bases of invidious discrimination in both the Senate and the House and violation of the equal protection clause of the Fourteenth Amendment to the United States Constitution.

---

[133] *Thompson v. Thomson,* 344 F. Supp. 1378 (1972).

[134] Davis, Miller and Novotny were senators. Representatives were Lockhart, Meier, Peck, Turner and Page.

[135] No. 5651 Civil, June 23, 1972.

Validity of the Court's 1965 Plan was established when it was approved by the United States Supreme Court.

The Court made short shrift of the invidious discrimination claim for the House.[136]

> We are of the opinion that the reapportionment of the House by the 1971 Act does not constitute invidious discrimination for the reason that the 1963 reapportionment of the House was not substantially altered and, therefore, the 1971 Act does not abridge the equal protection clause of the Fourteenth Amendment of the United States Constitution.

The Court looked at the charge of invidious discrimination for the Senate more carefully. They asked whether or not the 1971 changes to its 1965 Plan were great enough to cause concern.

They concluded the changes were not significant because their 1965 work had no invidious discrimination, therefore, there was none in 1971. Further, there was no violation of the equal protection clause of the Fourteenth Amendment because the only rearrangements had been to four senate districts.

The Court noted that the legislature used the 1970 Federal Census, which showed a .007% increase in the state's population. They agreed the population increase in Campbell had to be addressed by adding another Senate seat to Campbell-Johnson Senate district. It was reasonable to put Hot Springs with Washakie, using the seat from Fremont-Hot Springs.

They agreed with keeping the Senate at 30 seats. Regarding Fremont's Senate district with two senators, they found that "…[a]lthough this caused Fremont to be under-represented, this will be offset in time since its population is on the increase."[137]

The Court did not find fault with reducing the number of Senate districts from 17 to 16. They supported combining Goshen and Platte, "…since Goshen County was entitled to more than one Senator and Platte was entitled to less than one. By combining these two Districts the Legislature was able to offset the existing malapportionment." After referring to the practical impossibility of districts being the same size as discussed in *Reynolds v. Sims* they concluded, "…it is apparent on its face that the 1971 Act only made changes that reflect population

---

[136] *Thompson v. Thomson* 344 F. Supp.1378 (1972) at 1380.
[137] Ibid.

fluctuations. That is what this Court in its decision in 1965 intended the legislature to do...."[138]

The Court ruled the 1971 Act was constitutional. The Court dismissed the complaint and the cause. Then it directed the parties to pay their own costs.

The validity of some of the claims in the Court's Opinion, was open to question. First, the assessment of the Goshen-Platte Senatorial district was wrong. Goshen's 10,885 people did not entitle them to "one more senator" when the ratio was 11,500:1. And Platte's 6,486 people did entitle them to a senator. With words that obscured the facts, Wyoming's Federal Judges acquiesced to the Republican strategy to get rid of Ed Kendig.

James Thompson and Andrew McMaster of Niobrara saw the handwriting on the wall. They had lost "their" senator and they stood to lose "their" House member if or when representation was based on population. Niobrara's citizens wanted Thompson to "do everything" to prevent this outcome. John Turner, like Thompson and McMaster, represented a county with low population and faced the probability of losing his House seat.

Fremont legislators lost "their" third senate seat during the 1971 reapportionment. They concluded they were underrepresented and howled invidious discrimination.

EMERGING NATIONAL CASE LAW

After *Baker v. Carr*, a series of cases were presented to the nation's highest court seeking clarification of many elements of reapportioning, such as how much variation was acceptable to achieve equal representation. What was not acceptable was stated in *Reynolds v. Sims* (1964): "...any reapportioning containing gross disparities in population is unconstitutional per se and cannot be justified...."[139]

The five unacceptable justifications listed in *Reynolds* for gross differences in legislative representation were:

---

[138] Ibid at 1381.

[139] *Reynolds v. Sims,* 377 U.S. 533 (1964).

1. Any state's constitutional amendment that allowed any basis for apportioning other than population.[140]
2. Apportioning one chamber based on population and the other based on something else.
3. No state was to liken themselves to the United States Senate and the United States House where one was based on population and the other was not.
4. No state was to rely on what had been acceptable when they joined the Union.[141]
5. Arguments relating to differences in the U.S. electoral college cannot be used as a precedent for states to have differences between their chambers.

Reynolds did not give specific percentages of acceptable deviation range(s). That came in 1973 in *Mahan v. Howell*,[142] where the United States Supreme Court ruled that 16.4% was acceptable in the Virginia General Assembly. "[T]he reapportionment was shown by "uncontradicted" evidence to produce the minimum deviation possible while keeping political subdivisions intact."[143]

> *Mahan* clarified—somewhat—the rational state policy issue: [if all divergences are] unavoidably caused by conditions incident to a rational state policy a total maximum deviation above approximately 16.5% may be intolerable and unconstitutional per se."[144]

Thus *Mahan* set the ceiling for the acceptable deviation range to achieve equal representation under the equal protection clause of the Fourteenth Amendment. The *Mahan v. Howell* Opinion came the year after Pickett, Kerr and Templar ruled in *Thompson v. Thomson.*

Two other 1973 cases pushed the floor for the acceptable deviation range to below 10%. *Gaffney v. Cummings*[145] was a Connecticut legislative reapportionment case where the average deviation was 1.9% and the median deviation was 1.8%. Dense concentrations of population made these numbers workable.

---

[140] This closed the door to any new Wyoming constitutional amendment that distributed legislative seats on any grounds except population.

[141] That was then—this is now.

[142] *Mahan v. Howell* 410 U.S. 315 (1973).

[143] Ibid.

[144] Ibid.

[145] Ibid. at 640.

The other 1973 case was about districts for the Texas House of Representatives. In *White v. Regester* the deviation range was 1.82%.[146] This case took away the legitimacy of Wyoming Republican argument that open spaces worked against the possibility of any small deviation range. Wyoming's wide spaces were no different than those in Texas.

The National Conference of State Legislatures, other legislators and many legal scholars engaged in lively debate in their shared search for definitive parameters on equal representation.

However, this debate was an unintelligible foreign language to Wyoming's Republicans who clearly held political power. It was as if a moat surrounded Wyoming—keeping out ideas that were anathema to the majority in the majority party.

---

[146] Ibid.

9

Politics in the 1970's

When the dust settled after Pickett, Kerr and Templar dismissed *Thompson v. Thomson,* the politicians focused on the 1972 General Election. But the electorate did not tune in until after Labor Day.

It was a presidential year. Watergate happened but President Nixon succeeded in keeping that episode quiet during the 1972 campaign. Spiro Agnew was Nixon's running mate. George McGovern and Sargent Shriver were on the Democratic ticket for President and Vice President.

The United States Senate race in Wyoming brought four Democrats into the Primary: William Fritchell, Doyle Henry, Patrick Shanklin and Mike Vinich. Vinich beat *each* of his opponents by a 4 to 1 margin and faced the incumbent, former Governor Clifford Hansen, in the General Election.

Democrat Teno Roncalio was Wyoming's Congressman. The Republicans who wanted Roncalio's job were Bill Kidd, John Patton, Arthur Linde and Al Hamburg. That year Hamburg was a Republican. Bill Kidd won the Primary Election.

With significant races on both ballots, 37,072 Democrats, 54,695 Republicans and 1,237 unaffiliated voted in the Primary Elections. In the November election, 54% (151,541) of the statewide population voted. Nixon won. Hansen won. Roncalio won.[147]

---

[147] This was the closest race that year in the U.S. House. Roncalio won by 612 votes.

98

The constitutional amendment for annual legislative sessions, one of Governor Hathaway's proposals to improve government, was on the same ballot. Biennial sessions were changed to annual sessions and the number of days per biennium changed from 40 to 60. Statutory law provided for a Budget Session the second year of the biennium of about 1/3rd of the allowed days.

As the amendment was being written someone added "excluding Sundays." This addition prevented the legislature from doggedly staying in session deep into the wee hours of Sunday morning on the "last" day. Thus ended the practice of "stopping-the-clock" a few minutes before midnight Saturday and continue to work.[148]

In the 1972 November election the voter turnout in Campbell County was **slim.** Campbell's 1970 census found 12,957 people; yet only 3,836 voted. Granted persons under 18 years of age were counted in the census, but they were not 70% of the population. The Republican leadership was glad to have the additional reapportioned seats in recognition of their increased population, but if voting behavior was an indicator, the voters didn't care all that much.

Two years later, in the 1974 election, neither of Wyoming's U.S. Senate seats were on the ballot. In the House, the challenger to Teno Roncalio was Tom Stroock, a legislator from Natrona.

The most interesting race in 1974 was for the Governor's Office. Stan Hathaway did not seek a third term. Thereupon, political "heavies" from both parties filed their papers and paid their $100 to the Secretary of State.[149]

The Democrats who paid their filing fees were Senator Harry Leimback of Natrona and the veteran "pros" of legislative strategy, Ed Herschler of Lincoln and John Rooney of Laramie County. Ed Herschler won. Democrats cast 42,926 votes.

---

[148] During the 1977 Session significant severance taxes were placed on coal and other minerals. If any games had been played with the clock, the mineral interests were poised to challenge the legislation in court on the grounds of passage on a Sunday, which was contrary to the state's constitution.

[149] Election tradition in Wyoming allows any citizen who pays the filing fee to have his/her name on the ballot. The voters in the Primary election, not any political party, select the candidates for the November ballot.

The Republicans had a lively Primary. Those who wanted to be Governor were Clarence Brimmer of Laramie, who was Attorney General for *Thompson v. Thomson*; Dick Jones of Park, the politically savvy long-time chair of Ways and Means Committee who survived the Court's 1965 apportionment; Senator Roy Peck of Fremont, a plaintiff in *Thompson v. Thomson* (he and his brother Bob ran the *Riverton Ranger*—one of Wyoming's nine daily newspapers); and Senator Malcolm Wallop of Sheridan.[150] Dick Jones won. Republicans cast 59,884 votes (Table 28).

TABLE 28
1974 Primary Votes For Governor

Republican Candidates	Votes Received	% of Votes Cast
Dick Jones (won)	15,502	26.53%
Malcolm Wallop	14,688	25.14%
Roy Peck	14,217	24.34%
Clarence Brimmer	14,014	23.99%
Democratic Candidates		
Ed Herschler (won)	19, 997	46.6%
Harry Leimback	15,255	35.5%
John Rooney	7,674	17.9%

The State Canvassing Board certified the official returns. In Wallop's opinion, the race was "too close to call." He requested and paid for a recount. The recount did not find enough Wallop votes for him to win. Following good Wyoming tradition, he swallowed his disappointment. But he had "one more card" to play for this election.

After the November election, when Democrat Ed Herschler beat Dick Jones by 11.4 percentage points, Wallop went to the attic in the family home on his Sheridan ranch. There he dusted

---

[150] Later Harry Leimback became a District Judge in Natrona, John Rooney became Attorney General under Herschler then went to the Wyoming Supreme Court, Clarence Brimmer went to the Federal Bench in Wyoming, Malcolm Wallop became a United States Senator, Dick Jones retired from political office and Roy Peck died of a heart attack during a legislative session.

off and carefully packaged an ancient antiquated punch-key pull-lever adding machine—and sent it to Cheyenne as a Christmas present to Secretary of State and Chief Elections Officer Thrya Thomson.[151]

Ed Herschler's winning carried significant coattails for the legislative races. The State Canvassing Board certified 15 Democrats and 15 Republicans for the Senate.

Negotiations were needed to decide the leadership positions. Democrat J. W. Myers of South Lincoln-Uinta became President of the Senate; Ed Kendig of Platte was Vice President. Republican L. V. Stafford of Johnson-Campbell and Democrat David Hitchcock of Albany shared the responsibilities of Majority Leader. Each carried the title of "Floor Leader" and managed the General File on alternating days.

The State Canvassing Board certified 32 Republicans, 29 Democrats and one Independent for the House. With this slim majority the Republicans organized. Harold (Salty) Hellbaum of Platte was Speaker. Nels Smith of Crook was Speaker Pro Tem. Alan Simpson of Park was Majority Leader. Warren Morton of Natrona was Majority Whip.

For the Democrats Joe Stewart of Natrona was Minority Leader and Rodger McDaniel of Laramie County was Minority Whip. Bill Holland of Johnson—first a Republican then a Democrat—in 1975 was an Independent. His party caucuses were held on the House floor right in front of the Chief Clerk's desk.[152]

By 1975 the Legislative Service Office, under the direction of the Management Council, was fully operational. The chair of the Council was Nels Smith (R), the Vice-Chair was Senator David Hitchcock (D), and Joe Stewart (D) was Secretary. Other Democrats were: Senators O.R. "Bud" Daily of Carbon, Robert Johnson of Sweetwater, J.W. Myers of Uinta and Representative Don Scott of Goshen. The Republicans on the Council were Senator Percy Davis of Fremont and Representatives Alan Simpson of Park and Jack Sidi of Natrona.

---

[151] The legislature subsequently passed a law requiring an automatic state paid recount if there was a 1% or less difference between the top two contenders.

[152] One outcome of Bill Holland's Independent Caucus was the unanimous vote to have a container for facial tissues installed in each of the restrooms on the north side of the House Chambers.

Alan Simpson and Nels Smith were from the northern region. Jack Sidi, Joe Stewart and Percy Davis were central-region men. The remaining five were from the southern region. With Joe Stewart (central region) voting with the Democrats, political power shifted south.

The razor-thin majority in the House, the shared power in the Senate and the Management Council dominated by Democrats was a hard pill to swallow by those Republicans used to wielding unchecked political power. So they studied the Democrats—looking for someone(s) willing to switch parties.

They saw no one in the Senate amiable to their tactic. But they did talk Russell Zimmer of Goshen into leaving his House seat to run against Ed Kendig in the new Goshen-Platte district. Republicans needed an "experienced" campaigner because Kendig was well liked in both counties. But in 1976 the combined Republican votes in the Goshen-Platte Senate district were too great an obstacle for Kendig to overcome. The Madsen-Flitner-Jones strategy worked.[153]

Republicans also did not like Natrona's Senate delegation dominated by Democrats. So they recruited Deimer True—of True oil, gas, banking, trucking and ranching—to run for the Senate. The agriculture/mineral interests liked the idea of his moving from the House to the Senate. In 1976 he won Harry Leimback's vacated senate seat.

Senator-Pastor-Democrat Ray Nott from Park was also a thorn in the Republicans' side. Again, they raided the House for a popular legislator—this time Robert Frisby of Cody—to run against Nott in 1976.

With these three moves the Republicans succeeded in reducing the Democratic senate seats from 15 down to 12 for the 44th Session—a much better margin from the Republican point of view.

They were less successful in the House. Both parties targeted their usual plethora of races. In 13 races Democrats replaced Democrats or Republicans replaced Republicans. In six races there was a party switch. The switch from Republican to Democrat happened in Albany (out Joe Chasteen), in Niobrara (out Leslie ZumBrunnen) and in Platte (out Speaker Salty

---

[153] The allegation that Kendig lost because of the Democrats opposition to so-called "Right To Work" legislation is a smoke-screen Republicans have perpetuated to cover their fancy maneuvering to rid the Senate of as many Democrats as they possibly could.

Hellbaum).   The replacements were Dennis Stickley in Albany,[154] Ken Gropp in Niobrara and Doug Bryant in Platte.

The switch from Democrat to Republican happened in Laramie County (out Mary Kay Schwope), in Lincoln (out Nancy Peternal) and in Uinta (Hight Proffit to the Senate). The replacement Republicans were Bill McIlvain in Laramie,[155] Alan Stauffer in Lincoln and Ron Micheli in Uinta.

When the State Canvassing Board certified that election the count was the same as two years before: 32 Republicans, 29 Democrats and 1 Independent. For the Republicans' peace of mind this business of 32-29-1 had to stop. It was bad enough to have a Democrat sitting downstairs in the Governor's chair.

In 1976 Niobrara voters elected Ken Gropp as a Democrat. The House Democratic caucus gave him "tender-loving-care" with one of the much-sought-after seats on the Appropriations Committee. It was almost unheard of to allow a freshman legislator to sit on Appropriations. But Ken's presence as a Democrat was well appreciated in the (still) minority party.

The Democratic leaders considered the rest of the caucus members as "safe" and not vulnerable to party switching. Therefore, nothing "extra special" was done for them on committee assignments.

But the Republican political power brokers remembered that Gropp was a Democrat due to internecine Republican warfare in Niobrara County. In search of a "party switcher" they courted him. Political fences were mended. For the 1978 election he switched parties and was welcomed into the Republican caucus in 1979. His price for the switch: retention of his seat on House Appropriations. It was as unusual for a second-term Republican to be on the Appropriations Committee as it was for a first-term Democrat to be there.

After casting about for another Democrat, they found the receptive ears of Rory Cross of Converse. His father served in the Wyoming Legislature as a Democrat and never became Speaker. Rory's price for switching parties was committee chairmanship with the eventual possibility of becoming Speaker.

Rory was ambitious. In 1975 he was on Travel Committee. In 1977 he was on Agriculture and Transportation. In 1979 he

---

[154] Democrat Jim Boucher did not run for a 2nd term. The Democrats kept his seat and gained Chasteen's.

[155] The other Republican, Ellen Crowley, was returning. Republican Jim Van Velzor did not run again.

was welcomed into the Republican caucus with the chairmanship of Transportation. From 1981 through 1984 he chaired Agriculture, Public Lands and Water Resources. He went on Rules Committee when he became Majority Whip in 1985—the beginning step on his way to speakership. [156]

Besides the change to a Democrat for Governor, significant "upstairs" changes began in 1975. House Chambers and back rooms were restored and renovated to better use the space. The Speaker's podium was moved back against the east wall of the building to make more room for the chief clerk's and legislators' desks. Lighting was improved and a better sound system was installed. As the electronic age had arrived, an electrical outlet was available at each desk. The committees were reorganized to make them parallel in the House and Senate. [157]

Senator June Boyle, a legislator for 22 years, served both before and after the reorganization. She described the differences: [158]

> The bills began to reflect the wishes of a larger portion of the electorate.
>
> The legislators gained more control over budgeting.
>
> Those spending tax funds were held more accountable.
>
> State institutions were forced to account for *all* their spending.
>
> The mish-mash of everyone writing their own bills ended when the Legislative Service Office dictated the procedure and did the work.
>
> The title revision work brought order and understanding to archaic and confusing laws.
>
> The House and Senate staff was competently trained in the use of computers to handle the flow of words.

---

[156] Rory Cross became Speaker in 1991. What price may be paid for party switching? Cross had trouble getting bills passed where he was the prime sponsor. House Democrats discussed the situation. Democratic caucus decisions were never binding but the observation was made that if a Democrat really liked a Cross bill—go ahead and vote for it. But if a Democrat didn't really care about the issue in the bill, quiet unhappiness over his switching could be expressed by a "no" vote. Cross often "exclaimed" over his inability to get a bill passed. No one told him why—until now. Ken Gropp did not return in 1981.

[157] This, too, was part of the good work done by Speakers Harold "Salty" Hellbaum and Nels Smith during their early legislative years.

[158] Personal communication.

The Digests of the House and Senate Journals gave a
better accounting of votes and amendments.

Senate and House committee meetings were open to
any citizen interested in listening to any legislation
under consideration.

The executive branch was kicked out of all rooms on
the second and third floors of the Capitol.

Senate and House committees were *each* assigned
permanent rooms with off-session room
management under the control of the Legislative
Service Office.

Besides their desk on the Floor of their respective
chambers, each legislator was given one two-
drawer file cabinet placed in one of their
committee rooms.

Legislative salary increased from $15 to $30 per day.

The level of education of those elected increased. Everyone
had a high school diploma; many had university experience or
bachelor's degrees. Some had graduate or professional degrees.
Highly skilled union and non-union men and women brought
their valuable understanding and experiences as workers to the
debates.

There were seven women in the Legislature in 1975-76.
Esther Eskens of Big Horn, Matilda Hansen of Albany,
Catherine Parks of Campbell, Nancy Peternal of Lincoln, Mary
Kay Schwope of Laramie and Edness Kimball Wilkins of
Natrona were in the House; June Boyle of Albany was in the
Senate.[159]

A slightly embarrassing episode emerged at the 1975
Legislative Dinner of the Wyoming Association of General
Contractors—the first "fancy" dinner of the session. The
invitations specified "legislators only," meaning spouses were
not invited. So the men did not escort wives and the women did
not bring their husbands.

Not used to women legislators, the contractors allowed all
seven women legislators to sit at one table—without a contractor
host. The various speakers tried to be gracious to the women by
acknowledging, in an obvious appendage to their talk, "the wives
who were attending." After the third or fourth such reference the

---

[159] This was the most women legislators to serve in any session in
Wyoming's history prior to 1975. Verda James of Natrona had been
Speaker in 1969-70.

women-legislators had enough. At an appropriate time, almost in a chorus, they nearly shouted, "We are legislators."

Whereupon, the person speaking asked, "Are you wives?" The legislators replied, "Yes, but not to any of these men." The lobbyist for the Contractors realized the mistake. He shushed the speaker, then came to the table of women-legislators loaded with apologies. No lobbying group made this mistake again!

In 1979 sixteen women sat in the Legislature. June Boyle remained the lone woman in the Senate. Nancy Peternal was gone from the House, but the other five from 1975 were still there. Elizabeth Phelan returned in 1977.[160] Newcomers were Sheila Arnold and Patti MacMillan of Albany, Ellen Crowley, Cynthia Lummis, and Pat Tugman of Laramie, Nyla Murphy of Natrona, Peg Shreve of Park, Marlene Simons of Crook and Ann Strand of Sweetwater.[161]

The legislators in the late 1970's were men and women of stature in their home communities who were fully cognizant of the trust the public bestowed on them. The debates were lively but the underlying question was "Is what we are proposing in the best interests of the public?" The "watch dogging" legislators did of each other was conducted with dignity and respect, and it was consistent. Being a legislator then was a joy.

In the late 1970's Wyoming was booming with massive open-pit mines. Nuclear power plants were being built in other states and Wyoming's uranium mines were humming. The state became the leading exporter of low-sulfur coal.[162] Jim Bridger, Laramie River, Wyodak and Dave Johnson electrical power generating plants were fired with Wyoming's low sulfur coal. Electricity went "on the grid" to the rest of the nation. Extensive underground mining of trona[163] in the desert in Sweetwater

---

[160] She ran for State Treasurer in 1974. She served from 1971-1974 and 1977-1986.

[161] Ellen Crowley served from 1971-1974, then from 1979-1983. Sheila Arnold completed Dennis Stickley's term in 1978.

[162] Wyoming had more coal reserves than any other state. Only China had more coal than Wyoming.

[163] A sedimentary rock that consists of compounds of hydrous sodium-carbonate that include soda ash for the chemical industry, sodium-bicarbonate, sodium-carbonate monohydrate (water softener), and tripolyphosphate for use in many detergents. By the 1970's there was significant development of huge world-class deposits of trona in

became the major domestic source of soda ash for all commercial and industrial uses, including glass and detergents.

Governor Herschler's theme was "Economic Development On Our Terms." He wanted Wyoming—not the corporate boardrooms of America—to control its destiny.

For the first time *ever*, in 1974, severance taxes were collected[164] on the extraction of minerals—then followed by statutes passed under the leadership of Governor Herschler and those 32-29-1 Houses. The taxes were on oil, gas, coal, trona and other less abundant minerals.

Laws were passed on Industrial Siting that governed the placement of major mines or plants in Wyoming's sparsely settled counties. Better funding was given to the Department of Environmental Quality.

With severance taxes added to property taxes, the mineral industry was paying multiple millions into the state treasury. Rudy Anselmi[165] was granted "The Privilege of the Floor" to tell House members that the total statewide evaluation was expected to top $1 billion before Governor Herschler's first term ended.

After his tenure in the legislature, Rudy Anselmi was appointed to the State Board of Equalization. He possessed considerable understanding of the implications and ramifications of what was and what wasn't going on in the payment of taxes on Wyoming's extractive resources. The "minerals folks" didn't like the proximity of his expertise and talked the 1973 Session into eliminating the three-man board, instituting instead one "tax czar." This turned out to be a bad idea. In 1975 the three-man Board returned and Rudy returned as one of the three.

Jim Griffith, in his capacity as State Auditor, noted discrepancies in the reports on extractive resource production to the Oil and Gas Commission, to the Federal Mineral Royalty management people and reports to his office. His leadership was the impetus for multiple audits of the extractive resource industry both under the aegis of the State and of Wyoming's mineral-rich counties.

In the summer of 1978, the members of the Management Council discussed establishing the capacity to audit the Medicaid

---

Sweetwater County west of Green River, mined by underground mining techniques.

[164] Governor Hathaway succeeded in getting legislation passed to put the severance tax amendment on the ballot.

[165] Chairman of the three-member Wyoming Tax Commission.

and Aid to Families With Dependent Children programs. The "Feds" under President Carter were pushing the states hard to address the problem of fraud in these and other federal-state matching funds programs in the Departments of Health and Human Services.

Initially, the Management Council thought auditing these programs to go after fraud was a good idea. They were about to vote approval when Warren Morton said, "If we have in place the capacity to audit the massive Medicare, AFDC and Food Stamp programs we will have the capacity to audit mineral taxation." No one said anything more about auditing "people programs." Management Council moved to the next item on the agenda. Auditing of Wyoming's Medicaid program finally became a reality in 1995. It was one of the last states to do so.

The voters created the Permanent Mineral Trust Fund when they approved the first severance tax. Interest earned by the fund was directed to the General Fund. Succeeding legislatures added revenue streams to the fund to create a legacy for the future when the "bust years" came again.

There was enough money for every expenditure idea that received a majority of votes. In addition to the Permanent Mineral Trust Fund, investment was made in the state's capital facilities infrastructure with restoration and remodeling of the state capitol, improvements in highways, care institutions, the university and the community colleges. Annual appropriations for capital projects neared $50 million, creating hundreds of jobs for Wyoming workers.

The November 1976 issue of *The Mining Claim, Voice of Wyoming Mining Association* contained an editorial by lobbyist Bill Budd. He received "an assignment" from the Legislative Affairs Committee of the Mining Association to "run the numbers" in anticipation of the 1981 reapportionment.

He said if the 1971 House and Senate divisors were used with the State Planning Office's estimated population, the size of the Senate would increase to 35 seats and the size of the House to 74 seats. He cited the history of no reapportionment from 1933 to 1963. He identified the need for sub-districting—not a popular concept in Wyoming.

He said that he knew the "old arguments about gerrymandering," how it favored the party in power or protected the seat of "some good old boy." He just didn't agree with these arguments.

With the slim margin in the House and the Senate tied,[166] the gerrymandering issue is negligible. The people are the ones who suffer and are short changed when they are asked to vote for eleven out of twenty-two candidates in Laramie County, or ten out of twenty in Natrona County.

People should be able to identify their representative. He or she should come from the area they are to represent, and the legislator should feel a responsibility to the constituency he or she represents.

Legislators were elected in Natrona County in the last election with as few as 9,165 votes. This is 14.6% of the Natrona County population. It is true that the entire population doesn't vote or are even qualified to vote but for those legislators who like to talk about their mandate from the voters or the people they represent, even the top vote getters will have less than 20% of the population voting for them....

When Ed Herschler was in the middle of his second term it was time for the 1980 census—and a new reapportionment in 1981.

---

[166] 30 Republicans, 29 Democrats, 1 Independent in the House. 15-15 in the Senate. The issue that ran this editorial contained the answers to the Political Questionnaire sent to all legislative candidates for the 1976 election.

10

The 1980's

Wyoming's economy was booming. Jobs were here and people came. Some men left their families elsewhere and lived in "man-camps." Other men brought their families to the communities struggling to accommodate the influx of people. Social Services were swamped with the "three D's": depression, delinquency, divorce.

Sweetwater legislator Ann Strand told the story of standing one day on a corner of K Street in Rock Springs, waiting for her husband to pick her up. A cosmetic-heavy, scantily-clad woman aggressively sidled up to her and said, "Sister, this is *my* corner—get lost."

The 1980 Federal Census showed a population increase of 41.3%—from 332,416 to 469,557. Sweetwater's population increased by 127%—from 18,391 to 41,723—due to the Jim Bridger Power Plant, coal and trona mines.

Converse's population increased 135%—from 5,938 to 14,069—driven by expansion of the Dave Johnson Power Plant, coalmines, uranium extraction and oil fields. In that energy-rich county open-pit coal was mined from the surface, while uranium ore was scooped out from around oil derricks that reached deep for petroleum products. Thus severance taxes, based on market value of the product at the mine-mouth or wellhead, were paid on three separate minerals from the same location.[167]

---

[167] Many discussions, as well as litigation, took place over the meaning of "market value," where is the "mine-mouth"—at the face of the mineral or at the end of the conveyor belt—, just where in the pumping of oil is the "well-head," what were the allowable expenses for

Tourists continued to flock to Teton County to enjoy Grand Teton and Yellowstone National Parks. Nearly 3 million annual visitors came to northwest Wyoming. Teton's permanent residents increased 94%—from 4,823 to 9,355.

More coal mines and the Wyodak electrical generating plant accounted for Campbell County's 88% increase—from 12,957 to 24,367. Basin Electric's Laramie River Station at Wheatland brought an 85% increase to Platte County—from 6,486 to 11,975. Trona production and the opening of the Overthrust Belt[168] to natural gas wells were the reasons for the 83% population increase in Uinta County—from 7,100 to 13,021.

Casper, located in the geographic center of the state in Natrona, was the major center for service supplies and suppliers for all the mineral extraction resource activity. Population there increased by 40%—from 51,264 to 71,856.

Legislators of counties with extensive mining or electrical generating operations wanted sales tax revenues to be distributed to "point of use" cities and counties instead of "point of sale" cities and counties. This change had the potential to impact significantly tax revenues to the city of Casper and to Natrona County whose legislators loudly objected. Natrona's four senators and nine representatives prevailed! Sales tax revenues continued to go to the "point of sale."

---

equipment and extraction. The statute was so badly written there was even discussion over which verb applied where. This section of the tax code was deliberately written to confuse. Language-cleanup specialist Matilda Hansen tried repeatedly to rewrite this law into understandable English. Rick Robitaille, lobbyist for the Petroleum Association of Wyoming tried harder to defeat her efforts. Eventually she "won" when a legislative audit found the language unacceptable and "intended to confuse." In the session following the audit report the law was changed, clarifying the language.

[168] The Overthrust Belt is the area west of the Wind River Mountains in Sublette, Lincoln, Sweetwater and Uinta counties where the tectonic continental plates of interior North America collide to cause convoluted geologic formations in which natural gas is trapped.

TABLE 29
Population Changes by 1980

Northern Region Counties	1980 Federal Census	Net Increase Per County	% Increase Over 1970 Census
Big Horn	11,896	1,694	17%
Campbell	24,367	11,410	88%
Crook	5,308	773	17%
Hot Springs	5,710	758	15%
Johnson	6,700	1,113	20%
Park	21,639	3,887	22%
Sheridan	25,048	7,196	40%
Teton	9,355	4,532	94%
Washakie	9,496	1,927	26%

Central Region Counties	1980 Federal Census	Net Increase Per County	% Increase Over 1970 Census
Converse	14,069	8,131	135%
Fremont	38,992	10,640	38%
Lincoln	12,177	3,527	41%
Natrona	71,856	20,592	40%
Niobrara	2,929	5	0.2%
Sublette	4,548	793	21%
Weston	7,106	799	13%

Southern Region Counties	1980 Federal Census	Net Increase Per County	% Increase Over 1970 Census
Albany	29,062	2,631	10%
Carbon	21,896	8,542	64%
Goshen	12,040	1,155	17%
Laramie	68,649	12,289	22%
Platte	11,975	5,489	85%
Sweetwater	41,723	23,332	127%
Uinta	13,021	5,921	83%

TOTAL	469,557	137,141	41.3%
Yellowstone not included in reapportionment.			

Open-pit mines and man-made reservoirs made minor changes to Wyoming's physical geography.[169] But the demographic geography underwent massive changes. The additional people did not distribute themselves evenly around the state: 43% went to the southern region, 32% to the central region and 24% to the northern region (Table 29). The rural population dropped to 174,918 or 37.3% of the statewide population. The urban population climbed to 294,639 or 62.7% of the population. By 1980, urban population was nearly the same as the entire statewide population had been in 1950 (291,529).

Table 29 illustrates that a small increase in the total number of people can result in a large percent of increase in a county's population.

In 1981 the Republicans controlled both the House and the Senate. Don Cundall of Goshen/Platte was Senate President. Jerry Geis of Hot Springs/Washakie was Vice President. Eddie Moore of Converse/Niobrara was Majority Leader. All represented counties with small populations combined into districts in the 1965 Court intervention. The economies of these districts were based on ranching, dry-land farming and mineral extraction. The lobbyists for the agricultural/mineral interest power-elite were pleased—their men were in charge.

Democrat Dick Sedar of Natrona was Senate Minority Leader. Steve Majhanovich of Sweetwater was Minority Whip. Public school teachers and the labor unions were pleased with these Democratic leaders.

The Senate had 19 Republicans and 11 Democrats—enough Democratic votes to sustain Governor Herschler's vetoes.

In the House, Republican Bob Burnett of Albany was Speaker. Russ Donley of Natrona was Speaker Pro Tem. Dean Prosser of Laramie was Majority Leader. Pat Meenan of Natrona was Majority Whip.

Don Scott of Goshen was Minority Leader. John Vinich of Fremont was Minority Whip. Bill Edwards of Laramie County was Minority Caucus Chairman. There were 39 Republicans and 23 Democrats in the House—enough Democrats to sustain a veto by the Governor.

---

[169] The Surface Mining Control and Reclamation Act passed by Congress in 1977 has had a positive impact on reclaiming mining lands.

For the 1981 reapportionment, trucker Jerry Geis of Hot Springs/Washakie was the only northern-region man in the leadership.

Four central-region men were in the leadership: Senator Eddie Moore of Converse/Niobrara, Representatives Pat Meenan and Russ Donley of Natrona and Democrat John Vinich of Fremont. Moore was a rancher and mineral royalty recipient. Meenan owned a radio station in Casper, where Donley was a civil engineer. Vinich was from the near-ghost coal mining town of Hudson that hosted the excellent Svilar and Vinich restaurants.

Five of the leaders were from the southern region: Don Cundall of Goshen/Platte, Don Scott of Goshen, Bob Burnett of Albany, Bill Edwards and Dean Prosser of Laramie. Burnett was an insurance agent. Don Cundall and Dean Prosser were ranchers. Don Scott was in construction. Bill Edwards was on the faculty of Laramie County Community College.

Donley "carried water" for the agriculture/mineral interest lobbyists. Meenan never stayed "hitched" to any special interest lobbyists. Burnett represented the cosmopolitan electorate in the University town of Laramie. Prosser, the legislator whose home bedroom was in Colorado,[170] tried to manage the General File as a hand-maiden of the traditional Republican agriculture/mineral interests. With this motley collection of leaders with very disparate interests, the prognosis for a smooth session was not very good.

CHARLES SCOTT AND REAPPORTONMENT

Natrona's Charles Scott, a rancher with a Harvard MBA and previous experience as a federal employee in Washington, D. C., became a major player in reapportionment in 1980.[171] That year

---

[170] At the start of a previous session Prosser's Wyoming residency was challenged. The district court heard the case but ultimately said who sat in the legislature was the decision of those elected to that Chamber. Actually Prosser did live across the state line in Colorado but as no roads connected his place with anything in Colorado and all his personal and business affairs were conducted as a Wyoming citizen, the House seated him as a Representative of Laramie County.

[171] In 1981 Scott was a Representative. He was elected to the Senate in 1982.

he got Management Council approval to attend a seminar in Salt Lake City on reapportionment sponsored by the National Conference of State Legislators. In addition to Scott, Senate Majority Leader Eddie Moore and Legislative Service Office staffers Jerry Fox and Jim Orr went to the meeting.

Scott wrote the report, dated December 30, 1980, and distributed it to all legislators.[172] His "take" on reapportionment significantly influenced the final 1981 plan. Regarding multi-member districts he said,

> We [now] use multi-member Districts. ...[S]ome ... multi-member districts have been held to be unconstitutional [when used] as a device to discriminate against racial minorities.... [T]he Supreme Court has said explicitly that multiple member districts are not unconstitutional *per se....* Wyoming's...districts are clearly constitutional ... [I]n *White v. Regester* the Court held ... minorities [that] have not elected a member to a seat was not enough to show discrimination ... there must ... be evidence that the process is not equally open to minority members."

Then Scott described the normal interpretation of one man, one vote as "quite strict," with permissible variation not clearly defined. He said the consensus of the "experts" was that "...5% or at most 10% was all that normally would be allowed." He predicted application of this standard to Wyoming will "force [us] to wholesale splitting of counties."

Next Scott shared what he learned about meshing census data and voting behavior to draw political boundaries. He found that there was not enough correlation between census data and voters showing up at the November elections to use precinct-total-votes-cast as a defendable basis for drawing election districts. Only the use of census data was acceptable to the United States Supreme Court to draw boundaries to attain equal representation. In Scott's opinion breaking down the census data into smaller geographical units to obtain "rational political boundaries can be quite a problem, especially given the relatively strict interpretation of one man, one vote rule..."

In light of the federal voting rights acts and the "subsequent constitutional requirements" he warned his fellow legislators to

---

[172] *Report On A Reapportionment Seminar*, by C. Scott, December 30, 1980, distributed to House Members. Quotes are from Matilda Hansen's copy.

use "great care" with minority populations, especially Wyoming's residents of Hispanic heritage. He noted the additional expenses required because of the undeniable mandatory need for computers and statistical expertise in order to "stay out of legal trouble."

He closed his memo saying,

[T]he usual requirements that districts be contiguous and compact ... [is] a safeguard against the gerrymander but ... it has not proved effective *a perfectly good gerrymander can be done without them.*[173]

As Scott stated, "One Man, One Vote" was fact. In the opinion of many Wyoming legislators, the rulings of the United States Supreme Court were a sinister cloud hanging far too close. These legislators had no inclination to concede the interpretation (of equal representation) applied to Wyoming.

They were very comfortable with the time-honored, steeped-in-archaic-precedent of "major fraction thereof." They took comfort in the Court's approval of the 1965 deviation range. The case law on 5% to 10% deviation range, to them, was nonsense because this small variation left no wiggle-room for assigning a seat(s) to some counties and denying seat(s) to other counties. The power-elite of Wyoming was used to working within a 98% deviation range.[174]

Baker v. Carr made all the States conform to equal representation under the Equal Protection Clause of the Fourteenth Amendment to the United States Constitution. But Wyoming's Republican majority had their own criteria for legislative representation::

1. Ignore the fact the state's population was unevenly distributed.
2. Continue to define election districts as counties.
3. Use the large deviation range as approved in 1965.
4. Assign at least one representative to each county.
5. Continue to combine counties with low populations as per the Court's 1965 Plan.
6. Keep political power away from the southern region.

The movers-and-shakers—both legislators and lobbyists— knew that if they paid attention to the new ruling, their criteria

---

[173]Scott meant gerrymandering could be done even with "compact and contiguous" districts. Italic's are this author's.

[174] The range was plus or minus 49%.

were not workable. Therefore, "One Man, One Vote" and equal representation were ignored.

THE VOICES OF NIOBRARA COUNTY

In 1971 Niobrara County's one House seat survived reapportionment. In 1981 it set out to save it again. The citizens of Niobrara County could count. With their 1980 population of 2,929 they were below—more than 49% below—any ratio set by the legislature. Through their legislator, Russell Thompson of Lusk, the citizens sent the House a plea. Their letter, distributed by Representative Thompson said,

The people of Niobrara County are greatly alarmed at the results [in] this bill which would deprive us of any representation in the Legislature of the State...

"The Appalachia" of Wyoming deserves better treatment than this. The economy of Niobrara County is distinctly different from that of either Goshen or Converse, and deserves to be represented in the State Legislature. Niobrara County is strictly livestock. Goshen County is cash crop farming. While Converse County has livestock, the industrial activity is far out stripping this industry.

Whatever action is taken on reapportionment it faces the possibility of a lawsuit, but remember the U.S. Supreme Court decision concerning represen- tation dealt only with State Senators, not with State Representatives.

Wyoming has always been strong States' Rights. Witness the mineral severance tax issue in Congress. We believe that the Legislature agrees that States' Rights shall prevail.

We suggest to you that you apply the same principle to the Wyoming House of Representatives and leave Niobrara County with its small voice.... Even if sub-districting becomes law, it will not help.

PLEASE DO NOT DESTROY
OUR REPRESENTATION.

House members knew the battle lines were drawn when this letter arrived on their desks.

Charles Scott was the principal sponsor of House Bill 360. Co-sponsors were fellow House members Cynthia Lummis and Walter Urbigkit of Laramie County and Alan Stauffer of Lincoln.[175]

The bill contained no distribution of legislative seats—neither for the Senate nor for the House.[176] Unofficial sheets of paper with multiple columns of numbers and individual calculations based on unknown assumptions were placed on the desks of House members.

Historically, a bill draft set the number of Senate and House seats within the constitutional designation of the relative size of the House and Senate.[177] These numbers were divided into the statewide population. This gave the number to be divided into a county's population to determine the number of seats for that county—plus or minus "major fraction thereof." Anyone with rudimentary arithmetic skills was able to determine how many people each legislator represented and how close—or far—their district was to equal representation.

But, as introduced, there was no ratio in HB 360. Instead, it had a collection of formulas and instructions designed to fulfill the constitutional requirement for a ratio but without a ratio number to identify how many residents each legislator represented. In convoluted English, Wyoming Statute 28-2-109(a) provided:

> (i) The ratio for the apportionment of senators is the smallest number of people per senator which when divided into the population in each senate district as shown by the official results of the 1980 federal decennial census with fractions rounded to the nearest whole number results in a senate with twenty-nine (29) senators.

The language was the same in (ii) for the House except the last phrase read, "...results in a house with sixty-one (61) representatives." This was tricky wording. The operable words were "...the smallest number of people ... divided into the

---

[175] The legal ramifications of HB 360 are discussed in Chapter 12.

[176] State of Wyoming, 81LSO-701.01, House Bill No. 360 Reapportionment – 1981, sponsored by Representatives C. Scott, Lummis and Urbigkit.

[177] Article III, Section 3 "...at no time shall the number of members of the house of representatives be less than twice nor greater than three times the number of members of the senate...."

population in each (county)..." rather than the number of House or Senate seats divided into the statewide population.

This text allowed nearly unlimited flexibility in the number of residents per legislator per election district—so long as the total in each chamber did not exceed 29 or 61 respectively. The law did not require uniformity in the number of residents among the several districts. The text also made it difficult for proponents, opponents, the Press and observers in the Gallery to know what was being discussed.

At worst, the intent behind this formula was to obfuscate. At best, the intent was to allow as much flexibility as possible regarding which seats went to which election districts (counties).

HB 360 did not reach Speaker Burnett's desk until January 23rd. This was late introduction for a bill of this magnitude of importance. A third of the session-time had passed. Burnett sent it to Committee 7: Corporations, Elections and Political Subdivisions, where bill co-sponsor Alan Stauffer was chairman.

On Saturday, January 31st, the bill was considered in Committee of the Whole.[178] Stauffer's Standing Committee report made few changes except to add a section intended to be useful if there was a court challenge.

> If the validity of this apportionment is challenged in a lawsuit contending in part that the combination of counties in a single district violates the Wyoming constitution, the attorney general shall defend the suit <u>primarily on the grounds that the combination of counties into a single district is necessary to meet the requirements of the United States Constitution.</u>

The underlined words mandated the grounds the state's Attorney General was to use in any lawsuit filed with the intent of keeping Wyoming's county-based election districts. Support for this language was from members who were nearly paranoid in their resistance to change.

The amendment was divided at the underlined words. Non-paranoid House members prevailed. The underlined portion was defeated. Opponents said the rest of the amendment was dumb. No legislature can dictate to a court. The attorney general

---

[178] Saturday sessions were difficult. Everyone was tired from a week of intense work. Because those traveling home for the weekend—what was left of it—were anxious to be on the road, there was no lunch break. Saturday was counted as a full workday though only 4 to 6 hours elapsed between opening-gavel and adjournment-until-Monday.

defends the state anytime an act of the legislature is challenged. But this portion passed.

The substance of HB 360 designated counties as election districts. There was a Goshen-Niobrara House district. The combined Senate districts were: Converse-Niobrara, Campbell-Johnson, Crook-Weston, Hot Springs-Washakie and Sublette-Teton.

Nowhere did the bill say Platte and Goshen were separate districts each with their own senator. The Republicans quietly restored a senator to each county because they had gotten rid of Ed Kendig. The combination was no longer needed.

Likewise, nowhere was it stated that Lincoln was "rejoined" at Township 26 and 27 North, Sixth Principal Meridian, Wyoming, and given one senator. The obscurity of the formula and the "magic" number 29 made possible these invisible changes.

Representative Jim Roth of Sweetwater had the first Committee of the Whole amendment to increase the size of the Senate to 30 seats. Under the obscurity of the formula he realized the opportunity to get his county a third senator. Roth based his claim on the 127% population increase since the last census and on the pressures brought onto his county by the energy boom. His amendment passed with nothing written anywhere officially designating the seat to Sweetwater County.

The next amendments were from Cynthia Lummis. She successfully changed the size of the House, first to 62 then to 63 members, with no indication where the new seats were to go.

Before the vote was taken on one of her amendments she withdrew her version of "turning back the clock." The amendment read:

> The 46th session of the Wyoming Legislature, dedicated to maintain the integrity of its county sub-divisions and to promote the general welfare of all its citizens, has preserved established county boundaries as the foundation for representative districts in the Wyoming House of Representatives. Because Wyoming counties are actual communities, linking two counties in a single representative district will deprive the smaller county of representation and deny its citizens the equal protection of the law. We therefore hold the provisions of Article 3, Section 3 of the Wyoming Constitution as the determining standard of the reapportionment of the Wyoming Legislature,

which guarantees each county at least one representative.

It was a good thing this amendment was withdrawn for she was "spitting in the face" of the United States Supreme Court. Then Committee of the Whole closed and the members left for the weekend.

There were no amendments in Second Reading on Monday. In Third Reading on Tuesday, Dick Wallis tried to put in some divisor numbers to protect the counties with small populations:

> For the first five thousand (5,000) people, or major fraction thereof, residing in a county as shown by the official results of the 1980 federal decennial census, each county shall have one (1) representative.

This would have guaranteed Niobrara County a House seat. His amendment failed.

Peg Shreve offered the "delete the enacting clause" amendment allowing full debate on the entire bill. When the talking ended, she withdrew her amendment. The vote was 48 ayes, 14 noes. Republicans Dan Budd of Sublette, Doug Chamberlain of Goshen, Jack Winniger of Park and Russ Thompson of Niobrara voted no.

Democrats to vote no were H.L. Jensen of Teton, Ed McCarthy of Natrona, Jerry Michie and Tom Trowbridge of Carbon, Scott Ratliff and John Vinich of Fremont, Jim Roth and Ann Strand of Sweetwater, Don Scott of Goshen and Walter Urbigkit of Laramie.

The bill got to the Senate on February 4 and was sent to the Senate Corporations Committee chaired by L.V. "Neal" Stafford of Campbell-Johnson. Debate in the Senate began on February 18th.

The Standing Committee amendment did some "cleanup." The House had paired Niobrara with Converse in the Senate and Niobrara with Goshen in the House. Senators deemed this "nonsense" and paired Niobrara with Converse in both Chambers. Then the Standing Committee revived Lummis' withdrawn portion of her House amendment and added the sentence,

> Previous judicial decisions concerning reapportion-ment of the Wyoming legislature have addressed only multi-county senate districts. No county has heretofore been deprived of at least one (1) member of the legislature.

The first Committee of the Whole amendment was Stafford's. He didn't like the House section that directed the attorney general to defend any lawsuit. The Senate agreed with him. Tom Stroock of Natrona wanted to appropriate $200,000 to the Legislative Service Office to "defend the reapportionment formula contained in this act." Again the Senate agreed.

Second Reading was on February 19th. There were "cleanup" amendments. Then the bill was *laid back without prejudice for one day*. This allowed time for David Nicholas of Albany to prepare new (iii) and (iv) paragraphs to the formula. In (iii) he accomplished what Dick Wallis intended (assure Niobrara a House seat), without reference to "divisor number" or "major fraction thereof." In (iv) he directed that if a Court ruled that Niobrara was not entitled to a House seat, Niobrara was to be combined with Converse.

The Senate voted on February 23: 23 ayes, 6 noes, with Milton Nichols of Laramie County excused. Those voting no were Republicans Rex Arney of Sheridan, Jerry Geis of Washakie, Don Northrup of Park, Roy Peck of Fremont and Stafford of Campbell-Johnson. Democrat Dick Sadler of Natrona voted no.

The House disagreed with the Senate action: 21 ayes, 39 noes, 2 excused. With no record of this floor debate, the reasons are lost on why the House rejected the Senate changes.

The Conference Committee was appointed. House conferees were Rory Cross of Converse, Russell Thompson of Niobrara and Walter Urbigkit of Laramie County.[179] Senate conferees were Neal Stafford of Campbell-Johnson, Eddie Moore of Converse and David Nicholas of Albany.

Cross, Moore and Thompson were central-region men, there to "guard" Niobrara's House member. Lawyers Nicholas and Urbigkit were from the southern region; there to make sure the final version was a "reasonable effort." Stafford, a northern-region mineral industry man, was there to "guard" the interests of the Republican political elite.

On February 26th they requested designation as a "Free Committee."[180] This was granted. They reported back on

---

[179] Walter Urbigkit was counsel for the plaintiffs in *Schaefer v. Thompson* (1964).

[180] The first conference committee can negotiate only those provisions where the Senate and House disagree. Subsequent committees are "Free" to negotiate anything in the bill. Conferees cannot go beyond the parameters already in a bill.

February 28th, the last day of the Session, with a rewritten bill—House Bill 360B.

HB 360B was the Senate's cleaned up version of HB 360, adding sections (b) and (c) to the formulas in (a) in 28-2-109.[181] The reason for "Free committee status" was to specify in the bill the number of Senate and House seats assigned to each county election district. During the previous votes on HB 360, the majority of the legislators blindly approved a reapportionment plan with no designation of seats assigned to county election districts. Without specific seat distribution they abdicated their constitutional obligation to "...revise and adjust the apportionment of senator and representatives, ... according to ratios to be fixed by law."[182]

The conference committee did write a "reasonable final version" for the 1981 reapportionment. The ratios were named: the Senate at 15,652:1 and the House at 7,337:1.

The disparity in senate representation was considerable between the populations of Carbon and Park (21,896 and 21,639, respectively) and those of Big Horn and Platte (11,896 and 11,975, respectively). Yet each county was getting one senate seat. While these differences were within the historical range of "major fraction thereof"—equal representation they were not.

The other major change by the conference committee was to tinker with the purpose clause—a provision popular with many legislators. This new section combined the concepts in Stafford's version of the Lummis amendment, the Stroock amendment appropriating money for a possible court challenge, and commentary on the 1965 Court ruling on combined counties for election districts for the Senate but not for the House.

The language didn't suit Nicholas and Urbigkit.[183] There was no time for finely crafted words from either man. Someone "cut and pasted" words together. The result—a magnificent unintelligible muddle:

"Section 3. It is hereby declared the policy of this state is to preserve the integrity of county boundaries as

---

[181] Session Laws of Wyoming, 1981, Chapter 76.

[182] Wyoming Constitution Article III, Section 48.

[183] This author served many years on the House and Joint Judiciary Committee with both men. She knows first-hand their conscientious regard for appropriate words and their focus on the clear articulation of concepts.

election districts for the house of representatives. The legislature has considered the present population, needs, and other characteristics of each county. The legislature finds that the needs of each county are unique and the interests of each county must be guaranteed a voice in the legislature. The legislature therefore, will utilize the provisions of article 3 section 3 of the Wyoming constitution as the determining standard in the reapportionment of the Wyoming house of representatives which guarantees each county at least one (1) representative. The legislature finds that the opportunity for the oppression of the people of this state or any of them is greater if any county is deprived of a representative in the legislature than if each is guaranteed at least one (1) representative. The legislature finds that the dilution of the power of counties which join together in making these decalrations is trivial when weighed against the need to maintain the integrity of county boundaries. The legislature also finds that it is not practical or necessary to increase the size of the legislature beyond the provisions of this act in order to meet its obligations to apportion in accordance with constitutional requirements consistent with this declaration."

Walter Urbigkit did not sign the Joint Conference Committe. The other five conferencees signed (see Table 30 for final reapportionment).

The House voted 37 ayes, 23 noes. Pete Simpson of Sheridan was excused. The vote was essentially Democrats vs. Republicans, with five Democrats switching to vote "yes" and six Republicans switching to vote "no."

The switchers voting "aye" were Democrats Sheila Arnold of Albany, Doug Bryant of Platte, H. L. Jensen of Teton, Jack Pugh of Sweetwater and George Salisbury of Carbon.

The Republican switchers voting "no" were Tom Jones of Park, Cynthia Lummis and Dean Prosser of Laramie County, Carleton Perry of Sheridan, Jack Sidi of Natrona and Marlene Simons of Crook.

The Senate accepted the report: 20 ayes 9 noes. Ford Bussart of Sweetwater was excused. The Senate vote was more bipartisan. Democrats June Boyle of Albany, Win Hickey, Jim Norris and Bill Rector of Laramie County and Hight Proffit of Uinta voted "aye."

TABLE 30
Final 1981 Reapportionment

County	Senate Seats	Residents Per Senator	House Seats	Residents Per House Member
Albany	2	14,531	4	7,266
Big Horn	1	11,896	2	5,948
Campbell/ Johnson	2	15,533		
Campbell			3	8,122
Carbon	1	21,896	3	7,299
Converse	1	14,069	2	7,034
Crook/ Weston	1	12,414		
Crook			1	5,308
Fremont	2	19,496	5	7,897
Goshen/ Niobrara	1	14,969		
Goshen			2	6,020
Hot Springs/ Washakie	1	15,206		
Hot Springs			1	5,710
Johnson			1	6,700
Laramie	4	17,162	9	7,628
Lincoln	1	12,177	2	6,089
Natrona	4	17,964	9	7,984
Niobrara			1	2,929
Park	1	21,639	3	7,213
Platte	1	11,975	2	5,988
Sheridan	2	12,524	3	8,349
Sublette/ Teton	1	13,903		
Sublette			1	4,548
Sweetwater	3	13,907	5	8,345
Teton			1	9,355
Uinta	1	13,021	2	6,511
Washakie			1	9,496
Weston			1	7,106

Four Republicans voted "no": Roy Peck of Fremont, Cal Taggart of Big Horn, John Turner of Teton and Russ Zimmer of Goshen. It was the last day. The Speaker and the President signed the Enrolled Act.[184]

Everyone was tired. Saturday sessions had been held every Saturday in February and most of the Saturdays in January. This last day of the 1981 session was unlike any other last day.

Significant interim committee bills, reapportionment and major budget bills, "favorite and favored" bills of the House and Senate were on the docket for consideration.

Conference committee reports were rejected, one after another. The central region agricultural/mineral interest politicos[185] were exercising their political power. The southern-region legislators (and their friends) had their agendas.

The northern-region people were split—especially on the issues of severance taxes and education. Sheridan voters wanted increases in severance taxes for education so their legislators were voting with the southern region. On other issues the Sheridan legislators voted with the central region.

With this plentitude of legislation and conflicting agendas the system broke.

[184] Governor Herschler signed the Enrolled Act March 3, 1981.

[185] Legislators, citizens and lobbyists.

11

WHAT BROKE?

But what broke began on February 25th, the last day for consideration of bills on General File. House Majority Leader Dean Prosser[186] had all the bills with a "Do Pass" motion in his "basket." Each evening he authorized an Action Sheet that listed the bills to be considered the next day in Committee of the Whole in the order set by him; the bills on Second Reading in numerical order; and the bills on Third Reading in numerical order.[187]

The consideration of bills in Committee of the Whole continued until the Majority Leader stood and moved "The Committee of The Whole Rise And Report."

Both lobbyists and legislators anxiously scanned the Senate's "Board" and the House Action Sheet to see where "their" bill(s) were. Bills rose and fell in their positions as decided by the Majority Leader. Each day the order was different than the previous day.

In 1981, Majority Leader Dean Prosser of Laramie successfully moved 176 bills through Committee of the Whole. These included bills improving state employee's and judge's retirement. The laws on eminent domain were recodified. A tax

---

[186] Prosser was a Laramie County resident—where hundreds of state employees lived and voted.

[187] The Senate's procedure was similar except their General File bills were listed numerically. Each morning their majority leader wrote in black pen on a special board at the front of the chamber the number and order of the bills to be considered that day—very like hymns are listed for the congregation each Sunday.

increase of 2% "upon the privilege of severing or extracting oil and gas" was passed. There were 11 bills on mines and mineral affairs, eight bills authorizing millions for water projects. There were six changes to the tax code, six laws on labor and employment matters. Supplementary appropriations bills were passed.

The last day for General File was an anxious day. Everyone hoped "their bill" was high enough on the list to be one of the 20 to 30 bills considered.

On February 25th the Senate adjourned, having done those bills on General File their Majority Leader wanted to consider. The hour was getting late.

In the House lobbyists for state employees anxiously watched "their bill" restructuring their salary pay plan get closer and closer to the top. Initially it was "way down" on the General File, but it was rising and there was time for consideration. Legislators supporting the employees were also watching.

House members were tired and restless—many were away from their desks, though still within the confines of the Chamber. Six o'clock came and went as still more bills were considered. Then, just as the chairman of Committee of the Whole[188] was about to say, "The next bill for our consideration is the State Employee Salary Pay Plan," Prosser rose to his feet and made the motion for "The Committee of the Whole to Rise and Report."

This motion needed a second—usually a perfunctory request. Usually House members paid it little attention. But not this time.

House members supporting state employees were paying attention. They called "Division"—a request for a standing-vote-count. Politically astute members quickly saw what was happening. Members were challenging the Majority Leader and were trying to overrule him in order to continue with General File to consider the state employees bill.

Not all members stood in support of the Majority Leader's motion. An abundant number stood in opposition. Only a majority of those within the designated confines of the Chamber was needed. Prosser's motion passed by one vote.

---

[188] For alternating days each caucus leader designates a different member to preside. Some legislators considered this designation an honor. Others considered it a bother—it cut into much-valued desktime.

The House adjourned. Disappointment was nearly palpable over failing to even consider the much needed updating of the state employee pay plan. The disappointment was keenly felt by state employees and, to a lesser extent, by lobbyists, legislators and the public who supported them.

That evening senior legislators Mary Kay Schwope and Elizabeth Phelan of Laramie County and Matilda Hansen of Albany went to Poor Richard's for a late supper.[189] They wanted to rehash and recap Prosser's motion and other contentious matters of the day.

While Hansen was removing her coat before taking an outside seat in a booth, Senate President Don Cundall aggressively walked up to her and hissed, "You promised your vote and you went back on your word." Rather flustered she asked, "What do you mean?" Cundall walked to his table without replying. Hansen turned her attention to her dinner companions who asked, "What was that all about?" She did not know. She *never* (knowingly) "promised" her vote on any subject unless she had, after careful thought, arrived at her own conclusion.[190]

Cundall never told her what vote was promised. She never knew whether he wanted a "yes" or "no" vote. She never knew whether he was referring to just her vote or the votes of the Democratic caucus.[191]

Whatever, some highly charged issue was unresolved. That year tensions were high between the Senate "controlled" by agriculture-extractive resource interests and House, oriented towards labor, education, more-severance-tax issues. House

---

[189] One other woman was with them. It could have been Ann Strand, Ellen Crowley or Mary Odde. Memories and records are insufficient to specify the 4th person.

[190] There were issues she supported. There were issues she didn't. There were a multitude of issues on which she didn't decide how to vote until her name was called. Because she kept her own counsel, and did her own homework, she was never viewed as a "swing voter." Swing voters cast their vote "aye" or "no" depending on who was the last person (lobbyist, citizen or legislator) to talk to them.

[191] Democratic caucus votes during Hansen's legislative years were not binding. If a caucus member could not go along with the vote, there was the obligation to inform the caucus leadership so they could go find a vote someplace else. Except on rare occasions, getting all the Democrats to support a caucus position was like pushing a rope or herding ducks.

members espousing differing positions were jockeying to exercise maximum political control. Tensions of major proportions swirled about the two Chambers.

Then it was the last day, February 28th. All Second Readings were completed. The Third Reading and final votes were taken early in the day in both the House and Senate. One concurrence vote after another was taken. For non-concurrence, conference committees were named and met. It was a time of hurry-up-and-wait. Both the House and Senate often "stood at recess" meaning not in session (but don't go far—certainly not out of the Capitol).

Speaker Burnett followed Speaker Warren Morton's practice of again asking legislator Carroll Orrison of Laramie County to leave his RV at home.[192] Those who drank the Senate's coffee did so at their own risk.[193]

With state employees no longer having offices on the second and third floors of the capitol, no office was "a hospitality center" for thirsty legislators and lobbyists. Instead, a persistent person was able to "ferret out" which committee room(s) had "the good stuff." Sometimes their search took them to the Senate's fire escapes.

The long day continued. There was a break for supper—not time enough for dinner. The evening's entertainment came and left. The Chambers were called to order to watch the signing of Enrolled Acts (at least their cover page). Conference reports came and the votes were taken. When a report was rejected, that committee, or a newly appointed one, went back to work.

More wait time. More reports. More voting. More watching the signing of Enrolled Acts. More wait time. More reports. More…

Bodies were tired. Heads were fuzzy. Tempers were short. Near midnight the House learned the Senators were gone, left, adjourned the regular session, gone home. Neal Stafford was on his way to the golf courses in Arizona. June Boyle was headed home to her bed in Laramie. John Turner was on his way to Jackson. The Senators were "outa-here."

Consternation reigned in the House. Matilda Hansen told the Chief Clerk "her bill" on recodification of the lien laws was

---

[192] His custom was to park it in the capitol parking lot where invited guests "relaxed" and enjoyed his libatious hospitality.

[193] Usually it was spiked on the last night.

somewhere.[194] Worried Al Weiderspahn and Ellen Crowley reported their Limited Guardianship bill was *somewhere*. Then Hansen and Ed McCarthy realized their Conservation of Art bill cleaning the paintings in the House and Senate was *somewhere*.

Speaker Burnett turned to Chief Clerk Herb Pownall to ask, "What else is out?" What other bills were still *somewhere*—in limbo between the House and Senate with no final votes? Pownall began leafing through his stenographer notebook, reading aloud the numbers and titles of bills still *somewhere*.

Someone realized the Senate had committed the "worst sin of all": they left before all appropriations bills were passed. No act of omission was greater than leaving an appropriations bill "hanging." Then followed the worried question, "Which appropriations bill?" Scramble... Scramble... no final vote on appropriations for the University and the Community Colleges!

There was only one thing left for Speaker Burnett to do— end the session. The Constitution requires BOTH chambers to be in session to conduct business. The Governor was informed that the House was ready to quit, and it was time for him to give his closing-session remarks. It was late and the Governor's words were few. The House Digest reports:

> He thanked the Body for a lot of hard work and expressed his appreciation for all the kindness shown him, in the recent loss of his mother. He said he realized there probably were some "bloody noses" and realized this season had not been an easy one because of such important items as school finance, reapportionment and tax matters. He said he was sure no one in the Body had complete satisfaction, with the session.... [Then he] wished [everyone] a safe trip home."

It was early Sunday morning as House members went to their cars, then to the Hitching Post Inn. They called out to each other, down the long halls at the Hitch, as they identified first one bill, then another, that was *somewhere*.

By 2:30 am Speaker Burnett directed the Hitching Post Front Desk to put a message on House members' phones requesting legislators not to go home.[195] Eventually, he asked the Governor to call a Special Session for Monday morning.

---

[194] She chaired the Joint Interim Judiciary Committee on the lien laws.

[195] Except for the five from Laramie County, all Senators lived at the Hitching Post Inn during the session. Except for the 11 Laramie

At 6:00 am Hansen woke from a sound sleep of three hours remembering that Vern Shelton[196] left the House Chambers before midnight, to return to Laramie for an early morning meeting in Old Main with President Jennings and other top University administrators. He was to tell them about the University budget.

She reached for the phone beside her bed and called the President's Office. Vice President for Academic Affairs Alan Spitz, there early to put on the coffee, answered.

She told him the University budget did not pass. He asked, "How could that be? There was soon to be a meeting for Vern Shelton to give us the budget details."

She answered, "The appropriations bill did not pass. The Legislature adjourned. A Special Session is needed. Get in touch with Bob Burnett."[197] Then she hung up the phone and went back to sleep.

That morning the Coffee Shop at The Hitch served breakfast until noon as tired legislators and lobbyists gathered at the tables to commiserate, to figure out the mess they were in and to sort out how to untangle the legislation.

After sending his staff home to rest, Ralph Thomas[198] had them back in the Capitol by early Sunday afternoon tracking the bills: those in the backrooms of the Senate, those in the backrooms of the House and those in their offices. They made a list of 30 bills lacking final votes (Table 31).

The Speaker and the President each had a bill on the list. The recodification of Chapter 29 (Lien Laws) of the Wyoming Statutes was on the list. Management Council, the Select School, Judiciary and Labor committees had bills on the list.

County House members and 4 others, all House members lived at "The Hitch." A total of 74 legislators and a multitude of lobbyists enjoyed the amenities of "The Hitch" during the entire 1981 session.

In 1975 Harry Smith enticed the legislators to stay at his establishment with $5 per night rooms (Little America matched his price). In subsequent years the legislator's room rate gradually increased, as the legislators per diem increased from $15 per day in 1974 to $90 per day in 1994.

[196] Lobbyist for the University of Wyoming.

[197] Speaker Burnett was from Albany County. He confirmed Hansen's message. Vern Shelton was soon back in his car on his way back to Cheyenne.

[198] Director of the Legislative Service Office.

Non-passage of committee bills was particularly troublesome because of all the interim time and money invested in them.

TABLE 31
The Unfinished Business of the 1981 Session

Original Bill No.	Title	Sponsor
HB 31C	Commission on Aging	Labor
HB 276	County Attorneys	Urbigkit
HB 51	Involuntary Hospitalization	Judiciary
HB 237B	State Park System	Scott, Charles
HB 250	Limited Guardianship	Crowley
HB 285	Juvenile Court Records	Crowley
HB 316	Hospital Inspections	Burnett
HB 389	Farm Loan Board Loans	Sidi
HB 433	Sales Tax	Micheli
HB 20	Ports of Entry Operating Hours	Thorson
HB 448	Conservation of Art	Hansen
HB 522	Special Beverage Permits	Meenan
HB 229A	Office of District Attorney	Urbigkit
HB 223	School Bond Reserve Fund	School Comm.
HB 201	Farm/Ranch Electrical Exempt	Wallis
HB 251	Cigarette Tax Collections	Mgment Council
HB 260	County Salaries	Jensen
HB 149	Special Capital Const. Projects	Urbigkit
HB 98	Snowmobiles	Schwope
HB 63	Drivers' Licenses	Lummis
HB 21	Arrest Citations	Urbigkit
HB 9	Adoption	Jones
HB 7	Property Tax Relief Continue	Jones
SF 223B	Size/Weight Limits on Hway	Stafford
SF 213A	Institutional Health Services	Cundall
SF 86	Mineral Royalties-County Road	Stafford
SF 51	Architects	Nicholas
	Appropriations-Education	Appropriations

The bills sponsored by Crowley and Urbigkit made major improvements in the legal system. Schwope's bill on snow-mobiles was "landmark" legislation. Hansen's bill paid for the cleaning and preservation of the True murals in the Senate

133

Chambers and the two Gordon portraits. Nicholas' law improved the licensing of architects.

The missing appropriations bill contained supplemental funds for the University of Wyoming, the Community Colleges and the State Department of Education. Also outstanding, but not a supplemental appropriation, was the annual bill for capital construction projects containing $37,250,203. These annual investments in the state's infrastructure, made during the first 10 Herschler years, were a deliberate policy to leave assets for tomorrow while providing jobs for today as a wise utilization of severance taxes from non-renewable minerals.

The leadership of the House and Senate conferred on changes in the Joint Senate and House Rules to smoothly process the unfinished business of the 46th Legislature. The Governor issued the requested proclamation:

> WHEREAS, the House and the Senate of the Forty-sixth Wyoming Legislature, meeting in regular session, passed certain legislation; and
>
> WHEREAS, both houses of the Legislature adjourned upon the expiration of the forty (40) legislative working days provided by law for such session, before the legislation was enrolled or signed by the presiding officers of the Senate and House in the presence of the members of their respective bodies as required by Section 28, Article 3 of the Wyoming Constitution; and
>
> WHEREAS, the enactments are critical to the welfare of the state and critical to the effective operation of state government.
>
> NOW, THEREFORE, I, ED HERSCHLER, Governor of the State of Wyoming, pursuant to Section 4, Article 4 of the Wyoming Constitution, do hereby proclaim the necessity for an extraordinary session of the Wyoming State Legislature, and summon the members thereof to convene in special session in the legislative chambers of the State Capitol in the City of Cheyenne, Laramie County, on Monday, the 2nd day of March, 1981, at 12:00 o'clock noon, to perform such acts as are necessary and proper to consider legislation in full compliance with the Wyoming Constitution.

President Cundall called his senators back. They all came except Neal Stafford. He was on the golf course in Arizona and declined to return. Cundall excused him.

Speaker Burnett corralled his House members and found all accounted for except Alan Stauffer of Lincoln. This was Stauffer's third session. He spent the allotted 40 days away from his pharmacy and his family. He was home and he was going to stay there.

Burnett declined to excuse him, then went to the Governor for his help to bring Stauffer to the special session.[199] On Monday morning the sheriff of Lincoln County arrived at Stauffer's pharmacy, told him to pick up whatever he needed, then Lincoln County law enforcement escorted him to the Governor-authorized state plane to return him to Cheyenne.

Though the weather was fine along most of southern Wyoming, by the time the plane got to Albany County the airport in Cheyenne was socked in with a dense March fog. So the plane landed at the Laramie airport, where the Wyoming Highway Patrol met Stauffer. They drove him across the summit, escorted him into the Capitol, up the steps to the second floor and to the door of the House Chambers. Contrary to the dress code, when Stauffer arrived he was wearing denim blue jeans. But this time Burnett allowed him to take his seat dressed in jeans.[200]

By noon on Monday, March 2nd, all unfinished bills had new bill jackets and new numbers. They were introduced "en masse," the rules requiring three readings were waived, speaking time limits were extended in debate in Committee of the Whole, reconsideration votes had to be taken the same day as the original vote and suspension of the rules had to pass by a two-thirds vote of the members present.

The contentious atmosphere of Saturday was gone. Games were over. Concepts that had been the sand-in-the-wheels in the conference committees became "cleanup" amendments. Amendments were presented, debated, voted up or down.

---

[199]After taking the oath of being a legislator, unless excused by the President of the Senate or the Speaker of the House, it is mandatory to attend all official sessions. The Governor has the power to ensure compliance.

[200]During Stauffer's first year Burnett was majority whip. His duties included enforcement of the dress code. Men had to have jackets, matching pants, button-collar shirt and necktie. Stauffer came in jeans, a sports jacket, button-collar shirt and necktie. Burnett fussed. Stauffer wore suits. Matilda Hansen's desk was beside Stauffer's. She had a "ring-side-seat" for this episode in proper legislative dress.

Legislators were somewhat rested. Heads were no longer fuzzy. The atmosphere on the Floor of both Chambers was serious, down to business, let's get this right and let's go home.

The House and Senate staff and Ralph Thomas' crew focused on their respective jobs. As final votes were in, Enrolled Acts were prepared and placed on the leaders desks for signature.

The legislators and lobbyists left the Capitol at a reasonable hour for "one last night at the Hitch" while staff worked to finish the paper work.

On Tuesday, March 3[rd,] the Senate convened at 8am, the House at 8:15 am. The Enrolled Acts prepared since the previous day's adjournment were signed. With little fanfare the legislators were "outa-there" about 10:00 am.

PERSPECTIVES ON THE 46TH SESSION

It was the competing agendas of the southern region vs. the central region that underlay the "bloody noses" atmosphere of contention of the regular session of the 46th Legislature. The jostling for political power prior to the session illustrates the point.

In the elections of 1980, Bob Burnett won his Albany County seat and was in line to become Speaker. Word "circulated" that Russ Donley of Natrona was "testing the waters" to "leap-frog over and dump Burnett" to become Speaker for the 46th Session.

Rick Robitaille of the Petroleum Association of Wyoming really wanted Donley to be Speaker in 1981 because of reapportionment and because of the Governor's push to put new severance taxes on oil and gas. Burnett, whose Albany County voters *loudly* supported severance taxes, voted in response to his constituents *for* severance taxes. He declined to vote *against* severance taxes as the mineral interests requested.

While historical practice allowed the caucus of the majority party to designate the Speaker, in law the decision was that of the full House. Knowing this and knowing they were able to force a floor vote, the Democrats discussed the Donley-factor at their post-election caucus.

Prior to their caucus some Democrats, Matilda Hansen among them, talked with Burnett telling him their (and her) votes were for him for Speaker. At the caucus, in one of the

Democrats rare moments of unanimity, the decision was made to support Burnett over Donley, to let this decision *drift* among the politically astute and to engage in a Floor fight if necessary.

By December speculation over the speakership reached the media. When they asked Russ Donley if he were running for Speaker, he replied, "No."

Russ Donley became Speaker two years later. There were no more increases in severance taxes.

In the 1982 election Dean Prosser, in line to be Speaker Pro Tem, came in 13th in a field of 18 for 9 House seats in Laramie County. The state employees and their friends "paid him back" for closing General File without considering their new salary pay plan.

The passage of the 1981 reapportionment law did not satisfy everyone. While the 1982 voters were choosing the next crop of legislators, the League of Women Voters of Wyoming became the next set of "restless and concerned citizens" taking Wyoming into Court—*AGAIN*—because equal representation did not exist in Wyoming's legislature.

12

Ignoring the Supreme Court

The 46th Legislature ignored the United States Supreme Court by continuing to claim *Wyoming's* constitutional provision of counties as election districts superseded any ruling of any Federal Court.[201] Yet the legislators grudgingly continued the 1965 Court mandate to combine counties with low populations into Senate districts. They pointedly resisted combining counties for House districts in deference to the wishes of the citizens of Niobrara County.

The 1981 "movers and shakers" crafting Wyoming reapportionment seemed to ignore the concept of the *United* States of America. The Civil War ended four years before Wyoming became a Territory. That conflict welded the states into one nation.

But nearly 120 years later the Confederate concept of states' rights continued alive and well. These Wyoming Republicans thought the State had a right to *selectively* follow the rulings of the Nation's highest court. They did as they saw fit, resisting attempts to change any more of Wyoming's reapportionment practices.

On January 31, 1981, prior to consideration of HB 360 in Committee of the Whole, Representative Charles Scott distributed another document to House members. It was an

---

[201] The United States Supreme Court had directed the Legislature not to follow Article I, Section 28 of the Wyoming Constitution.

unofficial set of mathematical manipulations that ignored relevant Federal case law following *Baker v. Carr.*[202].

Mathematical Facts Relevant to HB360
With 61 Representatives and 29 Senators

House:

Overall range	96.7%
Mean deviation	8.5%
Ratio Largest to Smallest (Platte to Sublette	2.6:1

Senate:

Overall range	61.0%
Mean deviation	15.5%

House increased to 63 representatives:

Overall range	64.0%

House if Niobara is given a representative:

Overall range	118.0%
Ratio largest to smallest:	4.1 to 1

If ideal district size is 7,687, Niobrara County is entitled to 38/100th of a representative.

HB 360 was Scott's reapportionment bill—the only proposal considered by the legislature in 1981. The final version contained wide disparities between the county election districts. The deviation range between Niobrara's over-representation of 60% and Washakie's under-representation of 29% was 89%. This great a range of deviation made the 1981 reapportionment justiciable.[203]

---

[202] The rulings following *Baker v. Carr: Abate v. Mundt,* 403 U.S. 182 (1971), *Conner v. Finch,* 431 U.S. 407 (1977), *Gaffney v. Cummings,* 412 U.S. 735 (1973), *Kirkpatrick v. Preisler,* 395 U.s. 526 (1969), *Mahan v. Howell,* 410 U.S. 315 (1973), *Reynolds v. Sims* 377 U.S. 533 (1964), *Wesberry v. Sanders,* 376 U.S. 1 (1964), *Whitcomb v. Chavis* 403 U.S. 124 (1971), *White v. Regester,* 412 U.S. 755 (1973), *White v. Weiser,* 412 U.S. 783 (1973).

[203] An issue that the court deems worthy of consideration is defined legally as "justiciable."

While equal representation among county election districts did not exist, the regional voting strength in each Chamber in relation to the population in the respective regions almost met the equality standard (Table 32). Voting strength in the Senate shifted away from the northern region to the southern region. But Federal case law wasn't about *regional* equality. It was about equality among the several election districts in the state.

TABLE 32
1981 Legislative Voting Strength
and Statewide Population—1980 Census

	Southern Region		Central Region		Northern Region	
	Senate	House	Senate	House	Senate	House
Voting Strength	42%	43%	32%	32%	28%	25%
% of State Population	42%		32%		25%	

The Wyoming League of Women Voters was not interested in regional equity. They focused on Niobrara County's one representative for 2,929 people and Washakie County's one representative for 9,496 people and cried "foul."

Historically, fair elections and equal representation were the fundamental reasons for the existence of the League of Women Voters.[204] During the 1960's and 1970's the League had lobbyists at the Legislature keeping track of citizen concerns, testifying before Committees and influencing votes on the issues where League members reached consensus.

League lobbyists and Board members followed the progress of HB 360. They made a decision. If Niobrara County got a representative, they were going to Court. The 89% range of deviation was intolerable. It was an abridgement of one man, one vote. It wasn't fair. Margaret Brown[205] was president of the

---

[204] Access to the vote by women was a hard fought right won by ratification of the 19th Amendment in 1920. The League of Women Voters championed fairness in all matters pertaining to the vote as a fundamental right for every adult.

[205] Margaret Brown was a Carbon County Representative for the 1983-84 and 1985-86 sessions.

state league. On April 21, 1982, *Brown v. Thomson* was filed in Federal Court.[206]

Besides Margaret Brown, the other plaintiffs were Judy Knight of Albany, Jane Maxwell of Laramie County, Mary Shenefield of Fremont, Miriam S. Straughan of Sheridan, Sandra H. Shuptrine of Teton and Olive J. White of Campbell. Counsel for the plaintiffs were Sue Davidson and Edwin H. Whitehead of the Cheyenne law firm of Urbigkit and Whitehead.

Thrya Thomson, in her capacity as chief elections officer and Secretary of State, was again lead defendant. Others named in the suit were the members of the State Canvassing Board: Governor Ed Herschler, State Treasurer Shirley Wittler and State Auditor James B. Griffith. Defending the canvassing board were Attorney General Steven F. Freudenthal, Deputy Attorney General Peter J. Mulvaney and Assistant Attorney General Randall T. Cox.

Second-term governor Ed Herschler had no "fire burning in his gut" on this issue. The Attorney General presented a substantial but not flamboyant defense of Niobrara County's representative.

The people who were "hot to trot" were current and former Niobrara County citizens. Foremost cheerleader among them was Auditor Jim Griffith, publisher and former co-editor of the *Lusk Herald*, the weekly newspaper for Niobrara County.

Advocates for Niobrara requested, and were granted, intervener status. They were: James L. Thompson, Gerald D. Bardo, Russell Thompson, Kenneth A. Gropp, Richard G. Pfister, Peter M. Hansen, Gertrude Chamberlain, Betty Percival, Marl L. Burke as well as Louis L. Landkamer and Kenneth R. Freeman as individuals and as the Board of County Commissioners of Niobrara County. County Commissioner F. Everett Brooks was not an intervener.

Counsel for the intervening defendants was Richard J. Barrett[207] of the Cheyenne law firm of Hathaway, Speight and Kunz. Three Federal Judges heard the case: Circuit Judge William E. Doyle and District Judges Ewing Kerr and Clarence Brimmer.

---

[206] *Brown v. Thomson* 536 F.Supp. 780 (D. Wyo. 1982).

[207] Court observers reported that Richard Barrett, in his presentation to the Court, struck a "mournful pose and sadly entreated the Judges not to take away Niobrara County's *lone* representative."

BROWN V. THOMSON

The plaintiffs presented a two-part narrow challenge to the constitutionality of the 1981 Reapportionment Law:

1. The representative was given to Niobrara County despite its small population; and
2. The constitutional requirement that every county have at least one representative.[208]

The plaintiffs deliberately kept their challenge narrow because of the request in the 1972 ruling in *Thompson v. Thomson* that future challenges be specifically focused and include a single member district plan.[209] Plaintiffs and their counsel decided it was the legislature's responsibility to create a plan with single member districts rather than for the citizens to create a plan.

They sought a middle ground by asking specifically for Niobrara's representative to be found unconstitutional thereby setting aside Article III, Section 3 guaranteeing each county a House seat. Plaintiffs made Niobrara and Goshen counties a House district. The two counties already were combined in a Senate district. If approved, this precedent was to apply to future reapportionment plans. The defendants and interveners claimed that

> ...the statistical difference in allocating a representative to Niobrara County is insignificant and that any statistical discrepancies are more than out-weighed by a rational State interest in the current reapportionment.[210]

The case proceeded with all parties agreeing that:

---

[208] Article III, Section 3, of the Wyoming Constitution read: "...each county shall constitute a ... representative district ... [with] at least ... one representative..."

[209] Another reason for Sue Davidson's narrow focus in *Brown v. Thomson* was in response to the client's wishes. The State Board of the League of Women Voters was unable to reach agreement to address issues broader than just the disparity caused by Niobrara County's Representative. While the southern region was well represented on that Board, there were members from the central and northern regions. Even the League experienced the southern vs. central/northern region tensions.

[210] *Brown v. Thomson,* 536 F. Supp. 780 (1982) at 781.

1. Niobrara County was the least populous of Wyoming's 23 counties.
2. The 1981 population of the state was 469,557.
3. The 46th Legislature gave Niobrara County one representative.
4. The size of the House was increased from 63 to 64 to accommodate Niobrara County.
5. Niobrara County had had its own representative since 1913, when the county was created.

Judge Kerr wrote the opinion. Judge Doyle concurred and wrote an opinion of his own. Judge Brimmer voted with the others but did not write a separate opinion. The beginning of Judge Kerr's Opinion made no reference to plaintiffs' use of Federal case law developed between 1965 and 1982. He extensively referenced Wyoming case law that was stuck in the provincial concepts from the three previous considerations of reapportionment. He missed the opportunity to judge fairness in representation from the emerging new perspectives of national case law.

Judge Kerr did not see any of the "middle ground" the plaintiffs were trying to claim. He noted this was the fourth time the Court was considering Wyoming's reapportionment. He recalled the opinion in *Schaefer v. Thomson*[211] in 1965 when he and Judges Pickett and Daugherty found no invidious discrimination in the House even though four counties, including Niobrara, each got a House seat when their populations were below the 5,400-divisor level.

Nor had the Court found invidious discrimination in 1971 in *Thompson v. Thomson*.[212] Kerr wrote:

> We are of the opinion that the reapportionment of the House by the 1971 Act does not constitute invidious discrimination for the reason that the 1963 reapportionment of the House was not substantially altered and, therefore, the 1971 act does not abridge the Equal Protection clause of the Fourteenth Amendment to the United States Constitution....
>
> Under the 1981 Reapportionment Act ... five counties, Crook, Hot Springs, Niobrara, Sublette and Teton, fall below the population level of the official divisor (7,300 people). Each was given a repre-

---

[211] *Schaefer v. Thomson* 251 F. Supp. 450 D.Wyo (1965).

[212] *Thompson v. Thomson*, 344 F. Supp. 1378 (1972).

sentative under the 1981 law. ... None of the changes in the 1981 law are challenged herein with the exception of the allocation ... of a representative to Niobrara County."[213]

Judge Kerr also played with statistics.

Initially, the 89 percent relative range figure would appear to conclusively establish a prima facie case and possibly invidious discrimination ... other relevant statistics ... soon reveals the fallacy of relying upon only one statistic. Utilizing only the overall relative range figure distorts the picture. The population differential in Niobrara County between 1965 court-ordered reapportionment ... and the 1981 Reapportionment Law is the difference between 3,750 and 2,924 or 826 people.

The Court finds ... seven counties elect 28 out of 64 representatives or 43.75 per cent. The seven counties contain 56.3 per cent of the total state population [1980 census].... Comparatively, if the plaintiff's plan is adopted [combining Niobrara with Goshen] ... the seven counties ... would elect 28 representatives out of 63 or 44.4 per cent of the House.... Statistically, a .65 per cent change is trivial ... [and] is insufficient to constitute invidious discrimination. Rather, the effect ... is ... *de minimis*."[214]

Statistically, the "dilution" of the plaintiffs' votes is *de minimis* when Niobrara County has its own representative.... If Niobrara County continues to have its own representative, 46.65 percent of the population would elect 33 of 64 representatives. Thus 46.65 percent is the minimum population which could elect a majority of House members. This figure is comparable to the minimum population percentage of 47.52 percent of the Senate seats in the 1965 *Schaefer v. Thomson*.

This was curious reasoning. By comparing the *same district* in two *different decades,* the 826-population differential was meaningless if the issue was equality of voting strength among the election districts. Equally meaningless in 1982, and just as puzzling, was the relevance of the 1965 Senate "minimum

---

[213] *Brown v. Thomson,* at 782.
[214] Ibid at 783.

population needed to have a majority of senate votes" (47.52%) to the 1982 House "minimum population needed to have a majority of House votes" (46.65%). With these numbers, Judge Kerr concluded there was no invidious discrimination in the 1981 Reapportionment Plan.

The Plaintiffs' challenge was based on Federal case law. So what was the relevance of an opinion based on Wyoming case law?[215] Whatever the national precedent-setting implications, the opinion had considerable relevance to Niobrara County's retention of a House seat. The finding of no invidious discrimination may have been predictable given the narrowness of the plaintiffs' case.

But the Judges were not finished. They wanted to consider "rational state interest" as a justifiable reason for maintaining a House seat in every county. For this they did turn to Federal case law.

Judge Kerr quoted from *Gaffney v. Cummings*[216] stating that if a state plan had a large deviation, "The burden of proof shifted to the state to establish a rational justification and state policy...." Then he quoted from *Reynolds v. Sims*:

[T]he Equal Protection Clause requires a state make an honest and good faith effort to construct districts, in both houses of its legislature, as nearly equal population as is applicable ... so long as the divergences from a strict population standard are based on legitimate considerations incident to the effectuation of a rational state policy, some deviations ... are constitutionally permissible....[217]

Then he went back to *Gaffney v. Cummings* saying achieving fair and effective representation is a vital and worthy goal but to do so need not depend solely on gross population variations or mathematical equality among district populations. Kerr found in *Gaffney* justification for the legitimacy of other relevant factors and other important interests.

An unrealistic overemphasis on raw population figures, a mere nose count in the districts, may submerge these other considerations and itself furnish a ready tool for

---

[215] This curious rationale for a conclusion based on Wyoming case law reflected a singularly insular perception of Wyoming in our Federal system of government.

[216] *Gaffney v. Cummings*, 412 U.S. 735 (1973).

[217] *Reynolds v. Sims* 377 U.S. 533 (1964) at 565, 577 and 579.

ignoring factors that in day-to-day operation are important to an acceptable representation and apportionment arrangement.[218]

Thus the state and intervening defendants successfully established that a rational state policy did exist justifying the statistical deviations in the 1981 Reapportionment Law. Kerr agreed that if any of the 13 rational reasons were denied and a county lost a legislative seat, then citizen's rights would be abridged. The 13 reasons were:

1. Wyoming is unique among her sister states.
2. A small population is encompassed in a large area.
3. Counties have always been a major form of government.
4. Each County has its own special economic and social needs.
5. The needs of the people are different and distinctive.
6. Because Goshen County was larger than Niobrara County, the interests of Niobrara County would be "virtually unprotected."
7. The common interests of the people in a county are public facilities, government administration, work problems, personal problems.
8. Counties are the primary administrative agencies of State government.
9. Historically the state's policy has been to keep the counties as administrative agencies.
10. The taxing powers of the counties are constitutionally and statutorily limited.
11. The State distributes supplemental monies to the counties.
12. The financial requirements of each county are different.
13. Without representation, the people of Niobrara County will be forgotten.

Judge Kerr's three conclusions stated that the allocation by the State Legislature of a representative to Niobrara County: (1) is not unconstitutional; (2) is not statistically significant and does not constitute invidious discrimination; and (3) the integrity of political boundaries remains intact while a rational State policy continues to be maintained as it has been since 1913 in Niobrara County. Case dismissed.

---

[218] *Brown v. Thomson* at 784.

Though Judge Doyle concurred with Judge Kerr, he had a keen appreciation of equal representation expressed as one man, one vote. He noted the issue before them was very narrowly framed and about just one county. He thought the "over representation was noteworthy." The 1981 Plan added another seat rather than taking a House seat from elsewhere, whereby no county suffered at Niobrara County's gain.

Doyle said if the numbers approach were "religiously followed," districts would have to be merged to satisfy one man, one vote and Wyoming's representation by county would vanish. He agreed that Wyoming "has good reasons for clinging to the county as an (election) district" because by so doing the peculiar needs of each county can be represented. Although this approach "might not carry out fully" equal representation it came "close enough to be roughly fair."

Judge Doyle looked at whether disproportionate population in a single district was "injurious" to the remainder of the state. No discomfort seemed to be apparent just because Niobrara had a House seat.

> There is no indication ... the larger cities are being discriminated against ... Cheyenne, Laramie, Casper, Sheridan are not shown to have suffered in the slightest degree. There has been no preference for the cattle-raising or agricultural areas as such. [219]

Members of the Wyoming League of Women Voters were saddened by the Kerr and Doyle opinions. They were not deterred. They anticipated the possibility of the ruling going against them.

They took their challenge to the highest court in *Brown et al. v. Thomson, Secretary of State of Wyoming, et al.* No. 82-65. The United States Supreme Court took the case because it contained elements worthy of their consideration and it provided a forum for questions they wanted to ask.

On the vernal equinox, March 21st, State League President Margaret Brown appeared before the United States Supreme Court. Sue Davidson argued the League's case. Randall T. Cox argued for the State. Richard Barrett filed a brief for the intervenors. Announcement of the Court's decision came on the summer solstice, June 22, 1983.

---

[219] *Brown v. Thomson,* at 788.

Kenneth R. Buck, writing in "Case Notes" in the *Land and Water Law Review*,[220] succinctly identified the major points before this highest court. Buck reported that the League cited the violations of three equal protection clauses.

First, increasing the number of House seats to 64 in the 1981 plan was unconstitutional because it gave a county a representative solely because it was a political subdivision—a county—, without regard for population.

Second, in the opinion of the League, there were no overriding state policies to justify violation of the equal protection clause.

Third, there was improper dilution of the voting privileges of the appellants and other citizen/electors because of the 89% deviation.

Buck indicated the League belatedly "recognized the problem of limiting their objections to the one representative from Niobrara County" and suggested the court look at both the 64 and 63 seat plans.

The Defense presented three arguments in support of the 46th legislature's reapportionment.

First, there was no significant difference between the 64 and the 63 seat plans because it took nearly the same number of people to elect a majority of House members under either plan.

Second, the seven plaintiffs did not show they had been "purposely discriminated against."

Third, Wyoming traditionally used counties as the basic unit of local government and giving Niobrara County its one representative enhanced the state's rational state policy.

The Supreme Court affirmed the judgment of the District Court on a 5-4 vote.[221] Justice Powell wrote the Opinion of the Court joined by Justices Burger, Rehnquist, Stevens and O'Connor. O'Connor had a concurring opinion joined by Stevens. Justice Brennan wrote the dissenting opinion. He was joined by Justices White, Marshall and Blackmun.

Brown v. Thomson required the court to carefully address the very narrow issue of whether a 64-member Wyoming House of Representatives was bad enough to be invidious discrimination

---

[220] Volume XIX, Number 11984, pp. 253-69.

[221] *Brown et al. v. Thomson, Secretary of State of Wyoming, et. al.. Appeal from the United States District Court for the District of Wyoming*, No. 82-65. Argued March 21, 1983—Decided June 22, 1983, II-A, B & C.

and thus a violation of the Fourteenth Amendment while a 63-member House was not invidious discrimination.

JUSTICE POWELL

Writing for the majority, Justice Powell recognized that the Court previously allowed population deviations when "legitimate objectives" were pursued to "maintain the integrity of various political subdivisions" or "to provide for compact districts of contiguous territory" (*Reynolds*). Then he quoted from *Gaffney* about "unrealistic overemphasis on raw population figures" submerging legitimate objectives that became "a ready tool for ignoring factors" that are important to "acceptable representation and apportionment management." He said, "...minor deviations from mathematical equality among state legislative districts are insufficient to make out a prima facie case of invidious discrimination."

But Powell was talking about plans with "a maximum population deviation under 10%" as minor deviations. He said a plan with higher deviations did "create a prima facie case of discrimination."

The ultimate inquiry ... is whether the legislature's plan "may reasonably be said to advance rational state policy" and if so, "whether the population disparities among the districts that have resulted from the pursuit of this plan exceed constitutional limits."[222]

Justice Powell had no argument with Niobrara County's 60% deviation below the mean being "more than minor." He also did not question Wyoming's historical practice of using counties as election districts with at least one representative per county. He agreed with Circuit Judge Doyle that this practice was supported by "substantial and legitimate state concerns" and was applied "free from any taint of arbitrariness or discrimination."

He said "population equality is the sole ... criteria used" and the formula deviations encountered had been "no greater than necessary to preserve counties as representative districts." He saw no "built-in bias" that favored specific political interests or geographical areas. He noted that this case had a plan with population variations that were "entirely the result of the

---

[222] Powell's quote from *Mahan v. Howell*, 410 U.S. 315 (1973) at 328.

consistent and nondiscriminatory application of a legitimate state policy."

Then he said, "This does not mean that population deviations of any magnitude … are acceptable." In a footnote he explained the Court's prior decisions that invalidated other state plans were based on the "…lack of proof that deviations from population equality were the result of a good-faith application of legitimate districting criteria." He discussed the narrowness of the challenge.

> Here we are not required to decided whether Wyoming's nondiscriminatory adherence to county boundaries justifies the populations deviations that exist throughout Wyoming's representative districts. Appellants deliberately have limited their challenge to the alleged dilution of their voting power resulting from the one representative given to Niobrara County."

Thus the issue was not the constitutional permissibility of an 89% range of deviation. Instead, the issue became the permissibility of a 64-seat House or a 63-seat House in order to preserve county boundaries even though

> …considerable population variations will remain even if Niobrara County's representative is eliminated [because a seat for Niobrara County] … is not a significant cause of the population deviations that exist in Wyoming.

The Court found no violation of the Fourteenth Amendment when the legislature gave Niobrara County its own representative.

"The judgment of the District Court is affirmed."

JUSTICE O'CONNOR

Sandra Day O'Connor voted with the majority but she and Justice Stevens "recognized possible inconsistencies" between their ruling in *Brown et al.* and the Court's previous cases supporting population deviations in the 10% range. She said,

> [T]he relevant percentage … is not the 89% maximum deviation when the State of Wyoming is view(ed) as a whole, but the additional deviation from equality produced by … one representative to Niobrara County…. Even the consistent and nondiscriminatory application of a legitimate state policy cannot justify

substantial populations deviations ... where the effect would be to eviscerate the one-person, one-vote principle.

But the most important point made in the O'Connor concurrence was in the last paragraph. After referring to the suggestion in *Mahan v. Howell*[223] that a 16.4% maximum deviation "may well be within tolerable limits," she concluded:

I have the gravest doubts that a statewide legislative plan with an 89% maximum deviation could survive constitutional scrutiny despite the presence of the State's strong interest in preserving county boundaries. I join the Court's opinion on the understanding that nothing in it suggests that this Court would uphold such a scheme.

JUSTICE BRENNAN

In writing the dissenting opinion,[224] Justice Brennan seemed outraged. First, no justification existed to uphold "an 89% maximum deviation and a 16% average deviation from population equality."

Second, he seemed incensed the plaintiffs framed their challenge so narrowly so as to be empty of precedential value. He didn't want another case so limited in scope. He decried the plaintiffs' attack on only one small feature that denied the Court the opportunity to consider the "overall constitutionality of the entire scheme." He wanted *Brown* to be the end of challenges that exercised "moderation or restraint in mounting constitutional attacks."

He, too, reviewed the discussion in *Reynolds v. Sims*[225] and *Roman v. Sincock*[226] of "honest and good faith efforts" in constructing reapportionment plans with "population as nearly equal as is practicable." He discussed permissible deviation

---

[223] *Mahan v. Howell*, 410 U.S. 315 (1973) at 329.

[224] *Brown et al. v. Thomson, Secretary of State of Wyoming, et. al.. Appeal from the United States District Court for the District of Wyoming*, No. 82-65, 1983, II-A, B & C. at 850.

[225] *Reynolds v. Sims*, 377 U.S. 533 (1964) at 577.

[226] *Roman v. Sincock*, 377 U.S. 695 (1964) at 710.

ranges and certain factors that are free from any taint of arbitrariness or discrimination. He was very clear that

> [T]he overriding objective must be substantial equality of population among the various districts, so that the vote of any citizen is approximately equal in weight to the vote of any other citizen.

Justice Brennan used the four-step test from *Reynolds* to judge the constitutionality of redistricting plans.

1. A plaintiff must show that the deviations ... are sufficiently large to make ... a prima facie case of discrimination [using] a rough threshold of 10% maximum deviation ... below that level, deviations will ordinarily be considered *de minimis*....

2. A court must consider the quality of the reasons ... a State [uses] ...to explain the deviations. [Acceptable reasons] must be legitimate considerations incident to the effectuation of a rational state policy.

3. The state policy ... to justify the divergences... is ... furthered by the plan....

4. [I]f a state succeeds in showing ... the deviations are justified by their ... rational state policy, the court must ... consider whether they are small enough to be constitutionally tolerable....

When Brennan applied the four-step test to *Brown* he found it "manifestly unconstitutional." It was a "prima facie case of discrimination" because the 89% maximum deviation exceeded the Court standard of 10%.

He acknowledged that "one might reasonably" decide the State met steps two and three because of the "longstanding policy untainted by arbitrariness or discrimination." But in no way did Wyoming meet the standards in step 4 because "nothing can be allowed to negate the fundamental principle of one person, one vote...."

For the dissenters, Niobrara County's over- representation of 60% just could not be considered "any kind of a minor variation" because Niobrara's voters were given more than 2½ times the voting strength of the average Wyoming voter and more than triple the voting strength of voters in some other counties.

The sparse-population argument did not impress Justice Brennan. Actually, he said, "...sparseness of population, far from excusing deviations from equality, actually *increases* the need for equality among districts."[227]

Justice Brennan then got the 46th Legislature's reapportionment practice squarely in his sights and declared their work was an "absolute disregard" of the principle of population equality. In fact, Niobrara's seat was allocated "on a basis unrelated to population." Then he said the plaintiffs just challenged the "worst of many objectionable feature." Only nine counties were allocated seats within the 10% "population proportionality." In fact Sublette and Crook were "respectively 38% and 28% below the statewide average" and Teton and Washakie counties were "29% and 28%, respectively, above that figure."

Then Justice Brennan spoke plainly. He reproved the Court majority's attempt to escape the "stark facts" by using "two lines of reasoning based on unspoken legal premises that do not withstand examination" and called Niobrara County's House seat an example of "rotten borough politics." He said the Court "is mistaken" when it focuses on the "degree of vote dilution suffered by any one individual voter."

Whether over-represented or under-represented, each scheme was equally illegal because, either way, a very large number of people were adversely affected.

> It is the *principle* of equal representation, as well as the votes of individual plaintiffs, that a State may not dilute.... Just as the Equal Protection Clause does not permit a small class of voters to be deprived of fair and equal voting power, so does it forbid the elevation of a small class of *supervoters* granted an extraordinarily powerful franchise.

Justice Brennan was not impressed with Judge Kerr's statistical manipulations that showed *de minimus* between the

---

[227] *Chapman v. Meier* 420 U.S. 1, (1975) at 24-25 states: "Sparse population is not a legitimate basis for departure from the goal of equality. A state with a sparse population may face problems different from those faced by one with a concentrated population, but that, without more, does not permit a substantial deviation from the average. Indeed, in a State with a small population each individual vote may be more important to the result of an election than in a highly populated State. Thus *particular emphasis should be placed on establishing districts with as exact population equality as possible.*"

64-seat House and the 63-seat House. Brennan said that argument had been tossed out in *Tawes*.[228]

Brennan agreed with the Wyoming League of Women Voters that the nine justices should not have been "constrained by the initial narrow challenge" of *Brown*. The Justices had looked at "the scheme as a whole" in *Tawes*. They should have done so in *Brown*.

For Brennan, it just did not make sense to consider only one seat in a bicameral legislature—to look at one seat "in the abstract." He flatly stated that

> [T]he inequality created by Niobrara County's representative—a 23% increase in the maximum deviation from equality—is necessarily cumulative with the inequality imposed in the rest of the system.

He thought "artificial tricks" were played to say that fairness in the allocation of one seat should be considered as having no connection with any other seat. He further charged the Court with giving weight to and only looking at the inequalities that "favor the plan." He agreed they could not look at Niobrara County in a vacuum but he thought the inequalities ought to be considered as "undesirable features," not saving features.

In the opinion of Justice Brennan, "Wyoming's error in granting Niobrara County voters a vote worth double or triple the votes of other Wyoming voters" was compounded by the impermissible large disparities in voting power existing in the rest of the apportionment plan. He was astonished the Court managed to turn that damning fact *for* instead of *against* the State's favor. Finally, Justice Brennan said,

> It is senseless to create a rule whereby a single instance of gross inequality is unconstitutional if it occurs in a plan otherwise letter-perfect, but constitutional if it occurs in a plan that, even without that feature, flagrantly violates the Constitution. That, however, is precisely what the Court does today.

What Justice Brennan really wanted was for the Court to require "...Wyoming to devise an apportionment plan constitutional in its entirety."

The challenge to the 1971 reapportionment had been framed in broad concepts. Then the Court said it wanted a more narrow

---

[228] *Maryland Committee For Fair Representation v. Tawes,* 377 U.S. 656 (1964).

focus. The challenge to the 1981 reapportionment was a narrow focus. But the Court said it wanted broad concepts.

Thoughtful Court observers were especially interested in the opinions of Justice O'Connor and Justice Brennan. The search continued for clues on how to apply successfully the Equal Protection Clause of the Fourteenth Amendment to the United States Constitution to achieve Wyoming's constitutional requirement of equal representation in their legislature.

14

What Is at Stake?

Thus the United States Supreme Court upheld Charles Scott's HB 360, a "plan in obfuscation" that distributed legislative seats according to archaic assumptions and whims of political agendas.[229] Scott's plan was not the only plan prepared for the 1981 Session. Matilda Hansen created another reapportionment plan.

It was crafted to recognize Federal case law, to show clarity in the use of ratios based on census numbers and to reflect an understanding of the State's political realities.[230] A reasonable proposal was not wanted. The absence of "other state policy factors" and the goal of "equality in representation" were both anathema to the proponents of states' rights. Her amendment failed because it was crafted and presented by a Democrat.

The Court-approved Enrolled Act 111 kept the inviolability of counties as elections districts with deviations nowhere near the standard for one-person, one-vote. Citizens with an under-

---

[229] The "obfuscation" was the continued inequality in representation of the citizens of Wyoming among the several county-designated election districts.

[230] She used the preliminary census, made 62 House and 30 Senate seats with the Senate ratio at 16,652:1 and the House ratio at 7,541:1. She used counties as election districts, not in defiance of federal case law, but because no other districting option existed. She distributed legislative seats "strictly by the numbers". The plan *exactly matched* Enrolled Act 111 except for Goshen/Niobrara's House seat and the House seats in Park. She presented the plan in a 3rd Reading House amendment. It failed.

standing of Federal and state constitutional law were troubled. The Constitution of Wyoming clearly states the importance of equal representation:

> PREAMBLE: We the people of the State of Wyoming, grateful to God for our civil, political and religious liberties, and desiring to secure them to ourselves and perpetuate them to our posterity, do ordain and establish this Constitution.

> Article I, Section 1: ...All power is inherent in the people, and all free governments are founded on their authority, and instituted for their peace, safety and happiness;....

> Article I, Section 2: ...In their inherent right to life, liberty and the pursuit of happiness, all members of the human race are equal.

> Article I, Section 3: ...Since equality in the enjoyment of natural and civil rights is only made sure through political equality, the laws of this state affecting the political rights and privileges of its citizens shall be without distinction of race, color, sex, or any circumstances or condition whatsoever other than individual incompetency, or unworthiness duly ascertained by a court of competent jurisdiction.

If "all power is inherent in the people," then all the people in the state had the right to *equally* access, use and reap the benefits of that power. But for most of the 20th century the combined political power of the agricultural/mineral interests managed to retain archaic inequality, held in place through the use of counties as election districts, by intentional skewing of the federal or state census and by calculated distribution of legislative seats to attain or sustain control.

It was clearly about keeping economic and political power in the hands of the select few.

It was about maintaining privilege. The posterity of those who were here first, wanted to continue to be first. This eminent position was threatened if political equality—equal representation—was allowed.

It was about public resources used for private gain: lands, timber, deposits of state monies in banks that paid low interest.

It was about not paying taxes—yet wanting good roads.

It was about K-12 teachers not receiving professional-level pay—because they should work for the love of the job. It was about community college, university professors and public employees working for below-market salaries—because the ambience of life in Wyoming made up the difference.

It was about ignoring the less fortunate and disabled—for to recognize them "makes me sad" a Speaker once told the author.

It was about not trusting the blue-collar worker—because they always demanded good schools for their children to learn the skills to move up the ladder of economic success.

It was about Governor Cliff Hansen calling the National Guard to stand-by alert in the Capitol Rotunda in 1965—because the Democrats controlling the House wanted to repeal Wyoming's Right To Work law. The Governor feared a riot on the House floor. Those burly union members were not trusted to be gentlemen in *their* Capitol.[231]

It was about locking away felons and other people "we don't like"—and then complaining about the cost of corrections.

It was about taking away the treaty water rights of Wyoming's Native Americans—on the grounds that the white man knew best how to consume water.

It was about not funding abortions for poor women—thereby using the police power of the state to enforce church doctrine.

It was about denying life sentence without parole to anyone not a sex offender—thus denying equality before the Law to those who committed other capital crimes.[232]

It was about torpedoing potentially viable economic development initiatives designed to diversify the state's tax base with more jobs for the adult children of Wyoming residents— because more jobs meant more people, more schools, more streets, more hospitals, more roads to be financed through bonds on the real property of the agricultural and mineral interests.

As each decade in the second half of the 20th century came and went, many rank-and-file legislators chaffed at the band-aid attitudes generated during each session instead of reasoned long-range solutions for serious, real, long-standing issues of the constituents.

---

[231] Union members and their supporters were surprised at this expression of the Governor's fear. But he insulted them with his request the National Guard bring attack dogs into the Rotunda.

[232] The first "life sentence without parole" statute allowed this sentence only for those who committed a first-degree sex crime. It did not apply to any of the other capital crimes. In 2001 the law was changed to apply to all capital crimes.

Historical precedents and full comprehension of the structural challenge to equal representation was beyond the purview of too many of the 1981 legislators. Information was power. So those with the power controlled the flow of information.

Besides who controlled what information, the other deterrent to equal representation was the complacency of the general public. They understood election districts defined by county boundaries. They kept track of how many legislative seats their county was granted—decade-by-decade. Everyone knew Niobrara County was inordinately over- represented. Too many lacked the will or the inclination to demand fair representation in their legislature.

When the legal community outside Wyoming read the *Brown v. Thomson* opinion many were appalled. The author heard their expressions of disbelief in spirited conversations with members of the National Conference of State Legislatures.[233] Her appointment to the NCSL provided her the opportunity for interactions with professionals who focused on reapportionment matters of all the states. In seminars as well as in formal and informal discussions, she realized how out-of-kilter Wyoming's 1981 Plan was.

She also realized how the decisions in *Thompson v. Thomson* and especially in *Brown v. Thomson* continued to deny equal legislative representation to Wyoming's citizens. This denial was truly galling because of Wyoming's identity as the Equality State!

During the remainder of the decade, she worked to understand the issues surrounding reapportionment. The Executive Committee of NCSL appointed a Task Force on Reapportionment and assigned staff to do in depth research.

---

[233] NCSL is the organization of the legislatures of all the states and territories, established to share information among the several states, to lobby Congress and the White House on issues of common concern as determined by the members, to enhance networking among legislators, NCSL staff, leaders of both the Democratic and Republican National Parties and with the nation's major lobbying cadre of informed professionals. Membership in NCSL is by appointment by each state's President of the Senate and Speaker of the House. Matilda Hansen served on the Health, Human Services and Law committees of the State/Federal Assembly from 1979 through 1994. She was elected by the NCSL membership to a three-year term on the executive committee, July 1991- August 1994.

These specialists in reapportionment came from the disciplines of Law and Political Science. In October 1989, they published *Reapportionment Law: The 1990's*.[234] The document contained the case law generated by the Federal Courts and other writings pertinent to redistricting and reapportionment.

This growing body of knowledge—in the courts, in libraries and among legislative staffers in Wyoming's sister states—was solidly grounded. The focus was on how to provide and to protect equal representation, at 10% deviation range, as guaranteed by the Fourteenth Amendment.

Six Supreme Court justices in *Brown v. Thomson* clearly stated equal representation did not exist in Wyoming. In the "culture of legislators" Hansen felt like one of the "little kids" on the block. The "big kids," the other states, had seriously worked toward contiguous, compact, 10% deviation districts since 1963. Not only was Wyoming the single black sheep in the flock, we were all by ourselves on our mountain.

NCSL wasn't the only organization working on issues related to equal representation. In the April 1988 issue of *Government Executive*, the magazine written for legislators and others in state government, included an article on the census and its impact on legislative membership. The National Center For Policy Alternatives published *A State Report On Voter Participation*.[235]

THE PRELUDE TO 1991 REAPPORTIONMENT

Knowledgeable students of the legislative process expected the Speaker to refer election issues to Corporations, Elections and Political Subdivisions—Committee #7. Patti MacMillan of Albany chaired the House Committee from 1989 through 1992. Charles Scott of Natrona chaired the Senate Committee during

---

[234] National Conference of State Legislatures, Reapportionment Task Force, October 1989, Denver, Colorado. This readable half-inch document included chapters on: The Census, Equal Population, Racial and Ethnic Discrimination, The Voting Rights Act, Multi-member Districts, An Overview of Partisan Gerrymandering. The five chapters referenced 408 authors and excerpts from 75 United States Supreme Court cases.

[235] November 1989, NCFP Report Series, Vol 1, No 2.

those years. They co-chaired the Joint Committee (see Appendix B).

Serious work on 1991 reapportionment began with its 1990 Joint Interim assignment.[236] At the Joint Committee meeting in Cheyenne on January 26, 1990, reapportionment first appeared on the agenda. They reviewed NCSL's *Reapportionment Law: The 1990's* and asked Management Council for $50,000 in the "feed bill"[237] to hire outside counsel for legal assistance on reapportionment. At the June 11th meeting in Douglas Rick Miller explained:

1. Wyoming's county boundary multi-member districts were not a subterfuge to disenfranchise minorities because county boundaries had been used [as election districts] since statehood.

2. Wyoming was unique. All other states were redistricting, not reapportioning.

3. The 1965 Three-Judge Federal Court mandated multi-county election districts in the Senate but upheld Wyoming's tradition in the House where each county was an election district.

4. Carefully crafted legislation was needed to avoid difficulties if the seat of a "very popular legislator" was eliminated.

5. The ruling in *Brown v. Thomson* was not an endorsement of Wyoming's current system because the narrow question before the Court focused only on Niobrara County—not on the disparities among the rest of the counties that denied equal representation to the citizens.[238]

Senator Scott wanted two bills: a primary plan of counties as multi-member election districts and a back-up plan if the Court found the primary plan unconstitutional. He admitted the

---

[236] In Wyoming's legislature interim (out of session) committee work is done as a Joint Committee consisting of the respective House and Senate committees.

[237] The "feed bill," so named when the legislature met biennially, was the first bill of each session because it paid the salaries and expenses for the upcoming legislative session. With annual sessions, it became the appropriations bill for the Legislative Service Office and funded interim as well as session expenses for legislators and staff.

[238] From Minutes of the Joint Corporations, Elections and Political Subdivision 1990 Committee #7 Interim work.

purpose of the back-up bill was to influence the outcome of a court challenge and to prevent the Court from designing a reapportionment plan for Wyoming.

Because of the lack of a quorum to take action and with Scott's proposal on the table, Chairman MacMillan allowed free discussion. She asked, "Is there consensus on how a bill might be drafted for 1991 consideration?"

> John De Witt: "the current ... approach ... of county boundaries have served the state well. [My] concern [is] about a challenge.... The plan [should] be designed to avoid litigation but ... maintain the traditional approach.... If multi-county districts [are necessary] in the House ... those groupings should be identical with ... Senate multi-county districts.... [We should] ... set as a goal a plan ... [with] maximum deviation ... of 15-20% with a weighted average deviation ... of 10%.... Partisanship ... should be avoided ... [keep] the current size of the House and Senate ... only as a last resort ... split a county."

> Dorothy Perkins agreed with DeWitt: "...especially in ... avoiding partisanship and in the size of ... the House and Senate. [I] ... hope a plan can be developed [to] avoid litigation but I am fearful it could not."

> Della Herbst: "...retain the current county boundaries ... but if larger districts are required [this] to be done on a multi-county basis where entire counties are combined ... a court order would increase the size of the legislature. This would be difficult given the physical limits of the State Capitol and the difficulty [of more legislators] in the day-to-day operations of the ... session."

> Don Sullivan: "...it [is] not possible to avoid litigation. I believe the majority of the legislators want to maintain the current system. [I am] ... fearful ... a court would disapprove such a plan. Given political reality ... [a primary] plan should be developed but a backup plan should be prepared which would anticipate ... [a court holding of unconstitutionality]. If a court ... [chose] the backup plan ... the legislature would have ...

162

designated the reapportionment ... rather than ...
one designed by the courts."

Bruce Hinchey: "...urge a plan ... as close as possible
to the status quo ... not consider restructuring the
legislature by increasing the size to fit the
numerical requirements ... in Supreme Court
cases. I am fearful ... a House ... of that size
would ... be unworkable."

Patti MacMillan: "...[urge] the Committee not to
expand the size of either [chamber] and to reduce
them, if necessary. The overall range should be
reduced and the county boundaries should be
maintained ... gerrymandering ... be avoided. The
backup plan ... include multi-county districts as
necessary to reduce the range and average
deviations. [What is] ... the likelihood of a court
... [using] a backup plan should a primary plan be
held ... unconstitutional?"

Charles Scott spoke at considerable length: "[urge] the
Committee to maintain the current system ... all
systems which involve redistricting are
gerrymandered ... which is simply impossible
under the Wyoming system ... expansion of the
size of the legislative bodies is not feasible ...
House ... within a range of 58-65 members and the
Senate within a range of 29-31 members ...
litigation is extremely likely. A special interest
group could sue [or] ... a [frustrated candidate
who] feels he would have a better chance ... under
a different system ... a lawsuit may result as a part
of a profit motive since a law firm may ... recover
... fees."

Then Scott suggested: "[legislation be designed] to
reduce the range...use weighted average statistic
and ... a large appropriation to finance litigation to
make opponents understand that attacking
Wyoming's apportionment ... will be an expensive
undertaking ... concerned about gerrymandering
... which might make them more receptive to
Wyoming's ... gerrymander proof approach.
[Counties with] ... sparse and diverse population,
distinct interests, economics, demographic and the

integrity of county boundaries as a rational stable basis for deviations ... greater than 10%.

Do Palma, the lobbyist for the Wyoming League of Women Voters, said: "[The] League strongly believes in the one man, one vote concept ... some League members are deeply concerned about the disparities among the counties and the level of representation. [We] assure the committee the League will monitor your activities."

Chairman MacMillan reported that the Management Council put the $50,000 in the feed bill. She requested Niobrara's Mel ZumBrunnen[239] and the Wyoming League be placed on the list to receive meeting notices and copies of all materials distributed to the committee. Chairman Scott asked the Legislative Service Office to develop a generic statute specifying criteria for a "fallback position."

In a memo to legislators dated July 13, 1990, Richard Miller, Director of the LSO held "legislative school" for the committee, giving them the legal and tactical issues surrounding reapportionment.

At the July 30th Joint Corporations meeting in Laramie the Committee continued to "gnaw on the bone" of reapportionment. Observers were Kathleen Simon of Casper and Ruth Rudolph of Laramie for the League of Women Voters, Kreg McCollum and Steve Furtney from of the Department of Administration and Fiscal Control, Division of Research and Statistics, Clint Beaver of the Attorney General's office and Bob Beck from Wyoming Public Radio.

The LSO presented "Greatest Divisor" and "Float" plans.[240] Eli Bebout reported from an NCSL seminar, that "...the 10% deviation range limit was very firm and ... it will be very difficult to justify noncompliance."

Chairman MacMillan informally polled the Committee again, trying to determine if members still wanted to use the current reapportionment scheme as the basic approach for the 1991 committee bill.

Only Steve Freudenthal and Don Sullivan demurred, speaking in favor of single-member districts. Freudenthal requested the LSO to determine whether attorney's fees can be

---

[239] 1989-1992 Representative from Niobrara County.

[240] Miller's "Float" plan was a variation of floterial districting. See the Glossary for definitions of "floating member" and "floterial district."

recovered in a civil rights suit on reapportionment under 42 USC 1983. He requested the LSO to draft a bill with:

1. Single-member districts with the overall deviation not to exceed 10%;
2. Using estimates for the 1990 census and voter registrations from recent elections;
3. Respecting county boundaries to the maximum extent; and
4. Maintaining the 64-30 split between the Senate and House.

The November 16th Joint Corporations meeting was in Casper. Besides the committee, other legislators attended: Senator Allan Howard of Big Horn and Representatives Marlene Simons of Crook, Peg Shreve of Park and Rick Tempest of Natrona. Observers were Do Palma for the Wyoming League of Women Voters, Clint Beaver of the Attorney General's office, Lola ZumBrunnen of Niobrara and Duke Kessler of the Wyoming Education Association.

E. Mark Braden of Baker and Hostetler, a Washington D.C. law firm, was introduced as the new outside legal counsel. Braden saw two key issues: the Constitutional issue of one man, one vote and the possibility of a Voting Rights Act challenge. He said a fallback plan was not necessary because if Wyoming's initial plan were overturned in court, the legislature will have an opportunity to work on another plan. He said in his experience gerrymandering,

> [I]s far more sophisticated in this computer age. Gerrymanders do in fact work today. The approach is essentially to pack and fragment. Minority districts are formed so that the minority party has a super majority in some districts. Then the majority party has a majority in the remaining districts even if it is not a super majority. The fairness and integrity of the people who draw the lines in a redistricting situation is most important. In most states the majority party does draw the lines and it is a very partisan activity.[241]

The question surfaced concerning Braden's ability to be fair to Wyoming's Democrats considering his Republican credentials. The Minutes show Freudenthal spoke for the Democrats.

---

[241] Minutes of the November 16, 1990 Joint Committee Meeting. Braden was speaking from his experience as counsel for the minority Republicans in California redistricting.

He said he, "had no objections [to Braden's] political back-ground."

Rick Miller presented a "Float" multi-member reapportionment plan with the Senate deviation range of 7.37% and the average deviation 2.31%. The House deviation range was 9.60% and the average deviation 2.76%.

Committee members were unhappy with Senate District 5 of 31,028 people stretching from 45 miles north of Cheyenne to the Montana border and from 18 miles east of Casper to the Nebraska border. Even for Wyomingites used to long distances, this was considered extreme.

Each "Float" district had nearly equal population in the Senate and House. Within each "Float" district candidates ran "at-large" with no accountability to voters for their actions or inactions.

Committee members found "Float" hard to explain and feared it was too complicated for the county clerks to implement. Some counties were in a "Float" district for the Senate but were not in a "Float" district for the House. The more legislators, lobbyists and voters looked at "Float" the less they like it.

At the November 16th meeting, Mark Braden told the Joint Committee, that "Idaho rejected 'Float' districts because of perceived voter confusion with how candidates had to file, then run for office."

An editorial in the *Casper Star-Tribune*[242] championed single-member districts

> …because the current system of county-based districting blurs the capacity of the Legislature to reflect the populations, because of the effect the districting system has on election campaigns.
>
> For high-population counties, … Natrona … is a prime example, current districting means multi-member slates. The election campaigns for candidates on those slates are notoriously "beauty contests," where name recognition— and therefore, incumbency —too often decides the race.
>
> The legislative contests … do not involve debate between candidates over issues and voting records. Rather than prepare a focused campaign challenging an incumbent's views, would-be legislators must simply

---

[242] January 30, 1990.

outline their own virtues and hope to end up somewhere near the top of the heap....

We suspect that when everything including the court orders are over, we'll end up with single-member districts anyway. It would be better to do it now, and do it just because it's the right thing to do.

With the editorial page of the *Casper Star-Tribune* pushing the legislators where they did not want to go, other factors were buffeting them too.

14

Population Shifts—
The Busted Boom

By the mid 1980's the energy boom slowed. By the 1990's it was gone. The "bust" impacted 14 of the 23 counties especially hard. Uranium used in the nation's power plants, or for medical and research purposes, now came from Australia's close-to-the-surface, close-to-the-ports, high quality, open pit mines instead of from Wyoming.[243] The Soviet Union was dumping uranium from its stockpile into the United States market. Prices dropped. Some mining operations ceased.[244]

Construction was finished on three 1,500-megawatt power plants: the Dave Johnson at Glenrock, the Jim Bridger near Rock Springs, Basin Electric's Laramie River Station near Wheatland, plus Wyodak's air-cooled units near Gillette. Only the operating workforces remained.

The size of the workforce was a crucial factor driving population density and distribution. During Governor Herschler's first term, legislators were told "7" was the number of support people needed for each jobholder. Support people were the doctors and day care workers, the police and garbage collectors, the retail clerks and truckers—all the people who made a community viable. When 10 jobs evaporated and workers left town—the jobs of 70 other people were gone. With no work, they too left the state.

---

[243] An average 350 feet of overburden covered most of Wyoming's uranium deposits.

[244] *Wyoming Quarterly Update,* Winter 1991, Vol 10. No. 2.

The mineral industry accounted for 68% or 62% or 57% of the state's income from property and severance taxes. The percentage varied depending on who did the talking and what year (or decade) was counted. Whatever the percentage, Wyoming was 2nd among the states in dependence on the mineral extractive industry for revenues to the state's coffers.[245]

The petroleum industry was very, very sensitive to the actions of OPEC. When OPEC sneezed, Wyoming's producers trembled. Therefore, with lower prices, less oil was pumped from existing wells and wildcat drilling slowed to a crawl. The legislators were asked to lower the severance tax on stripper wells and to give tax breaks for slant-drilling into oil "pools."

Legislators with the political agenda to "cut government" used the state's economy to engage in doom rhetoric. Sometimes they were justified. Other times they were "crying wolf." No one assigned credibility to statements made during debate. It was hard to discern truth. It was a "toss-up"— depending on which lobbyist's information was to be trusted.

The legislature made its own contribution to the constriction of the economy. Under the guise of "belt-tightening," no longer was $20 to $50 million *annually* appropriated to improve the infrastructure of Wyoming's educational, correctional and care institutions. This decrease in capital construction money resulted in massive elimination of jobs—of workers, suppliers, retail and wholesale outlets and of community infrastructure.

Each of the minerals reacted to its unique market conditions. Each county had its mix of extractive minerals. Not all minerals "busted" at the same time. Teton, and by 1990 Platte, had no mineral industry. Depending on the market for coal, or oil, or trona or bentonite, each county experienced its own bust cycle. Short-term or long-term contracts and spot-market selling dramatically influenced jobs and population, taxes and the state's budget.

---

[245] Alaska was first.

THE NORTHERN REGION COUNTIES

In the northern region, only Teton and Campbell had significant economic "engines" driving the state's economy. Park had a healthy economy. For other counties in the region, the loss of people and the loss of economic prominence portended a possible loss of political power for their historically dominant intertwined agricultural and mineral interests (Table 33).

TABLE 33
Northern-Region Population Shift—1980 to 1990

County	% of Increase	Number of People	% of Decrease	Number of People
Teton	19	1,817		
Park	7	1,536		
Big Horn			12	1,371
Hot Springs			16	901
Washakie			12	588
Johnson			8	555
Sheridan			6	1,486
Campbell	21	5,003		
Crook				14

In **Teton** growth was due to tourism—people came to see the beauty of Grand Teton National Park and Yellowstone. People with wealth built showcase homes there, thus strengthening the property tax base, attracted by Wyoming's lack of an income tax.

Park had substantial activity in oil, gas and bentonite. The 10-year annual average oil production was 20.7 million barrels. The natural gas production was 7 million MCF. Gypsum, used to produce cement for their regional market, including Montana, was the county's fourth mineral. Tourism to Yellowstone was good for Cody. Extensive irrigated multi-crop agriculture, made possible by the lower crop-friendly altitude, provided jobs and a stable workforce.

For many decades oil was pumped out of **Hot Springs**. Production steadily declined from 9 million barrels in 1980 to 6.7 million barrels in 1989. The decade high for natural gas was

296,000 MCF in 1984, with a low of 217,000 MCF in 1989. Not much coal was mined there; the average was only 38,000 annual tons. The hot springs at Thermopolis delighted visitors and the cowboys watched over the range cattle. By 1990 the county lost 16% of its 1980 population.

The 1980 oil production in **Big Horn** was 5.7 million barrels, dropping to 3.8 million barrels in 1989. The annual average natural gas production was 3 million MCF. The county's population dropped 12%.

In **Washakie** the average annual oil production was 2 million barrels with natural gas production averaging 2.8 million MCF. The county's population dropped 12% as adult children of ranching and irrigated farm families sought jobs elsewhere.

Johnson, sandwiched between Natrona on the south and Sheridan on the north, had grass and more grass, lots of sky, more sheep than people and some minerals. Uranium mining was minuscule until 1988–89 when 513,000 tons were mined. Average annual oil production was 2.7 million barrels. Natural gas production was 920,000 MCF.

The Decker coal mine in Montana impacted **Sheridan** because it was "home" to those construction workers and miners. Tax revenues from Decker went to Montana with no money to Sheridan for the living amenities infrastructure. At the beginning of the 1980's, Sheridan coal mines produced 4.3 million tons of coal, but by 1989 they were down to just 111,293 tons. Natural gas was a "sometimes recovered" asset. None was produced in 1983, 1984, 1987, 1988, 1989 but in 1981 there were 32,639 MCF and in 1986 6,638 MCF. Oil production was at 231,000 barrels in 1982, then down to 127,000 barrels in 1989. Ranching, polo, homes of the wealthy and the community college sustained the economy. Sheridan experienced only a 6% decline in population.

The growth in **Campbell** was due to mining low-sulfur coal from open-pit mines. Some coalfaces were 40' high; others were greater than 90 feet. The depth of the overburden, the dirt on top of the coal, was not a problem because the coal was so near the surface. The county also had substantial oil and gas production. The annual average production during the decade was 23.4 million barrels of oil and 23 million MCF of natural gas. Coal production was 58.2 million tons in 1980 that increased to 144 million tons in 1989.

Oil production increased in **Crook**, from 2.7 million barrels in 1980 to 5.5 million barrels in 1985, then down to 4.7 million barrels in 1989. Small amounts of natural gas was recovered, an annual average of 892,000 MCF. Only 14 fewer people were found in the 1990 census.

THE CENTRAL REGION COUNTIES

The Central Region essentially dropped out of economic importance because of lost jobs, reduced retail or field supplier sales, less local and state tax revenues. While Sublette and Lincoln experienced 7 and 4 percent population growth, respectively, this increase was only 784 people. There were 19,919 fewer people in the region (Table 34), accounting for 4% of the combined county-by-county population decline from the 1980 census of 469,557. Apprehension was palpable over the possible political consequences of the population shift.

TABLE 34
Central-Region Population Shift—1980 to 1990

County	% of Increase	Number of People	% of Decrease	Number of People
Lincoln	4	488		
Sublette	7	296		
Fremont			14	5,330
Natrona			15	10,630
Converse			21	2,941
Weston			8	588
Niobrara			15	430

Sublette and **Lincoln** benefited from the natural gas activity in the Overthrust Belt. The average annual oil production for the decade in **Sublette** was 2.8 million barrels. The 1980 natural gas production was 43.9 million MCF and in 1989 it was 157.5 million MCF. There also were lots of cows in Sublette County.

The ten-year annual average oil production in **Lincoln** was 442,000 barrels; gas production averaged 27.3 million MCF. The economy in the Star Valley of northern Lincoln was based on agriculture—with its ebb and flow of workers—and three manufacturers: cheese, handguns and light aircraft.

The bust in the minerals economy hit **Fremont** hard. All taconite (iron ore) production ceased in 1983 from the mine at South Pass City. Uranium production plummeted from 2.1 million tons in 1980 to *238* tons in 1989. With the decrease in mining on the Wind River Reservation, the royalty payments to the Shoshone and Arapahoe dropped. Merchants in Riverton, Lander and the smaller retail centers felt the reduction in buying power of the Native Americans. Oil production dropped from 6.4 million barrels in 1980 to 3.5 million barrels in 1989. Natural gas dropped too: from 50.1 million MCF to 30.9 million MCF. Jobs evaporated. The population decline for the decade was 14%.

Natrona was hit in multiple ways as the steam went out of the energy boom. Large road construction companies were headquartered in Natrona County making Casper the only source for really big heavy equipment. Because business was down for Casper-based suppliers of goods and services to mineral extractors, the ripple of the multiplier-effect was significant. Three-week advance reservations at motels were no longer needed. Fewer people were dependent on restaurants. Uranium production in Natrona ceased in 1984. Annual average natural gas production hovered at 7.1 million MCF. Oil production topped in 1985 at 10.8 million barrels. Casper was the state's second largest city but its mineral-based economy was not diversified enough to withstand the economic depression—15% of the population left.

In mineral-rich **Converse** it was not uncommon to remove seams of coal, then go deeper for uranium, with an oil well pulling black gold from still lower levels—all in the same open-pit. At the Dave Johnson plant three 500-megawatt units were operational, fed by nearby coal deposits. In 1980 3.2 million tons of coal were produced, in 1989 3.1 million tons. Uranium mining petered out: from 542,000 tons in 1984 to 41,000 tons in 1987. Natural gas reached a production high in 1986 of 34.2 million MCF, then dropped to 18.3 million MCF by 1989. Along with the uranium miners, the construction workforce left and 21% of the population was "outa-there."

The first Wyoming oil well was a hand-dug one in **Weston**. Oil production was 1.8 million barrels in 1980, 2.8 million barrels in 1983, then 2.7 million barrels in 1989. Suppliers for the oil business were located in Moorcroft. Grass and more grass, both for cows and wildlife, dominated the landscape. The population dropped 8%.

The legislature sent the new women's prison to Lusk in **Niobrara**, partly as a way to keep the town from dying. The average annual oil production for the 1980's was 1.1 million barrels and natural gas averaged 420,000 MCF. The grasslands fed cows and sheep, not buffalo. Hunters came for game birds, deer and antelope but there were few other tourists. The population continued to drop—the county lost 15% of its people in the 1980's.

THE SOUTHERN REGION COUNTIES

TABLE 35
Southern-Region Population Shift—1980 to 1990

County	% of Increase	Number of People	% of Decrease	Number of People
Platte			32	3,830
Goshen	3	333		
Laramie	7	4,493		
Albany	6	1,735		
Carbon			24	5,237
Sweetwater			7	2,900
Uinta	44	5,684		

Platte lost one-third of its population. With the closing of the Sunrise Iron Mine[246] at Guernsey, ranching, dry land and irrigated farming employed most people. The construction force building the Laramie River Power Plant, three 500-megawatt coal-fired units, put the county through its own boom/bust cycle. With the iron mine working, the census found 6,486 people in the county in 1970. With the power plant construction, the 1980 census found 11,975 people. With the mine gone and construction finished, the 1990 census found 8,145 people. In

---

[246]Sunrise was the source of iron ore shipped to Colorado Fuel and Iron in Pueblo, Colorado. The closing of this steel plant ended mineral production in Platte County.

the 1981 Reapportionment, Platte was given two House seats in anticipation of still more people by 1990.[247]

The land of **Goshen**, where the North Platte River left Wyoming, experienced little change during the 1980's. Oil production was a "mere drop" at 12,500 barrels annually. Cows and more cows, grass and more grass, winter wheat, sugar beets, irrigated cornfields dominated the landscape. The job market remained stable. Population grew 3% during the decade. The placement of missile silos by the Air Force, in 6-mile checkerboard patterns, vastly improved the county roads.

Mineral extraction did not dominate the economy of **Laramie** —government did. The jobs connected with the seat of state government in Cheyenne and the Federal jobs drawn there by the agencies wanting to be in the capital city were public-sector jobs. Private sector jobs were in retailing, wholesaling, tourism and to staff the Union Pacific Railroad. Cheyenne was a division point for the nation's major east-west railroad and a point of intersection for two interstate highways—I-25 and I-80. However, by the 1980's the Colorado and Southern Railroad was gone. Burlington Northern, with a presence in Cheyenne, was a major north-south railroad.

Education, not minerals, dominated **Albany**. An early natural gas field brought cleaner heating fuel to Laramie in the 1920's but by the 1980's the annual average oil production was only 133,000 barrels. The University of Wyoming, the state's only four-year baccalaureate and graduate school, was the economic engine for the community.

Carbon, as its name implies, was dominated by minerals. Uranium production in 1980 was 1.3 million tons. For the rest of the decade the annual average was 342,000 tons. Coal declined too: from 9.7 million tons in 1980 to an annual average of 4.3 million tons. Oil and natural gas production remained steady, with an annual average of 2.7 million barrels and 41.9 million MCF, respectively. The men's penitentiary in Rawlins contributed to the economy.

With the drop in uranium and coal production main street businesses were vulnerable. By 1990 many retail or office buildings and warehouses were empty. The 24% decline in population was of no concern to the majority party, for those

---

[247] This was the excuse of the majority party for giving this agriculture-dominated county more political power than their population justified. The political games of the Kendig era continued.

175

legislative seats, historically held by Democrats, reflected the strength of the labor and public employee vote.

The good news in minerals in **Sweetwater** was trona, which, when refined, is soda ash used in glass, detergents and many, many other products. Trona existed in thick underground layers deep below the desert west of Green River from where 111.2 million tons were taken during the decade. The Union Pacific carried unit-trains of trona to the nation's manufacturing plants. There were good trona-patch jobs and good railroad jobs. The other good news was that coal production remained steady at an annual average of 11 million tons. Coal was mined for the three 500-megawatt units of the Jim Bridger Power Plant east of Rock Springs. Some coal was shipped to power plants in the Midwest. Again, good jobs.

The bad news was that by 1984 the uranium miners were gone. Part of the natural-gas-rich Overthrust Belt was in Sweetwater but production was on a rollercoaster: In 1980 it was 135.4 million MCF, 61.5 million MCF in 1986, then 104.8 million MCF in 1989. Oil production in the Great Divide Basin was 9.98 million barrels in 1980 then slowly dropped to 6.84 million barrels by 1989. Rock Springs and Green River were supply centers for the extractive industries. By 1990 the boom had come, gone and "washed away" 7% of the population—a net loss of 2,900 people.

In **Uinta** drilling for and the processing of natural gas from the Overthrust Belt brought jobs and more people. The Overthrust Belt, the old Idaho/Utah Territory, stretching from the Tetons south to Colorado, is where the earth's tectonic plates push against, then override, each other. A driller, going down thousands of feet for natural gas found alternating layers of high-sulfur and low-sulfur gas at the same drill site. Oil was the only other extractive mineral in Uinta, with production averaging 10 million barrels a year during the 1980's. Production of natural gas was 24.1 million MCF in 1980 and 186.1 million MCF in 1989.

Uinta County was the significant "engine" driving the economy in the southern region. Strong economic factors of trona, coal, power generation, higher education and government lent strength and stability to the region's work force. The region lost 11,967 people, but gained 12,245 people, for a net population gain of 278 people (Table 35).

176

Historically and traditionally under-represented in the legis-lature, the southern region was ready to exercise political muscle that reflected its population and economic strength.

But the numbers comparing the 1980 census with the 1990 census identify only part of the decade's demographic changes. During the debate for the 1981 Reapportionment, Representative Dick Wallis of Campbell, distributed a document projecting the state's population to soon exceed 500,000.

An article in the *Laramie Boomerang*[248] reported, "Wyoming lost more than 42,000 residents from mid-1980 through 1988." If the news article was correct, at the height of the boom the state's population topped-out at 511,000.

The 1990 census takers found 453,588 people: 64.9% or 294,465 urban residents and 35.1% or 159,123 rural residents. For the decade, the range of change among the several counties was 76%: from 44% more people in Uinta to 32% fewer people in Platte. While the number of people coming to or leaving each county may seem insignificant, the impact on those small communities was massive.

The preliminary discussions on reapportionment were completed. The 51st legislature was elected in November—to convene on January 8, 1991. Legislators, lobbyists and the public began the next round of reapportionment.

---

[248] July 28, 1989.

15

Reapportionment 1991 Attempt #1

Mineral-man Deimer True of Natrona became the President of the Senate.[249] He was one of four sons of wildcat oilman Hank True. Near the end of the Great Depression, after finding more dry holes than he wanted, the elder True found the black gold.

By 1991 the True companies were one of Wyoming's major employers with oil fields, ranch lands, trucking and two banks. The agricultural and mineral interests were pleased that "one of their own" held the top leadership position in Wyoming's Senate.

Rancher Boyd Eddins of the Star Valley in Lincoln was Senate Vice-President. He was a Major General in the United States Air Force Reserve, a Commercial Pilot and Master Navigator.[250] He understood well "the proper order of things" and what it took to achieve success.

The Senate Majority Leader's business was trucking—closely tied to the "oil patch." Jerry Dixon of Weston spent his University of Wyoming years in Petroleum Engineering. He was a past director of the Wyoming Trucking Association.

---

[249] See Appendix G for the complete list of legislators of the 51st Session.

[250] The source for personal information included in this section is from the publication of the Wyoming Trucking Association, *Lawmakers of the Fifty-first Wyoming State Legislature 1991-1992.*

In the opinion of the agricultural/mineral interests, the Senate leadership was in good hands controlled by central-region Republicans: Eddins of the Star Valley in Lincoln, True of Natrona, and Dixon of Weston.

Senate Minority Leader was Frank Prevedel of Sweetwater. He was a people-man, an educator who was Director of the Sweetwater Board of Cooperative Services, part of that county's adult education.

Minority Whip was rancher and businessman John Fanos of Uinta. The mineral interests knew he was not "a man in their hip pocket." There was disagreement between Uinta Commissioners and the companies over the amount of taxes owed. As one of Unita's three county commissioners he challenged the energy companies'[251] assessed valuations given to Uinta's assessor and to the state Department of Revenue.

Fanos was consistently vocal in his advocacy for fair and full payment of taxes. Another factor that made him a problem for the mineral interests was the high respect this maverick held among his peers—both at home and in the legislature. In 1991 the Senate had 20 Republicans and 10 Democrats.

In the 1990 election Democrats Mike Sullivan and Kathy Karpan won second terms—he as Governor and she as Secretary of State. The Senate Democrats were short one vote to sustain any vetoes by Governor Sullivan.

The ranch of Yale-educated House Speaker Rory Cross was the historic family spread in mineral rich Converse. The agricultural/mineral interests considered Cross "one of their own."

Speaker Pro Tem Ron Micheli was a 4th generation rancher in Oregon Trail country near Fort Bridger in Uinta. His agricultural credentials were impeccable.

Douglas Chamberlain of Goshen was Majority Leader. He was a trucker, farmer, rancher, real estate broker and school-teacher. He was acceptable because he seldom let his educator proclivities show.

Sheepman John Marton of Johnson was Majority Whip— again a man acceptable to the agricultural/mineral interests.

The regional leadership in the House was split: Micheli of Uinta and Chamberlain of Goshen were southern-region men.

---

[251] Extracting natural gas, both high sulfur and low sulfur, from the Uinta portion of the Overthrust Belt.

Cross of Converse was from the central region. Marton of Johnson was northern region.

The Minority Floor leader was lawyer Fred Harrison of mineral-rich, public-employee-saturated Carbon. The Assistant Minority Floor leader was Matilda Hansen, an educator from University-dominated Albany. The Minority Whip was homemaker Mary Kay Schwope of government-dominated Laramie County.

The leaders of the Minority Party in the 51st Legislature were from Union Pacific Mainline southern-region counties. They were savvy, experienced legislators. While often unable to prevent actions of the Majority Party, they were knowledgeable observers with clear understanding of what was, or was not, being done.

The 42 Republicans controlled the House. There were 22 Democrats. The Democrats did have enough votes to sustain a Governor Sullivan veto—if they agreed to do so.

Republican rancher Charles Scott of Natrona again chaired the Senate Corporations Committee. The other members were Democrats James Applegate, an attorney of Laramie and Della Herbst, a homemaker of Sheridan; Republicans Tom Kinnison, a businessman of Sheridan and Gary Yordy, physician/attorney of Laramie County.

Republican Patti MacMillan of Albany, a realtor/retailer, chaired the House Corporations Committee. The other Republicans were John DeWitt of Park, an educator, Bruce Hinchey of Natrona, an environmental engineer, April Brimmer-Kunz, an attorney from Laramie County, Bruce McMillan, a horticulturist from Fremont and Carol Jo Vlastos an educational nursing consultant from Natrona. The Democrats were Eli Bebout, Vice President of Nucor Drilling, from Fremont, Don Sullivan, an attorney, from Laramie and Matilda Hansen, an educator, from Albany.

Southern-region members were Applegate, Yordy, Brimmer-Kunz, Sullivan, MacMillan and Hansen. Central-region members were Scott, Hinchey, Vlastos, Bebout and McMillan. Northern-region members were Herbst, Kinnison and DeWitt.

With the northern and central region's focus on retaining the status quo and the southern region's focus on gaining voting strength to reflect their population dominance, the balance of power in the Joint Committee was even at 7-7. Democrat Herbst, of the northern region, usually voted with the six southern-region members.

180

Watching over legislative shoulders were the lobbyists of the agricultural/mineral interests who "walked tall" in the Halls of the Capitol.

The dean of mineral lobbyists was Rick Robitaille. With him were Wendy Frueauf and Cheryl Feraud of the Petroleum Association of Wyoming; John Atkins of Pathfinder Mines; Ed Brophy of Phone-Poulenc (trona); Brian Dunphy of Exxon; Dick Hartman of Union Pacific Resources; Douglas Johnson of AMOCO; Marion Loomis and Jack Ratchye of the Wyoming Mining Association; Jay Lyon and Jim Fitzgerald for FMC (trona); Walt Maguire of Chevron; Luyle Randen of Thunder Basin Coal; Don Coovert, Dan Sullivan and Steven Youngbauer of AMAX Coal and Grover Wallace of Tg Soda Ash.[252]

The agricultural lobbyists were Larry Bourret and Buddy Livingston of the Wyoming Farm Bureau; Bob Budd, Rod Smith and Cindy Garretson for the Wyoming Stock Growers; Carolyn Paseneaux for the Wyoming Woolgrowers and Jeff Lundberg for the Wyoming Wheat Growers Association.

OUTSIDE LEGAL COUNSEL

Because the 1990 Interim Committee hired Republican Mark Braden as outside legal counsel,[253] it was a "done deal" for the 1991 Committee. They had no say about his suitability for the upcoming—supposedly bipartisan—reapportionment. So the reconstituted Corporations Committee studied his resume and listened. Speaking to the Committee, Braden said,

---

[252] This listing for both mineral and agricultural lobbyists is from the Wyoming Capitol Club, Membership Directory 1991. Headquarters for the Capitol Club was in the basement of the Capitol, Senate side, in the hall and in the conference room of the Civil Department of the Attorney General. Lawyers may also have lobbied for agricultural or mineral interests but the directory only listed the names of their firms, not who paid them to lobby.

[253] The 1990 Interim Committee sent Rick Miller of the LSO, Attorney General Joe Meyer and Senator Charlie Scott to Denver in the summer of 1990 to select outside counsel. Eleven firms responded to Miller's RFP. They interviewed 3 and unanimously selected Braden's firm. According to the minutes of November 16, 1990 meeting, "preliminary agreement for legal services through the end of the Session...provides for a ceiling of $25,000 in legal fees, $5,000 in expenses and $5,000 in technical advise outside the law, e.g. statistics, political science etc."

I have … represented … the Wyoming Republican Party.[254] I worked as counsel to the 1988 Republican National Convention's Rules Committee when … Dick Cheney was chairman.… I currently advise the Republican Caucus of the New York Assembly on redistricting.… I was a member of the California Redistricting Task Force.…

My office [prepared materials] … in … *Thornburg v. Gingles, Bedham v. Eu* and *Davis v. Bandemer*.… The principal aim of the Republican National Committee's Counsel Office … [in] the 1980's was to expand the basis on which a political minority could attack redis-tricting plans.… *Badham v. Eu* … [created] a new cause of action—partisan gerrymandering. Fathered in my office, this new cause of action is generally viewed as the key judicial redistricting development of the 1980's.

Davis v. Bandemer established the justiciability of partisan gerrymandering. I … assumed a significant role in supporting the North Carolina Republicans in *Thornburg v. Gingles*.… Our aggressive position brought my office into direct conflict with the Department of Justice and the Assistant Attorney General for Civil Rights, but we did not permit their mistaken interpretation of these amendments to block our assistance to the North Carolina Republicans. The Supreme Court … supported our view resulting in significant political gains for the North Carolina Republican Party.

I have played a variety of roles in the redistricting process … from California to New York, Mississippi to Massachusetts, Florida to New Jersey. Two of the three chairmen of the Republican National Committee, for whom I served as chief legal counsel, … are available to offer knowledgeable recommendations regarding my legal abilities.… I am retained by the Republican Governors' Association as counsel on redistricting issues.… I am drafting a memorandum on redistricting for the National Republican Congressional Committee.

---

[254] Neither the documentation nor his testimony gave details of when or the circumstances pertaining to this representation.

Before formulating legal arguments, the Legislature will want to focus on tactics that may deter potential plaintiffs... In [1981] the limited scope of the plaintiff's action combined with a saving clause, permitted Wyoming to maintain its current system ... but it is unlikely that any future plaintiff will be as narrow in their action.

There are many methods to measure deviation. Assistance from the more creative statisticians may provide you with different analysis of population deviation that may be more attractive ... an examination of registered voters versus actual population might provide a lower deviation between your districts.[255]

What attracted Scott and other Republicans to Braden was his ability to "think outside the box" in his work with minority Republicans when Democrats were drawing the lines.

In 1990 Steve Freudenthal "had no objections to Braden's serving as counsel to the Committee in light of his political background."[256] The Democrats in 1991 viewed Braden's work as too partisan. They listened with skeptical ears and questions in their minds. The possibility of hiring outside legal counsel for the Democrats was "outlandish" and given no consideration by the majority Republicans.[257]

REPUBLICAN PHILOSOPHY FOR 1991

An unsigned memorandum appeared on desks in the House delineating Republican philosophy.[258] The statement was on behalf of the entire legislature. It declared that the object of the 1991 reapportionment was "... to achieve fair and effective

---

[255] September 5, 1990 letter from E. Mark Braden of Baker & Hostetler, Counselors At Law, Washington D.C., included in the Minutes of the November 16, 1990 meeting of the Joint Corporations Committee.

[256] Ibid, p. 5.

[257] The Republicans dealt with the partisan issue by proclaiming all their work on HB 295 was nonpartisan—which it wasn't.

[258] Documents distributed by the Pages to members' desks on the House floor required authorization of a House member.

representation for all Wyoming citizens ... best accomplished [by preserving] county boundaries [for] ... legislative ... districts." It claimed that Wyoming's counties were

> ...accurate representations of divisions between social, economic and political communities and interests ...[and that] ... a legislator cannot properly represent his constituents, nor can voters ... exercise the ballot franchise intelligently when a legislative district is nothing more than a fragmented unit ... [separated from] ... and ... possibly in conflict with ... [other political communities because] counties are vital and effective units of Wyoming local government.

The memorandum claimed historic reapportionment practices kept district boundaries constant, with the number of legislators in each district changing, while redistricting kept the number of legislators constant, with the district boundaries changing.

> Wyoming's reapportionment system significantly reduces the opportunity to manipulate legislative districts in a discriminatory manner against minority political, cultural or economic interests.

> Wyoming's consistent and nondiscriminatory policy ... avoids the evils of partisan, ethnic or racial gerrymandering.

> [There is] the obligation to comply with both ... the constitutions of the United States and of Wyoming ... [with] ...Wyoming's Constitution ... subservient to ... the Constitution of the United States.

> Each county [has] its own representative as required by the Constitution of the State of Wyoming except for the combined district of Converse and Niobrara counties ... [to] insure that all of the people of Wyoming have effective representation within the Legislature.

"Other Relevant Factors" were listed to justify a representative for each county: long distances between population centers, unique Wyoming weather and geography, the unique social, economic and political identities of the communities. The statement included the belief that,

> [B]ecause the reapportionment system used generates a relatively small weighted average deviation in population per representative, the considerable range between the largest and smallest populations per representative does not reflect discrimination against

184

any Wyoming citizen. [But] ... neutral and rationale criteria for representative districts such as county boundaries can result in very large population disparities between districts.

We have determined that providing a separate representative district to Niobrara County with a total population significantly smaller than any other legislative district may be interpreted as an emasculation of a goal of this process as articulated by the United States Supreme Court, substantial equality of population for representative districts.

This statement, intended as the intent of the legislature, articulated in convoluted, enlightening and somewhat obfuscating language the philosophy of the Wyoming Republican leadership.

HOUSE CONSIDERATION OF HB 295

HB 295 was introduced on January 18. It went to Corporations, Elections and Political Subdivisions. The final census numbers came on January 25th. Public comment was heard; minor adjustments and $300,000 were added to the bill.[259] On January 29th it was reported out of committee, placed on General File and scheduled for debate on January 30th. But first the Appropriations Committee held a short, noon meeting and deleted the money, then sent the Bill back to the Floor.

Dennis Tippets of Fremont chaired Committee of the Whole.[260] Committee Chair Patti MacMillan's "technical

---

[259] HB 295, Section 4: "(a) There is appropriated to the attorney general from the general fund ... ($250,000) to be used for legal and technical costs incurred in litigation of the apportionment plan contained in this act. (b) There is appropriated to the legislative service office from the general fund ... ($50,000) to be used upon recommendation of the legislative reapportionment oversight committee and with the consent of the legislative management council for purposes of consultation, technical support, or administrative support necessary to carry out the provisions of W.S. 28-2-115 as created by section 1 of this act."

[260] Matilda Hansen retained her working copies of the 1991-1992 bills and all amendments. The dates for consideration of the bills are from the 1991 and 1992 Digests of the House and Senate. In 1991 Jeanne Rideout, House Democratic Aide, sat in the House Gallery taking notes

cleanup" amendment passed. In her explanation of the bill she said:

> "This bill is gerrymander-free. Ask yourself if you can be reelected in a single-member district plan? The current way is better. The people support it."

John DeWitt of Park explained the transition provisions for the senators in the middle of their 4-year terms.

> Appropriations Chair Dick Wallis, of Campbell explained: "We stripped the funding away so you could pick what you want. And, we have the attorney general to defend us."
>
> Les Bowron, of Natrona asked: "Can't we do better than this?
>
> MacMillan: "The appropriation is to defend a lawsuit. [The House denied the funds because] "inclusion of the $300,000 means we are casting doubt on their own work."
>
> Chris Plant, of Sweetwater asked, "Will the court send the plan back to us or will the court reapportion if we lose?"
>
> MacMillan: "We would probably get another chance."
>
> Plant: "What documentation do you have to support your contention that Wyoming people support this [HB 295]?"
>
> MacMillan: "As many as you think."
>
> Plant: "Wouldn't single-member districts make us all sacrifice rather than the committee proposal which makes Niobrara[261] sacrifice?"
>
> MacMillan: "I dun no."

---

of the debate during all readings of HB 295. She was hired by the House Democrats who paid her salary from "their own pockets" to do research and to follow legislation of special interest to Democrats. The Republican House leadership finally funded this position in 1993.

In 1991 the House Democrats also hired a stenographic reporter to record the reapportionment debate under standards acceptable in a court proceeding. All direct quotes are from this collection of notes.

[261] In the original bill Niobrara was linked with Converse for their representative and with Crook and Weston counties for their senator to make the respective districts more equal in the number of people per district.

The next amendment was Les Bowron's.[262] His purpose was to keep all court challenges out of the state courts and away from the federal three-judge panels. He wanted to require the attorney general to take reapportionment to Federal Court under W.S. 9-1-603 where constitutional questions were asked, where there was a body of case law and where there was a higher certainty of remand. One of the state justices already had expressed his opinion on reapportionment.

> Fred Harrison of Carbon: "It is inappropriate for us to try to run a lawsuit. The state court will at least look at our constitution."
>
> Carroll Miller of Big Horn supported Bowron: "If a claim is filed in state court we cannot force it into federal court. We cannot deprive the judiciary of the authority to review our acts. It is a separation of powers issue."
>
> Don Sullivan of Laramie County: "We can't declare in advance how to run a lawsuit. If a judge has expressed an opinion, he will recuse himself. Our state constitution essentially requires one person, one vote 'as nearly as may be according to the inhabitants.'"[263]

Bowron's amendment passed with 36 aye votes.

The Niobrara citizens again were lobbying for their House seat. By 1991 they were skilled, proficient citizen-lobbyists. Talking and watching in the lobby, House and Senate galleries, leaning on the railings around the rotunda, appearing in the social centers at the Hitching Post Inn they stated their case. They *really had to have* their own House seat. They lost their senator in 1965. They kept their House seat in 1963 and in 1971. In 1981 their House seat pushed the range of deviation to 89.5% and was clearly vulnerable to a challenge. They worked even harder.

---

[262] Text of Bowron Amendment read: "In defending the state in any civil action which challenges this act, the Attorney General shall take all actions necessary, including removal pursuant to applicable federal statutes and rules of civil procedure, to ensure that the action brought is first tried before the United States District Court for the District of Wyoming" (HBO295HW2).

[263] Sullivan is quoting from Article III, Section 3 Wyoming Constitution.

The next amendment was by Niobrara's Mel ZumBrunnen. He unhooked Niobrara from Converse and gave Niobrara a seat of its own—for 2,929 people. He quoted from the purpose clause in the 1981 Plan where the "legislative finding" on denying Niobrara a seat showed,

"... the opportunity for oppression.... We should go as we did 10 years ago, give Niobrara a seat and only give it up if a court makes us. Our one representative is like Wyoming's one representative in the United States Congress."

Chris Plant: "The amendment makes the bill consistent."

Dick Wallis: "The basic amendment is right to have House representation for Niobrara County. The bill without the amendment is even worse for it gives them different House and Senate representation."

MacMillan: "The different House and Senate districts resulted from the numbers. It is possible to do combinations of Crook-Weston and Niobrara-Converse districts but this will drive the range up to some extent.

Carroll Miller: "We are flying in the face of the United States Supreme Court for what we think are good reasons."

Don Sullivan supported ZumBrunnen: "This case is weak, but it is stronger if we have Niobrara County in. With it in we have consistent policy."

Clyde Wolfley of Lincoln in support: "It was lonely when Lincoln County didn't have our own senator."

April Brimmer-Kunz of Laramie: "It will blow our best argument if we don't give Niobrara a seat."

Dan Budd of Sublette commented on the federal analogy. He interpreted "representative government to mean sticking to county lines and political subdivisions."

John Rankine of Hot Springs: "United we stand, divided we fall."

MacMillan, in opposition, closed the debate: "The federal constitution is supreme, even our state constitution says so. Equal protection is the important principle. Another county with only one

188

representative has three times the population of Niobrara County. We have to be fair."

The amendment passed on a voice vote. The citizen-lobbyists of Niobrara won again.

THE SINGLE-MEMBER SULLIVAN PLAN

Don Sullivan made the first serious attempt at single-member districts. As a member of the 1990 committee he requested the LSO to get county road maps and information on voting districts/ precincts from the 23 county clerks.

His database was flawed because the count he used was of those who voted in the last general election and all adults did not vote. Neither did persons under 18 years of age. Therefore the non-voters were not given House or Senate representation in his plan. Information from the county clerks was not comparable from one county to another. It ranged from the verifiable, to the unreliable, to the absurd. Some precinct maps were out-of-date. One county clerk sent a restaurant placemat that showed a map of her county.

In 1991 each county clerk was the *supreme and final authority* for all election matters in that county. The only authority over them was the Court. The Secretary of State or the County Attorney tried to influence them through interpretations of the law with in-depth discussions, the use of logic and by jawboning. There was no uniformity from county to county concerning the conduct of elections.[264]

All Sullivan's legislative districts were as contiguous and compact as Wyoming's open spaces allowed. He did not use the community of interest criteria.[265] He had 30 Senate and 65 House seats. In some of his districts Senate/House seats were

---

[264] After the election of 1994 the legislature required uniformity of election procedures in addition to their previous requirement of "uniform application of Election Law."

[265] For instance: In Albany County, Sullivan's House District 14 included all the rural residents south and west of town, the blue-collar service workers and railroaders in Laramie west of the Union Pacific tracks and the horse, chickens, gardens, backyard car-fixit residents of West Laramie. The ethnic mix was Anglo, Hispanic and African-American.

nested, in most districts they were not. The problem of over-representation in Niobrara was not solved in the Sullivan Plan.

Even with this handicap, Chris Plant and Matilda Hansen cosponsored Sullivan's plan because it was a serious attempt to create single-member districts. The debate on the Sullivan plan proceeded.

Chris Plant: "This is one person, one vote. There is equality of sacrifice."

Pat Hacker of Laramie County: "Our system already is gerrymandered by historic accident. Both the House and Senate are now under-represented. Five chairmen of House committees were unopposed in the 1990 election and they come from over-represented counties. Two of the three leaders are from over-represented counties. Only one committee chairman in both houses comes from an under-represented county. Let's do it right."

Then Majority Leader Doug Chamberlain interrupted: "It's 4:00 pm—time we usually stop debate. But the rest of the leadership doesn't want to stop. So, keep going."

MacMillan asked Sullivan about the timing of his amendment. He replied: "The work was done by DAFC[266] six weeks ago."

MacMillan: "The amendment won't pass constitutional muster because it doesn't use actual census data. It is not the will of the people to move in the direction of gerrymandering."

Sullivan acknowledged that she was right about the census data, "…but we still don't have final census data processed into voting districts. We just have to trust the majority party will draw districts fairly. Gerrymandering is a big issue in the courts because every other state observes one person, one vote. We don't."

Fred Harrison: "People in Wyoming wouldn't support our system if they realized how watered down their votes are. We have passive gerrymandering now in favor of incumbents. This is the only thing that

---

[266] By the Division of Economic Analysis of the Department of Administration and Fiscal Control.

will help Niobrara County and still survive in court."

Matilda Hansen: "I am a cosponsor of this single-member district amendment because it is the right process. The right numbers will come along later."

MacMillan: "...Niobrara County cuts up Converse County."

Hansen justified combining the counties: "The fairness is in the community of interests in the shared ranching economy of the two counties."

John Rankine thought it was a terrible amendment. "It puts Hot Springs County with part of Fremont County."[267]

John DeWitt objected because the counties were torn up: "Park County is a mess."

Eric Alden of Platte: "It is a fallacy that people will be well represented in single member districts. Single member districts disenfranchise the minority."

The amendment failed on a voice vote. The hour was late but the House had one more amendment.

FLOTERIAL DISTRICTS AND THE BEBOUT PLAN

The floterial method had multi-member legislative districts encompassing more than one county. Within the district, some members represented a single county their county of residence—while others "floated" and represented everyone in the multi-county legislative district. Eli Bebout of Fremont presented a floterial district plan.[268]

He kept county election districts. He used the 1990 census. He created 10 multi-member Senate districts with 30 seats and 10 multi-member House districts with 64 seats—all fully nested (Table 36).

---

[267] Rankine spoke from experience because the 1965 court plan put Hot Springs with Fremont.

[268] The "floating member" concept is discussed in relation to land law in *Wisconsin 133 US 496, 10 CT 341, 33 L.Ed 687.*

TABLE 36
Bebout's Floterial Districts

Election District	Counties in District	Census of District	Number of Senators	People per Senator	Number of Repres.	People per Repres.
1	Albany Carbon	47,456	3	15,819	7	6,779
2	Big Horn Washakie Park Hot Springs	46,900	3	15,633	5	9,380
3	Campbell Crook Weston	41,182	3	13,727	5	8,236
4	Converse Natrona	72,354	5	14,471	10	7,235
5	Fremont Sweet-water	72,485	5	14,497	10	7,485
6	Goshen Niobrara	14,872	1	14,872	3	4,957
7	Laramie Platte	81,287	5	16,257	11	7,390
8	Lincoln Uinta	31,330	2	15,665	7	6,764
9	Sheridan Johnson	29,707	2	14,854	4	7,427
10[269]	Sublette Teton	16,015	1	16,015	House Seat with Lincoln & Uinta	

---

[269] Floterial House Districts 8 and 10 returned to the confusion engendered by the geography of the Old Utah/Idaho Territory. The House seats were similar to the Territorial apportionment of District 5 in 1887—7 seats. Candidates again would be forced to campaign from Yellowstone to the Colorado border across mountain ranges and

In floterial districting, some candidates campaign only in their county of residence while the "floating" candidate has to campaign "at-large" in all the counties in that district. In the Bebout Plan candidates running only in their county of residence clearly had the cost and logistics advantage over candidates campaigning in all counties within the same House or Senate district. Another disadvantage for the "floating" candidates centered on geography: having to campaign over a larger area—often challenged by the barriers of Wyoming's deserts, roadless mountain ranges or large reservoirs. Bebout stated,

> The amendment maintains both the Bowron and ZumBrunnen amendments. It follows county lines. It is constitutional. It brings the Senate within the *Mahan*[270] range of 16% deviation. It is intended to be the legislature's Plan because I don't like the idea of the court redoing reapportionment for us. I like multi-member districts.

Bebout claimed the deviation range for his Senate was 16%, acceptable according to *Mahan*. But by 1991 the *Mahan* standard was no longer accepted by the United States Supreme Court. Therefore, the constitutionality claimed by Bebout was nonexistent.

By 1991 standards, Bebout's House deviation range was an abomination. The widest spread, 94.4%, was between House District 2[271] in the Big Horn Basin, with an under-representation of 24.5%, and House District 6 in Niobrara and Goshen counties with an over-representation of 69.9%. Here too, county boundaries as election districts failed to reach equal representation. Fairness was absent.

MacMillan: "How big are the districts going to be?"
Bebout: "Big."
Macmillan: "All the way from Yellowstone to Uinta County?"
Bebout: "Yeah."
MacMillan: "This amendment has drafting problems. We should not reject it on the concept, but we

---

portions of the Red Desert. Bebout's seats in the Senate reverted to nearly the same north/south split as the Court imposed in 1965.

[270] ZumBrunnen was referring to *Mahan v. Howell*, 410 U.S. 315 (1973).

[271] The "ideal" number of people per House district was 7,087.

193

should reject it because of the bugs that need to be worked out. We could debate this more but it is 4:30 pm. If we have a Plan B, it will send the signal that we don't really support our first plan."

The amendment failed on a standing vote. Chairman Tippets moved adoption of the Committee of the Whole report. HB 295 moved to Second Reading—the next day.

The hour was late. Lobbyists and citizens were quietly waiting for the after-session committees to convene. On the evening's social calendar was the reception hosted by the Independent Telephone Association. It had been a long day.[272]

---

[272] Matilda Hansen's day began at 7am in the Governor's office with the House Democratic leaders. Corporations Committee met during lunch—with Committee secretary "gofering" sandwiches. Minerals, Business and Economic Development Committee met from House adjournment to nearly 7pm. She "put in an appearance" at the reception. Her legislative day ended soon after 9pm.

HOUSE CHAMBERS - AFTER HOURS - 1994

In The House Chambers

Della Herbst-Sheridan County Douglas Chamberlain
Goshen County

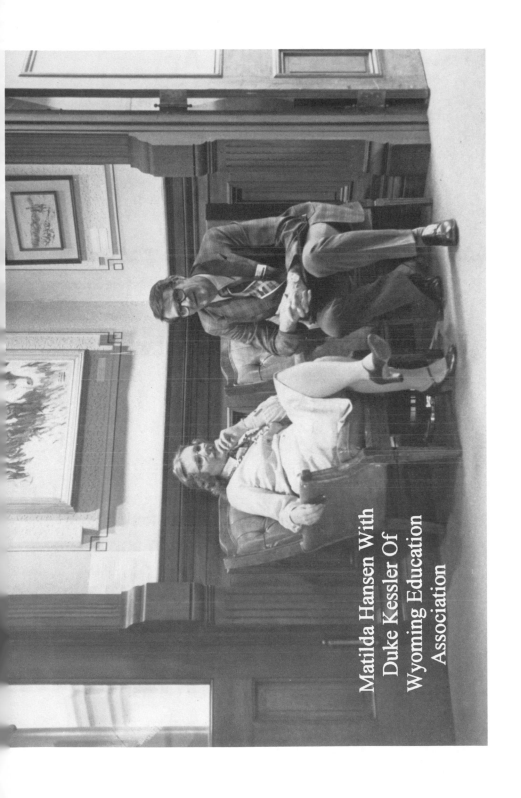

Matilda Hansen With
Duke Kessler Of
Wyoming Education
Association

There's An Important Message

Do You Hear It?

A church hired a new minister. They were very impressed by the first Sunday's sermon. The next Sunday, he preached the same sermon. And the following week, the message was identical.

The chairman of the board called him aside and said, "Look, that's a good sermon, but don't you have any others you can preach?"

The minister replied, "Why should I? You haven't done anything about this one yet . . . "

Maybe you want a new *"sermon"*, but we're waiting to see what you do with this one.
Eliminating our seat
*isn't fair
*isn't reasonable, and
*isn't constitutional.

There are other important matters besides reapportionment facing this session and future legislative sessions.
But unless you recognize the truth in our *"message"*, Niobrara will never have a voice in deciding them.

REPENT AND
SAVE NIOBRARA

Kathy Karpan and Matilda Hansen
Before Portrait of Governor
Nellie Tayloe Ross

Sarah Gorin Of Gorin v. Karpan

Governor Sullivan Delivering His Message

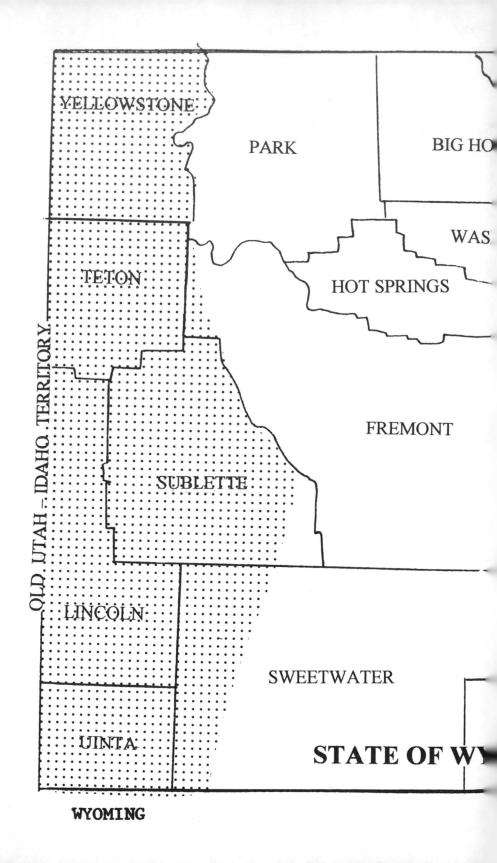

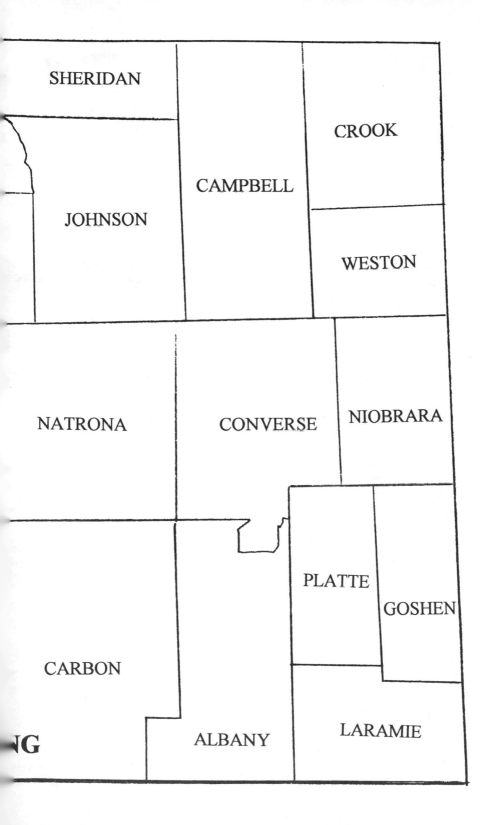

FRED HARRISON
Holds Democratic line

House uph
veto of reap
Override attem

By CHARLES PELKEY
Star-Tribune capital bureau

CHEYENNE — Voting strictly along party l.
the House of Representatives on Tuesday uphel
one vote Gov. Mike Sullivan's veto of a reap
tionment plan the Legislature approved last we

All 22 Democrats in the House voted agains
override measure. The solidarity of the Democ
Party meant the House's 42 Republican mem
fell one vote short of the two-thirds majorit
quired to nullify the governor's veto.

Sullivan on Monday rejected a reapportion

Tribune

Founded in 1891   Casper, Wyoming

Sullivan's
rtionment

s by one vote

pted last week by both houses of the Legis-
ullivan said the measure was both unfair
esented the Legislature's desire to protect the
ncumbent lawmakers.

e role of the Governor must be to assure
and that there is no overreaching in the leg-
rocess. In this plan, I am not convinced that
was accomplished," Sullivan wrote in a ve-
ge to House Speaker Rory Cross, R-Con-

ay afternoon, Sullivan offered no reaction to
e Democrats' success in upholding his veto.

Please see HOUSE, A14

PATTI MacMILLAN
Angry assault on veto

bruary 19, 1992

Margaret Brown of *Brown v. Thomson* Addressing The House Members

Peg Shreve – Park County
At The Back Podium

Waiting to Address The House

Louise Ryckman
Sweetwater County

Behind The Glass
House Chamber

Pat O'Toole and Fred Harrison
Carbon County

Music For Your Ears!

Let's __All__ Sing Along

(to the tune of "Five Foot Two")

22
Counties who
Vote on bills for me and you,
But have you seen old Niobrar'.

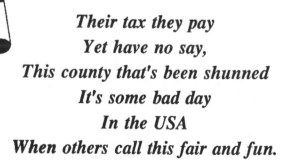

Their blood's so blue
These 22
They don't need help with what to do
From any hicks in Niobrar'.

Their tax they pay
Yet have no say,
This county that's been shunned
It's some bad day
In the USA
When others call this fair and fun.

Shame on you,
You 22
There's hair as fair and eyes as blue,
And brains as good as you in Niobrar'.

SAVE OL' NIOBRAR'

17

HB 295
Second & Third Reading

Thursday morning's Second Reading began with Watson-Lummis Amendment #2. Both Carol Watson and Cynthia Lummis were Laramie County legislators. Their plan combined three reapportionment methods: smallest divisor,[273] controlling population and floterial. Watson described their plan:

> It has a 63 member House and a 30 member Senate. Election districts do not cross county lines. The plan sets up seven nested House and Senate floterial districts. In each district some legislators will be elected at-large—only within their county of residence. Other legislators will be elected at-large in all the counties in the district. We have provided for the transition of Senators whose terms have not expired. The plan is gerrymander-proof. The deviation range in the House is 35.7% and in the Senate is 25.7%.

Co-sponsor Lummis added:

---

[273] First the 16 counties with the smallest populations were combined to create 7 groups of contiguous counties. These 7 and the 7 counties with the largest populations were each designated an election district and assigned 2 House seats. The 2 districts with the smallest population were dropped and 14 seats were distributed among the remaining 12 districts. Two more lowest population districts were dropped and 14 seats distributed to each of the remaining 10 districts. The districts with the largest populations got the most seats.

This is an appropriate compromise. The range in HB 295 is unacceptable. The range in this amendment is still too high to meet the 1991 Supreme Court standards. Because yesterday we rejected the Sullivan and Bebout plans, this amendment may forestall a lawsuit.

TABLE 37
Watson-Lummis 2nd Reading

Election District	House Seats Per District	Persons Per House Seat
Laramie	10	7,341
Natrona	8	7,653
Sweetwater	5	7,765
Big Horn, Park	5	6,741
Fremont	5	6,732
Converse, Platte, Goshen	4	7,912
Lincoln, Uinta, Sublette (split)	4	7,833
Albany	4	7,699
Johnson, Sheridan	4	7,427
Campbell	4	7,343
Carbon	3	5,553
Sublette, Teton	3	5,338
Crook, Weston, Niobrara	2	7,156
Washakie, Hot Springs	2	6,599

Table 37 shows the combinations of low-population counties needed to almost reach the deviation range of the counties with larger populations. The anomalies were Carbon and Sublette-Teton.[274]

Watson-Lummis ended the rural northern-region domination in the Senate. With the southern region's 16 senators or 53.3%

---

[274] Political boundaries again mirrored the 1869 Territorial House District 5. The southern part of Sublette was with Lincoln and Uinta and the northern part of Sublette was with Teton.

of the Senate representing 229,347 people or 50.01% of the statewide population, Watson-Lummis shifted the senate's voting strength into their own political turf. With only geography and census numbers driving their work, their plan got closer to equal representation. But it, too, fell short of the United States Supreme Court's threshold of 10%.

But their mix of smallest divisor, controlling population and floterial methods was too much for House members. Speaker Cross of Converse was agitated. His constituents were shifted from their half-century privileged position of "greater voting weight" to their votes having less weight—down to dead last!

Majority Leader Doug Chamberlain's voters were in the same district. He, too, was unhappy with the Watson-Lummis amendment. Because of opposition from the two men in the most powerful House positions, the amendment got little debate. It failed on a division vote[275]: 21 ayes, 36 noes.

BUDD AND THE BOWRON AMENDMENT

Dan Budd and Fred Harrison did not like the Bowron amendment.

Budd: "The Committee of the Whole amendment is not a good idea. You don't pick your courts before you know what your lawsuit is. It makes it look like you have something to hide."

Fred Harrison: "The Attorney General is the one to make this decision."

Bowron: "You are the client. You want to keep things the way they are. We know it will be litigated. Let's send it to the court that upheld us before."

Dick Honaker of Sweetwater supported Budd: "Do you want to play on the wrong turf?"

Carroll Miller supported Bowron: "All the information we got was about federal court decisions. Let's put

---

[275] A division vote is taken after a voice vote to question the ruling of the chair. Upon the "call for division" the person in the chair asks for all those voting aye to stand. The clerks at the front desk count heads. Those people sit down. Then the chair asks those voting no to stand. Again the clerks count heads. The clerks compare numbers; the chief clerk announces the result. Then the person in the chair rules "passed" or "failed" according to how the majority voted.

it [litigation on HB 295] where it belongs, in state court."

MacMillan: "When the referees have already decided who the winner is, do you want to play there?"

Fred Harrison: "All of us are potential witnesses in federal court. We can be deposed. Under the state constitution in a state court that wouldn't happen."

Budd: "I am not arguing on legal grounds but on common sense grounds. Justices have to stand for retention. Trust them to uphold Wyoming's Constitution."

Bowron: "The United States District Court for Wyoming are Wyoming judges. They live here. They interpret Wyoming law every day. Fred Harrison is wrong about being deposed in federal court. You can't be questioned in any other place. Federal judges will consider the state constitution. I think federal judges will support the Wyoming position."

Eli Bebout: "We can go from state to federal court but not federal to state court, right?"

Jim Perkins of Sheridan: "Pass this amendment—it doesn't make sense to tell the attorney general where to go."

Eric Alden: "If the Wyoming Supreme Court decides the issue on federal constitutional grounds, the case can be appealed to the federal system. If it decides on state constitutional grounds, that's the end of the road."

Bill Rohrbach of Park: "Defeat the amendment."

Pat Hacker had the last word: "The federal judges are not obligated to recognize the immunity of legislators. They may or may not in this case. If suit is filed in federal court on both state and federal grounds, it could end up on both. If the plaintiff files on state law, the suit cannot be sent to federal court. Defeat the amendment. The plaintiff picks the forum and the theory." [276]

---

[276] Six lawyers debated the Budd/Harrison amendment: Fred Harrison (D) of Carbon, Les Bowron (R) of Natrona, Dick Honaker (D) of Sweetwater, Eric Alden (R) of Platte, Bill Rohrbach (R) of Park and Pat Hacker (D) of Laramie counties.

The Budd-Harrison amendment failed on a division call: 21 ayes, 39 noes. There were no more second reading amendments.

THIRD READING, FEBRUARY 1, 1991

Encouraged by 21 aye votes and acknowledging the displeasure of the leadership, Carol Watson and Cynthia Lummis revised their amendment for 3rd reading. They kept 30 Senators and 63 House members but they reconfigured their county combinations to soothe the feathers of Cross and Chamberlain.

This time they made 17 election districts instead of 14 (Table 38). Goshen, Johnson, Lincoln, Sheridan and Uinta counties got their own districts. Converse was combined with Platte and, Sublette with Teton, making two districts.

TABLE 38
Third Reading Changes to Watson-Lummis Amendment

Election District	House Seats Per District	Persons Per House Seat
Laramie	9	8,127
Sheridan	3	7,854
Converse/Platte	3	6,424
Uinta	3	6,235
Carbon	2	8,008
Lincoln	2	6,313
Goshen	2	6,187
Sublette/Teton	1	8,008
Johnson	1	6,145

Sheridan County lost one of its 4 seats to Johnson County. Speaker Pro Tem John Marton's feathers also were soothed with the allocation of a seat for his sparsely populated county. The gainers were the counties represented by the leadership: Converse and Cross, Goshen and Chamberlain, Johnson and Marton.

The losers were Laramie and Carbon—both strongly Democratic counties. Minority Leader Fred Harrison of Carbon was not pleased!

In debate on this second version of Watson-Lummis Marlene Simons of Crook was the first to the podium:

"Do reject this amendment. You should know what it is like not to have representation. In the Crook/Weston combination, it is always a Weston person, not a Crook person, who is elected. Both former senator Earl Christensen and current senator Jerry Dixon are from Weston County."

MacMillan: "Reapportionment is about addressing Wyoming's needs. The courts have gotten into it because the legislators proved unable to take care of the task themselves. I recognize we are in the 1990's and we have to comply with Federal court dictates. Let's do this ourselves instead of having a court dictate to us."

Dan Budd: "Look at what equal protection means. It means having representation. Sublette County depends on multiple-use to survive. There are a bunch of environmental nuts in Teton. They will override the Sublette people."

John Hines of Campbell: "How many representatives does Carbon get—2 or 3? The map is different from the text."

Lummis: "Things have changed from yesterday. We dropped Laramie County from 10 down to 9 and Carbon from 3 to 2. The range drops to 29%. But Carbon[277] objected. Then we added back the Carbon seat for a 63 seat House and a 35% range, which explains the disparity between the map and the amendment. In all honesty it was an attempt to compromise with Carbon."[278]

Don Sullivan: "I applaud the attempt to build consensus but there are still problems with this, so defeat it. We can only hope to get away with a deviation range of 16%. This bill as it stands is 300% unconstitutional. The Watson-Lummis amendment only gets it to 200% unconstitutional."

Peg Shreve of Park: "Counties are too important to the state but we have to address the problem. I want

---

[277] In 1991 it was not acceptable to use the names of House members during debate. Lummis uses "Carbon" to mean Fred Harrison. This Rule Of The House is intended to defuse potential animosities.

[278] In explanation of this 3rd reading amendment Lummis said, "…the range is still high, but maybe doable. We need to get the range down."

counties, not election districts. This amendment doesn't make a lot of us happy but it isn't bad."

Mel ZumBrunnen: "Resist the amendment. We had this same argument in 1980. The Supreme Court upheld the 1980 plan. Why do we want this plan now?"

John Hines: "The sponsors are failing to get to the heart of the matter. It doesn't make sense to give Carbon another representative for 2,500 people."

Eli Bebout: "*Chapman, Connor, Connor* all got tossed with ranges lower than this. Let's use this as fallback rather than Plan A because if this gets tossed we have nothing left."

Eric Alden: "It's not our role to anticipate court rulings. We should do what we think is right and see what they think. We can do it over if the court doesn't like it. We can give them the message of what we want."

Dan Budd: "*Reynolds* says equal protection is not flexible. Equal protection has to be equal. The Warren Court Doctrine is not supported by anything. We can't get equal protection in the Sublette-Teton combination."

Don Sullivan: "We have multiple responsibilities. The United States is not a hostile foreign power. We took the oath to uphold the United States Constitution. In fact the United States Constitution is put first by our own Wyoming Constitution."

MacMillan: "He [Sullivan] was quoted in the paper as saying he supported it. The Constitution doesn't say you can't have more than a 16% deviation. I think the range in the proposed amendment, combined with no gerrymandering, may make it stand."

ZumBrunnen: "New thinking is going on in upper echelons of legal circles. Robert Bork's work on one-person, one-vote is an example which I read from a Harvard public policy article given to me by Walter Urbigkit."

John DeWitt: "The amendment is in the spirit of bipartisan cooperation.[279] It embodies the combi-

---

[279] Carol Watson was a Democrat. Cynthia Lummis was a Republican.

201

nation of democracy and republicanism referred to in the Harvard article. No counties are torn apart. The range may be a bit high but it is a lot better than other plans."

Lauris Tysdale of Weston: "The courts are supposed to disperse justice. What minorities are we hurting with the current system? If we start down the road to compromise, it will get worse. I oppose the amendment."

Watson had the last word: "Some of my fellow Democrats support single-member districts. I don't. I like multi-member districts. We can save money defending a lawsuit if we pass this amendment. We can show the two parties can work together and do it ourselves."

The amendment failed on a division vote: 41 ayes, 23 noes.

ZUMBRUNNEN AND NIOBRARA'S LOBBYISTS

Niobrara's lobbyists wanted their 1983 purpose clause from *Brown v. Thomson* in HB 295. ZumBrunnen agreed:

The state of Wyoming, as a sovereign state, hereby declares that the Wyoming Constitution does provide for a fair and rational method of apportionment given the uniqueness of the state in view of the sparseness and distribution of the population over a large geographic area, of its geographical features and its varied social, economic and political communities."

ZumBrunnen said,

I want to make the best better. I have been advised by legal counsel to put everything in the bill. I want to establish the states' rights position. This sentence brings out the sparseness and distribution of our population."[280]

With little discussion, the amendment passed on a voice vote.

---

[280]The concept "the sovereign state of Wyoming" indicated the arrogance of legislators who seriously thought they could impose their *will* by making a simple declaration and attempt to exercise state's rights in opposition to the United States Constitution. In 1991 these were the opinions of a majority of the House of Representatives.

LUMMIS/BRIMMER-KUNZ AMENDMENT

Cynthia Lummis teamed up with April Brimmer-Kunz for the 4th amendment to delete all of HB 295, conduct a study of different apportionment methods and present a bill in 1992. It required three public hearings and to the "extent practicable" to maintain county boundaries, have compact districts, consider geographical features and the highway system, use the 1990 census and have a population deviation of no more than 8.2% or a 16.4% deviation range.

> Brimmer-Kunz: "This amendment is not proposed as an alternative to the committee bill. If this amendment passes it is okay to keep the Bowron amendment. I don't agree with it but if the body likes it, so leave it in."

> MacMillan: "The Constitution requires we reapportion now. We can't leave it to the interim. Nothing's going to change."

> Ron Micheli of Uinta: "Wouldn't it make sense to vote on the amendment and then address the lines about the Bowron amendment? I think overall the amendment will fail."

Speaker Cross directed the House to vote on keeping the Bowron amendment. The vote was no.

> Bowron: "What did we do? We don't know what we're doing." (Laughter)

> Hacker: "The Voting Rights Act issues are not applicable. The Hispanic population is our largest ethnic group. Rural areas of counties with big cities are just as bad off as Niobrara. This is the last chance you have to consider important issues."

> Brimmer-Kunz: "The amendment sends the interim study to the Corporations Committee. *Chapman* dealt with North Dakota, which is much like Wyoming. It is going to be hard to justify differences between Wyoming and North Dakota. The Supreme Court wouldn't even accept Hawaii's islands as subdivisions. Our other neighboring states like Montana, Idaho and Arkansas got their deviation range down. How do you think the Supreme Court will react to bringing counties together in the Senate but not in the House?

In the 1990 primary in Laramie County 28 people were on the ballot. Rural Laramie has 2 ½ times as many people as Niobrara. A Democratic rural candidate carried every rural precinct in Laramie County and yet didn't make it through the Primary.

If you want accountability, get rid of this system of electing people. Look at statistical methods. Compare Laramie and Natrona counties. The former will have 12,000 more people but the same number of senators. Our previous debate shows how many options there are. We should study them."

Fred Harrison: "It is impossible for this group to do the right thing. We are too attached to county lines to give people equal representation. We are on the course to self-destruction. The courts will draw the lines."

Mark Harris of Sweetwater: "Basically I agree with Fred, but a year isn't going to help. Let's get on with it."

Brimmer-Kunz: "The amendment instructs the committee to come up with a solution within the 16% range. We won't re-hear debate about Niobrara. I disagree with the concept that we *have* to do reapportionment now. We just got the census data. We don't adjourn sine die until the end of the budget session; so technically, we're still in session. What would the remedy be for anyone filing a lawsuit now? The worst that could happen would be a special session."

John DeWitt: "The first question we [Corporations Committee] asked was about the Voting Rights Act. Be assured the Committee didn't ignore it. The Committee considered a plan close to a 16% range involving floterials. Ten counties had floterial districts. The Committee abandoned it because voters couldn't understand it. Defeat this amendment."

The House did, overwhelmingly on a voice vote.

CARBON HAS A PLAN

The men from Carbon—Pat O'Toole, Bill Vasey and Fred Harrison—decided the under-representation in HB 295 was unacceptable for Carbon and Washakie. The 5th amendment increased the House size to 66 and gave Carbon and Washakie each another seat.

Pat O'Toole: "All lines are arbitrary. If we go with the bill as it now stands Carbon will lose a representative at a critical time. My amendment has a House of 66 members. It keeps the representation in Carbon, Niobrara and Washakie."

MacMillan: "I don't want to see the House get bigger. More folks make it harder to debate, harder to find space for desks, harder to move around in the chamber. For these reasons the Committee decided not to bring more representatives in unless one is needed for Niobrara. This is special legislation and gerrymandering. My county, Albany, lost a representative last time [1981]. That's the way it goes. Oppose this amendment or there won't be any end to this."

Fred Harrison: "I don't like this position but there hasn't been any opportunity to address equity. Carbon will have $1/6^{th}$ the voting power of Niobrara under the existing bill. Likewise in the existing bill Big Horn will have 5,000 people per representative compared to Carbon with 8,000 people per representative."

ZumBrunnen: "Vote against this. Statistics get in the way of reality. I wish I had 6 times the voting power as the rest of you."

O'Toole: "Expanding the House by 2 seats won't make it unworkable. It's fair."

The amendment failed: 24 ayes, 40 noes. The vote followed party lines except Republicans Ray Harrison, April Brimmer-Kunz, John Marton and Bill Rohrbach voted aye and Democrat Matilda Hansen voted no.

Fred Harrison joined Don Sullivan, Matilda Hansen and Chris Plant for a recorded vote on single-member districts. It was the same plan he presented in Committee Of The Whole.

> MacMillan: "It is not a constitutional plan because it was drawn on the basis of voter registration, not population. Vote no."

> Sullivan: "The plan was drawn on the basis of population apportioned proportionately to voting strength."

The roll call vote was: 16 ayes, 48 noes.

In the next amendment Sullivan gave reapportioning to the county commissioners in the 23 counties. His intent was to "take the monkey" off the backs of the legislators. He directed the commissioners to create individual member districts in multi-member counties with districts as nearly equal in population as "reasonably practicable."

> Sullivan: "If the county commissioners did the sub-districting, it will be done according to the same number of House seats as HB 295 gives to each county. Gerrymandering by 23 county commissioners will make everything come out in the wash."

> MacMillan: "You will have to subdistrict on the basis of population. This will require breaking county lines within Senate districts. Oppose this amendment."

> Sullivan: "The amendment doesn't require gerrymandering but if it's done, it won't be so bad."

The amendment failed on a voice vote. Debate on amendments ended. Chris Plant moved to delete the enacting clause, thus allowing full debate on the entire bill.

> Plant: "We have met the enemy and he is us. The bill represents the will of this body but it is antiquated. The Equality State should embrace equal representation. Asking the courts to accept county lines as more important than equality makes no sense. The bill doesn't address minorities. The bill favors incumbents."

> ZumBrunnen: "I read from the Hawaii case that the Supreme Court found the policy of preserving

island boundaries rational. That apportionment was tossed due to the use of voter registration as the basis for counting people and because of the failure to be consistent."

MacMillan: "The bill gets the range down. The Committee looked at the Voting Rights Act. We find the bill OK. Gerrymandering and single member districts are the height of incumbent protection. We'll get litigation."

Plant: "The first United States Constitution counted blacks as 3/5ths of a person. This bill is not at all acceptable."

Debate was over, the vote was taken: 40 ayes, 24 noes. Two Democrats—Sheila Arnold and Richard Honaker—voted "aye." Four Republicans—Eric Alden, April Brinner-Kunz, Bruce McMillan and Rory Cross—voted "no."

The 1991 House attempt at reapportioning was a rehash of the old arguments on the sanctity of county lines for defining election districts. Don Sullivan and his single-member district cosponsors were heralds of what was to come. They "saw the handwriting on the wall." With vast geographical distances between population concentrations, Sullivan found that it was imperative to ignore county boundaries in order to get election districts of equal populations.

To thoughtful students of reapportionment his struggle with voting returns clearly indicated:

1. For legislative districting the only constitutionally acceptable database was the census blocks; and

2. Wyoming had to get the technical capacity to match census blocks (head count) with voting precincts (geographical political space) for all election districts.

The House finished the bill. Next it went to the Legislative Service Office for engrossing and printing on green paper. The Senate received the engrossed bill on February 1st. The President referred it to Committee 7: Corporations, Elections and Political Subdivisions chaired by Charles Scott of Natrona.

Scott, James Applegate and Gary Yordy of Laramie County, Della Herbst and Tom Kinnison of Sheridan were ready to begin committee hearings.

17

Senate Committee Struggles with HB 295

The Senate approached the work of the House with interest and with caution. There was sufficient time for Committee hearings—a full month before the end of the session. On Monday, February 11th Chairman Scott laid the bill jacket on the table and invited Do Palma, lobbyist for the Wyoming League of Women Voters, to begin the testimony. The League's statement was available to everyone.

> The League of Women Voters of Wyoming urges the state legislature to adopt a reapportionment plan that divides the state into districts in order to represent the one-person-one-vote principle articulated in the Fourteenth Amendment of the United States Constitution.
>
> A population standard is the fairest and most equitable way of assuring that each vote is of equal value in a democratic and representative system of government. County lines alone cannot produce a reapportionment plan which is based substantially on population.[281]

Do Palma urged the committee to consider the constitutionality of one-person-one-vote and to produce a document as free as possible from gerrymandering. Because of the

---

[281] Position Paper, January 30, 1991 League of Women Voters of Wyoming: *REAPPORTIONMENT: HOUSE BILL 295*, archived at the American Heritage Center, University of Wyoming, Laramie.

complexity of reapportionment the League recommended a committee be set up to work during the "forthcoming summer, then come back next session with a plan."

Applegate: "Do you (the League) have a plan?"[282]

Palma: "We recommend you create a committee to make a plan. It is too late now to make a plan. When a mistake is found, everything else in the plan is shot. Take the time during the interim and get a reapportioning plan right."

Scott: "The Constitution requires the legislature to act promptly with the new census figures."

Palma: "When the new committee reports, it will still be the 51st Session. It is better to set the process in motion to achieve one-person, one-vote than it is to pass HB 295 this year."

Scott: "Hot Springs County has 4,000+ people. Washakie County has 8,000+ people. Under HB 295 they each have one representative, but they would make a good combined district. Are they better off with one representative each or to share two representatives?"

Palma: "Each representative should represent the same number of people. The votes are the same."

Scott: "Why do people up there say they want a representative for each county?"

Palma: "It is a natural reaction. Those counties need leadership here in the legislature."

Scott: "Is your group going to sue?"

Palma: "I cannot say now."

Listening to Chairman Scott probe about a possible lawsuit from the 1981 plaintiffs were two Republican lawyers: Mark Braden, the man hired in 1990 as Wyoming's expert counsel on apportionment, and Gordon Baker, who successfully challenged the Democrats' reapportionment of the California legislature. Scott turned to their testimony next.

---

[282] The quotations from testimony before the Senate Corporations Committee are from Jeanne Rideout's notes. House Democrats directed her to attend all committee meetings and to take notes. Matilda Hansen retained Rideout's work in her legislative files. Matilda Hansen collection, American Heritage Center, University of Wyoming, Laramie.

Baker: "One person, one vote doesn't mean precise mathematical equality. The Supreme Court took *Mahan's*[283] 16.4% as approaching tolerable limits. I don't know where the limit is. The problems of gerrymandering vastly outweigh problems with substantial population equality. If any state can justify reliance on political subdivisions, Wyoming probably stands the best chance. The Courts should adjust to local circumstances."

Herbst: "How does what you say about recognizing local conditions square with the Hawaii case?"[284]

Baker: "The Hawaii case was not a Supreme Court case."

Mark Braden, answering Herbst: "The Hawaii case could be persuasive in another court but it has no precedent value. This case also involved minority representation, making it complicated."

Mel ZumBrunnen: "The Court said maintaining islands was okay but they ran into the problem of using voter registration as the base and subdividing one island."

Scott: "For history's sake, what conditions preceded the reapportionment revolution?"

Baker: "Honor the statistics. *Reynolds*[285] involved an apportionment on a federal plan."

Scott: "What standards do you think should be applied?"

Baker: "The 'fair and effective representation' phrase from Warren's *Reynolds* opinion.[286] Obviously

---

[283] *Mahan v. Howell,* 410 US 315 (1973).

[284] It is unclear which Hawaii case Herbst referenced: 1-*Dyer v. Kazuhsia Abe,* 138 F. Supp. 220 (D Hawaii 1956) on the legislature's failure to obey the fundamental law of Hawaii was equivalent to affirmative electoral legislation which operated to discriminate against a class of persons (no reapportionment since the Organic Act of 1900); or 2-*Travis v. King*, 522 F. Supp. 554 (D. Hawaii 1982) that ruled their plan unconstitutional based on the number of registered voters in an election district.

[285] *Reynolds v. Sims* 377 US 533 (1964). It is the equal protection clause of the 14th Amendment that requires states to construct legislative districts that are substantially equal in population.

[286] Warren said: "...each citizen has the inalienable right to full and effective participation in the political process (at 565 *Reynolds*) and

this is open to interpretation. It is not right for him [Warren] to tell Wyoming what it should do. If the legislature wants to maintain counties, Wyoming can make more rational justification than most [states]."

Applegate: "What do you recommend?"

Baker: "You are trying to anticipate judicial reaction. You have to accept the possibility that your plan will fail. Your percentage is not close to what they've accepted before. But I don't anticipate that the Court would get into gerrymander, which it did in *Bandemer*.[287]

Scott: "The approach for the Committee has been to do what we think is right for Wyoming and then worry about the legalities. From a democratic standpoint, how would you judge a plan?"

Baker: "The representation should reflect diverse interests yet enable the majority to prevail. Don't build in minority blockage. Don't submerge the minority political party."

Scott: "How important is the degree of competitiveness?"

Baker: "A significant degree of competition is important."

Scott: "Is the geographic ability of people to have access to legislators important?"

Baker: "It is important, but you can't carry this beyond a certain point. You shouldn't submerge the population principle."

Scott "Single-member districts or combined county plans make for some large districts with population concentrated in different parts of the district."

Baker: "You have to look at transportation links."

Scott: "We have a high sense of county identity. In districts do people know who their representatives

---

"...the clear standard for vote dilution cases, 'equal representation for equal numbers of people' (at 560 *Reynolds*). "...mathematical nicety is not a constitutional requisite (at 569 *Reynolds)* and "...the overriding objective must be substantial equality of population among the various districts (at 579 *Reynolds*)."

[287] *Bandemer v. Davis,* 603 F. Supp 1479 (S.D. Ind. 1984).

are? Do people have trouble identifying with their representatives?"

Baker: "I don't know of any research although I am sure it is a problem."

Scott: "If we have large multi-member districts are the problems the same as in single-member districts?"

Baker: "Your problem is to keep the county intact and avoid gerrymandering. In states where partisanship is bad, large multi-member districts disadvantages the minority party. But I understand in Wyoming this is not a problem."

Scott: "Our experience is with large multi-member districts that gets representatives from both parties. Small counties are locked in."

Baker: "Large multi-member districts present problems with racial minorities."

Scott: "We do fine here."

Baker: "Yes, this is what makes Wyoming interesting because problems you might expect don't occur here."

Scott: "Are there other things that distinguish Wyoming?"

Baker: "You have a small number of counties. If you had more counties your proposed plan would be unmanageable from the one person, one vote standpoint. [Scott seemed to prompt Baker]. Wyoming has small numbers of people involved. The citizen legislature meets for a short time which makes simplicity a major concern."

Scott changes the direction of his questions: "We haven't had experiences with drawing lines. How is it done?"

Baker: "A consultant to the California Masters was hired to actually do the reapportionment. Legislators look at printouts. You look at the political results, at the effect on incumbents, at past voting patterns, at voter registration. Partisans can work the system to advantage."

Kinnison: "California went to state court?"

Baker: "Yes."

Applegate: "Do you think HB 295 meets the criteria you laid out?"

212

Baker: "I am not familiar with the Wyoming proposal, but with the documentation available to me, my criteria have been met in general."

Herbst probes further: "What happens to our bill if we have to make minority districts?"

Baker, "It does not look like you face any Voting Rights Act issues. I heard about Niobrara County at the last hearing. You did a great job. I would've voted to put them in. But to put them in makes the population badly skewed."

Scott returns to his question: "But you think our plan is fair in representing the people of Wyoming?"

Baker: "Yes, generally. You have the Supreme Court's 1980 decision, a weird one, with Niobrara called de minimis."

Scott: "If we had more counties like Niobrara, things would be worse?"

Baker: "Yes."

Kinnison shifts the questions. "Our plan will be challenged. I don't want the state Supreme Court drawing our lines. What if we include an alternative plan or set up a committee?"

Baker: "A challenge can go to federal district court. I understand that an interim group is included as fallback. I am not a fan of commissions making reapportionment decisions. I have seen it simply project partisanship into another forum."

Braden: "The California situation was an impasse, nor did it invalidate the plan. The preponderance of jurisprudence means the courts will give the legislature a second shot."

Kinnison: "Our plan could be held up in court. The constitution requires us to move. Would that mean the Wyoming Supreme Court would have to reapportion?"

Braden: "I don't know."

Scott: "Did I understand you to say that commissions invariably turn partisan?"

Baker: "That is too strong a statement. But experience has not met expectations. A commission can be partisan or ignore politics entirely, which can be just as bad."

Applegate: "What about the judges on the Supreme Court?"

Baker: "I can't predict but Brennan is gone and he was the stiffest advocate for mathematical equality. There is no indication in their earlier careers how Kennedy, Scalia or Souter might go. The most important justice probably is White who has advanced more play in the joints. But he also wrote *Swann*, a Texas case."

Applegate: "Have you had a chance to look at our census to see if we have Voting Rights Act problems? Or, maybe I should save this question for Mark Braden."

Yordy: "Were any of the new justices quizzed on this during their confirmations, like Bork was quizzed?"

Baker: "Bork was quizzed about this because he had been a prominent critic of the Warren Court. He attacked reapportionment."[288]

Applegate: "Are there any cases which draw a distinction between reapportionment as opposed to redistricting?"

Baker: "Reapportionment is rare now, since the 1960's. In most places reapportionment won't work. This is the last bastion."

Scott: "I think we are the only ones. Am I right in thinking no cases other than the earliest ones bear on this?"

Baker: "Yes."

Scott: "I ask you the same question regarding Hot Springs and Washakie counties. Are those who wish to have one of their own, a rational means to fair and effective representation?"

---

[288] Bruce Shawver Glenn of KGWN TV, Cheyenne, a station owned by The Great Western Broadcast Services of Stauffer Communications, Inc. sent a letter marked PERSONAL CORRESPONDENCE to Mel ZumBrunnen dated January 24, 1991 telling of the "...masterful job of exposing the fraudulent nature of judicial intervention in re-apportionment matters..." in *The Tempting of America, The Political Seduction of the Law* by Robert Bork. ZumBrunnen distributed copies of the letter and Bork's article to all legislators.

Baker: "I agree with the League of Women Voters. It is natural to adhere to the status quo and to resist change. This is an interesting question."

Mark Braden testifies on the Voting Rights Act. "The *Thornburg*[289] case is the only Supreme Court interpretation we have. For multi-member districts the Court has a 3-prong test: 1-A minority community has to be large and geographically compact enough to make an electoral district; 2-The minority group must be politically cohesive; and 3-Is there racial block voting? Does the white bloc always vote down the minority candidate?

The census bloc data for Wyoming show it is not possible to make an Hispanic district in Cheyenne. It is possible to make an Indian district in Fremont County. Fremont County meets criteria #1 and moves on to step 2. There is very little litigation on Indians and the Voting Rights Act.

Evidently there are conflicts between the two tribes there but I cannot offer an opinion on political cohesiveness. Maybe we don't have to be concerned because it clearly falls on criteria 3. There is no racial block voting. In fact all minorities in Wyoming are disproportionately represented in the legislature. You have an Indian representative who runs well, has been in the legislature a long time. [290]

There is no obvious divergence between Indian and non-Indian precincts. People who are not Indians vote for him. He gets elected. So, there is no need to worry about making Fremont County an Indian district. Obviously other issues are involved here, namely Indian sovereignty, taxation, etc."

Scott: "Would giving them a district have an adverse effect?"

Braden: "There might well be an effect. You might lose your Indian representative. If the legislature ever goes to single-member districts, then the

---

[289] *Thornburg v. Gingles,* 478 US 30 (1986).

[290] Scott Ratliff of Fremont County served from 1981 to 1992.

Voting Rights Act comes back. You might have to make Hispanic and Indian districts."

Herbst: "Does the Voting Rights Act override the population equality issue?"

Braden: "No."

Applegate: "If a 3-judge panel sends HB 295 back to us, could we appeal to the Supreme Court before we re-draw the election districts?"

Braden: "Yes, and I assume that would happen. The losing party will almost surely appeal."

Applegate: "Should the county commissioners draw the lines?"

Braden, "There are no neutral ways to draw lines. A zero-sum game really isn't zero-sum. The use of neutral criteria can have different impacts. The Voting Rights Act will lower the number of Democratic Congressional people by making urban minority districts. Some commissions have been bad and some have been good, it depends on the people on the commission. You don't want apolitical people doing it. It's a very political process once you get into it. A commission seems to have worked well for majority party control of the commission. The party that controls the commission will control the legislature."[291]

Scott turns the questions to bill drafting: "I don't sense a desire on the part of the committee to mess with the House plan. Would there be virtue in having a backup plan to strengthen their case?"

Braden: "You would like to go to federal court with the same plan as last time so you can say it's just the same."

Scott: "What about the Watson Plan as an alternative?"

Braden: "Having a backup plan doesn't change the litigation strategy that much. Your plan should be driven by what you think is the best policy. I would prefer the 1980 setup."

Herbst: "What about the Senate?"

---

[291] Braden's answer was about special commissions assigned to draw the lines. He was not answering Applegate's question about having Wyoming's county commissioners draw the lines.

Braden: "You are not asking the Supreme Court to overrule *Reynolds*. You are asking them to consider Wyoming as a special case. It takes so few people to move the percentages in Wyoming. Using range analysis is a bad way for the court to analyze this but the court does it consistently. So, you will have to make the Supreme Court get sophisticated regarding their analysis. The boom and bust cycle of Wyoming's population is a reality. Yet the census is just a one-day, one-year snapshot that shouldn't be determinative for the next 10 years."

Yordy: "Since the basis of our argument is going to be the need for stability based on county lines, we should stick with counties in the Senate instead of districts to be consistent?"

Braden: "Yes."

Applegate: "Did the *Brown* court express any concern regarding Senate combinations?"

Braden: "The dissenters did."

Applegate: "What about the majority?"

Braden: "I think Powell would have sustained your plan on a broader base, but the others didn't. I am not saying you will prevail."

Applegate: "The current bill doesn't have the fallback we had in 1980. Do you recommend this?"

Braden: "Yes."

Scott: "What about messing with the Senate combinations?"

Braden: "Go ahead and mess with them to minimize populations deviations. Lowering the population deviation has to be a goal."

Yordy was thinking about logistics: "Can plaintiffs, whoever they may be, get consolidated? We don't want stuff going all over."

Braden: "You can combine the federal filings, no problem. But the combining of federal/state filings presents problems."

Yordy: "Even with this language [Bowron amendment], do we accomplish what we want? If we're trying to send a message, we can write a letter."

Scott: "I want to add something regarding adherence to county lines that prevents gerrymandering. We can put out a formal committee report for judicial record."

Braden: "Wyoming is somewhat lacking in a legislative record here. It would be useful to have a report laying out the rationale."

Kinnison: "I suppose you have it written?"

Scott: "It's being kept up to date."

Kinnison: "Do you want it in the Journal?"

Braden: "Yes."

Herbst: "If we want a record, why don't we report the debate? That'll give you what you want."

Yordy: "The House killed that."

Scott: "This should be a committee report. I'll exercise my prerogative as chair to have it prepared, then you can do as you will."

Then the Committee heard testimony from Bern Hinckley, a citizen of Albany. [292] Salient points from his prepared statement were:

It seems instead of asking how the people of Wyoming can be best served through the reapportionment process, we have fallen prey to an "us against them" mentality and are asking, "what's the least we can do and still get away with it.... There is a much larger constituency to consider—the people of Wyoming. If we cannot accommodate the wishes of the 2500 people in Niobrara County without violating the fair and equitable representation of the 450,000 people of Wyoming, there should be no argument about which constituency should take priority.

Hinckley asked five questions:

1. Do county lines divide the state into well-defined, homogenous communities? No.
2. Do county-based legislative districts ensure everyone ready-access to their representative? No.
3. Does the use of county lines save us from gerrymandering? No.
4. Does inclusion of more than one population center in the same legislative district preclude the smaller from ever being represented? Obviously not.

_____

[292] For Hinckley's full testimony see Appendix C.

5. What's broke that needs fixed? His answer: "Basic fairness."

Hinckley continued:

> While the voice of Niobrara County is increased by the present disproportionate levels of representation, the ability of Senators and Representatives in Sheridan, Laramie, Uinta and Teton counties to represent the views and aspirations of their constituents is significantly compromised....
>
> The mission of this Legislature ... should be to provide what's best for the people.... The specific interests of each component ... must be taken into proportionate consideration, but reapportionment is a statewide issue. Let us not compromise the integrity of the whole in our attempts to preserve the status of a few parts.... Wyoming is the Equality State. Let statewide fairness and equality be our guides. Let's assert our uniqueness through responsible legislation. Rather than looking for the least you can get by with, strive to do the best you can for all the people of Wyoming.

The testimony concluded. The Committee began its work. Chairman Scott presented several plans but he was not advocating for any. He asked: "What kind of mechanism do we want in place to meet litigation? Do we want the original joint committee bill? Do we want the Watson Plan?"

The discussion then focused on Crook-Weston, Niobrara-Converse, Goshen-Platte, Sheridan-Johnson. Scott wanted to talk about the added cost of a 31-member Senate with Kelly Mader, Senate Appropriations Chairman.

Kinnison looked at the transition for senators who were in the middle of their 4-year terms—especially for the Sheridan-Johnson district.

> Kinnison: "Maybe two of our Sheridan people get elected for 2-year terms with Herbst, Perry and myself all on the ballot at the same time running for 2 seats. Everybody would get an equal chance."
>
> Herbst: "It will all come out in the wash."
>
> Scott: "You three decide."
>
> Yordy: "Do we discuss mine? Are we going that way?"
>
> Kinnison: "Not now, but let's don't throw it away."

Scott: "How should the legislative oversight be conducted?"

Kinnison: "Like standing committees, but the House Committee is so large the joint committee gets unwieldy."

Yordy: "Cutting down the House committee makes real problems as far as picking them."

Kinnison: "I don't like the idea of the President and Speaker appointing a committee. If we're going to do that, then let's put a fallback plan in the bill."

Yordy: "[My plan] doesn't include even the word 'district.' Let's give [reapportionment] some flexibility."

Scott: "Bring your plan back as an amendment. Miller[293] has drafted language to put the original committee bill in as a backup."

Kinnison: "I'm not sure I want the Bowron amendment."

Scott: "The Bowron amendment will be gone." [Turning to Miller]: "Draw up an amendment for a 31-seat senate using the combinations discussed previously and make a good transition provision. Don't make a 32-seat senate because that pushes the House to 64 and might make problems if Niobrara is tossed." [Then turning to the committee]: "Do you want a declarative judgment?"

It was 10:00 am—time for the Senate to convene. They adjourned, to reconvene in two days.

Wednesday morning, February 13, all committee members were present. No public comments were allowed. Observers were welcome. Mark Braden, the committee's outside legal counsel was there.

Yordy: "I move to delete the Bowron amendment, create a legislative reapportionment oversight committee, add an appropriations and make the effective date immediately. My choice for the oversight committee is the Joint Corporations Committee. We need it in place to oversee

---

[293] Rick Miller, Director of the Legislative Service Office and lead LSO staff on reapportionment.

litigation and other matters as they will surely occur."

Discussion ensued over adding gubernatorial, secretary of state and judicial members to the oversight committee. Then the decision: "...if these other folks were interested they could show up at the meetings if they wanted."

Scott: "What if someone on the floor asks who needs it [the oversight committee]?"

Yordy: "This will show the court we've thought about it. This will take the decision away from the Management Council."

Applegate: "This is probably a better idea than a Plan B."

Scott: "This is not a substitute for at least a mild Plan B, but I think we need it."

Yordy: "This gives specific direction but no criteria."

Scott (to Braden): "Is this okay?"

Braden: "Okay by me. It doesn't affect the litigation. I would like to have it. It gives liaison with the legislature to consult with in the course of litigation."

Yordy: "It centralizes the discussion of the issue."

Yordy's motion passed 5-0, but with no appropriation.

Applegate: "I move adoption of an amendment to make identical senatorial and representative districts using the Watson-Lummis Plan and to have a Park-Big Horn senate district with 2 seats."

Scott: "Is this going to be a new backup plan or a new substitute plan?"

Applegate: "We'll offer it as a substitute. If that fails then I propose it as a backup."

Scott: "Then let's look at the concept and trust you on the language."

Applegate: "Okay." (He explained Watson-Lummis 3rd reading, amendment #2 and his change that gave Laramie County 10 House seats.)

Yordy: "Can the Senate and House be separated?"

Applegate decided to withdraw his original motion and asked the committee to vote on the concept.

Scott (to Braden): "Will giving Laramie County another seat create a problem?" (Braden does not reply.)

Yordy: "It will on the floor."

Scott: "Maybe we should look at a 29-seat senate."

Yordy: "Maybe we should throw out all the Senate alternatives and then vote."

Scott: "Okay then, I move my amendment for a 31-seat senate with Crook-Weston, Converse-Niobrara, Goshen-Platte with 2 seats and avoid removing Sweetwater's 3rd senator."

Herbst: "Is the 31-member senate permanent or transitional?"

Scott: "Permanent."

Yordy: "What kind of range does that create?"

Scott: "58%, actually 57.7%."

Yordy: "What difference will it make to have a difference of 25.8% to 57.7%?"[294]

Braden: "It is always easier with smaller deviations but with rational policy considerations, fair and effecttive representation involves more."

Herbst: "Will it help you as far as defending the case with regard to Niobrara since Scott's senate district is more compact?"

Braden: "Niobrara is not going to be a significant issue in the litigation. We are going to approach this as *de minimis* as was done before. The key issue is the underlying plan."

Yordy: "If it's true that deviation difference is not a big deal, then let's discuss policy."

Applegate: "Do we want to offer a change to the senate plan in HB 295?"

Scott: "I have problems with 3 counties in a district. Voters wouldn't get the degree of communication needed for fair and equal representation. I want to correct these."

Herbst: "There is no consideration of single-member districts, nor of one person, one vote here. If we can't have that, then I prefer your plan."

Applegate: "I want to adjust senate districting in a substitute move."

Yordy: "Me too."

Scott: "What if we put my plan in as the new Senate in HB 295 and Watson plan as the substitute?"

Yordy: "I like those 5 senate seats in Laramie County."

---

[294] This difference gives a deviation range of 83.5%.

Applegate: "I have to go with that."

Yordy: "But I think in terms of overall best representation, I'll go for Scott's amendment, and then come back on the floor with an amendment to add another seat for Laramie County."

The committee voted to use the Scott Plan as the new senate plan: 4 ayes, 1 no. Applegate voted no. Kinnison moved the Watson-Lummis Plan as Plan B with 4 senators for Laramie County and a 29-seat senate.

Applegate "Will this skew up the deviation?"

Rick Miller of the LSO: "I'll have to re-run it."

The vote was 2 ayes, 3 noes—Herbst, Applegate, Yordy. Applegate moved the Watson-Lummis Plan as Plan B with 5 senators for Laramie County—it passed unanimously.

Yordy: "Should we pass the Watson-Lummis Plan for Plan B for the House?"

Applegate: "I so move."

Scott: "We need to give Mel the best possible case. We have two alternatives: the original committee bill with a 63-seat House or the Watson Plan with a 62-seat House."

Applegate: "I move the 63-seat plan."

Scott: "I suggest you move the 62-seat plan."

Yordy: "How smart is it to include an alternative plan? Will the court say we've already taken 2 bites of the apple and draw the lines for us?"

Braden: "I don't see backup as a significant part of litigation. It doesn't endanger you. The court will still probably either accept the backup or remand, perhaps with directions."

Scott: "Does it help? Or are you better off without it?"

Braden: "If you're asking me what I prefer, I'd rather have nothing because it's another issue to muck around with. But I don't really care."

Yordy: "I'm leaning toward keeping it out of the bill, just on the shelf."

ZumBrunnen: "Won't having a backup that crosses county lines weaken our primary argument?"

Braden: "Might, but not likely."

Yordy: "Put the backup in the files, assuming the court buys off on our underlying philosophy. I am concerned that having a backup plan will cause the court to reject Plan A because they'll think the legislature wasn't serious."

Braden: "The more I think about it, the more I'd rather have no backup."

Yordy moved the committee reconsider its earlier vote and delete any backup. Motion passed 4-0. Applegate was absent.

Scott: "We need to return to the purpose clause. We have to work on it because it assumed passage of the Watson plan as a backup. I want to remove the 'sovereign state' phrase."

Yordy: "I object. Isn't this one of the issues? What rights do the states have to check the feds?"

Scott: "John C. Calhoun has been dead for years."

Braden: "This is a kick in the sand at a bully."

Yordy: "That's what I want."

They voted to remove "sovereign state": 3 ayes, 1 no (Yordy). Applegate was absent.

Scott: "We need to insert language about consideration of plans crossing county lines. We reject crossing county lines as the basis for not giving in to the evil of gerrymandering."

Herbst: "There has been no floor discussion yet. Isn't it presumptuous to say we've considered it?"

The vote on Scott's purpose clause: 2 ayes, 2 noes (Yordy and Herbst).

Yordy explained his vote: "I don't want to put it on because it's kicking sand in the face of the court again."

Herbst: "I think it's premature. Put it in on the floor if we actually do it."

Scott (to Miller): "Delete the Bowron amendment, direct the attorney general to seek a declaratory judgment, make the standing committee report into divisible parts to better explain the committee's work."

The final vote on the Standing Committee report (SS1) was along party lines: Scott, Kinnison, Yordy aye and Applegate, Herbst no.

Rick Miller wrote a understandable standing committee report. The bill was on the Chief Clerk's desk on February 14th. There was no referral to the Senate Appropriations Committee.

224

THE SENATE WORKS HB 295

It was the 29th day of the 51st Session, February 15, 1991, when the Senate "took up" HB 295. They did not touch the House reapportionment. The Senate was all they cared about. Chairman Scott began by explaining the Standing Committee's amendment.

They took a seat away from Park, made Majority Leader Jerry Dixon's district just Crook-Weston, put Niobrara with Converse and retained the anti-Ed Kendig, anti-Democratic, combination of two senators for Goshen-Platte.

The central-region men exerted their power. They took a seat from the northern region and gave it to the eastern region[295] and made the deviation range worse—from 53.8% in the original bill to 85.4% in the Standing Committee amendment. Because the 1981 Court accepted 89% range in *Brown v. Thomson*, the senate majority saw nothing wrong with 85.4%.

The transition for senators with 4-year terms remained unresolved for Johnson-Sheridan—both seats were still in the "Herbst wash."

The Senate liked the legislative oversight provision. They created the committee to consist of the members of the Joint Corporations Committee charged with keeping track of any lawsuits filed against HB 295, giving summaries of what was happening "on a timely basis" to the Management Council, developing alternatives or plans, should the 1991 reapportionment be unconstitutional. They were to meet "as often as necessary," hold public hearings and take public testimony.

On the purpose clause the Senate agreed to delete "sovereign state of Wyoming" and accepted Scott's language:

> The legislature has considered a variety of plans where districts cross county lines. The legislature finds that preserving the integrity of county boundaries is necessary to minimize the potential of the gerrymander.

They tossed the Bowron amendment, then added their own preemptive move to forestall all lawsuits by Wyoming's restless and concerned citizens:

> (b) The legislature directs the attorney general to immediately seek to resolve any issue regarding the

---

[295] Took away from Park; gave to the reconfigured districts comprising Converse, Niobrara, Goshen, and Platte. Goshen was over-represented by 32.1% and Park was under-represented by 53.3%.

compliance of this legislation with relevant federal constitutional and statutory provisions in a judicial forum competent to decide such issues.

This was a curious directive because Attorney General Joe Meyer was directed to immediately sue the legislators whose districts were under-represented. Yet in his official capacity, he had to defend those same legislators who were acting in their official capacity.

After passing the Standing Committee report, Scott tried to adjust the transition for the Sheridan-Johnson seats—the Herbst "wash." Then a Yordy/Scott amendment restored $300,000 for expenses, should HB 295 be found unconstitutional.

After Applegate made an initial presentation of his single-member district plan, the Senate adjourned for the weekend.

Second Reading was on Monday. Scott still stirred the "Herbst wash" for the Sheridan-Johnson seats.

Lawyer Applegate held a "deep concern" over the 85.4% deviation range—a clear violation of federal case law. He proposed his plan based on population, used county boundaries for nested Senate and House seats in a floterial distribution similar to Watson-Lummis. He took senate-county mixes from the original bill, then added Big Horn-Park and Lincoln-Uinta.

Applegate: "The purpose of this amendment is to get a supportable deviation range. Everyone has agreed to use county lines to define election districts. In order to get to 25%,[296] we need to make combinations of 16 of the 23 counties. In 1965 the Court changed the Senate, not the House. In 1971 the Court looked at the House, not the Senate. If we present this Senate plan, the court more likely than not will support it. The deviation in the House is 83%. If we have a viable Senate plan, the Court will probably focus on the House—25% is supportable."[297]

Boyd Eddins of Sublette: "My silence doesn't mean I'm not interested. This bill [without the

---

[296] He used the preliminary census to get 25%. In the official census his plan had a deviation range of 38.3%.

[297] Quotations during debate in the Senate on Second Reading are from Do Palma's notes, who was the lobbyist for the Wyoming League of Women Voters. Matilda Hansen Collection, American Heritage Center, University of Wyoming, Laramie.

Applegate amendment] is a good bill. The amendment is not needed. I would like Senator Applegate to try to be in my county. It is 200 miles long. There is tremendous diversity in agriculture and in religion. The amendment doesn't allow for proper representation."

Scott: "I want the Senate to pay careful attention. This is a responsible amendment. It reduces the range, which I don't think is a relevant measure of a reapportionment system. The percentage needed to elect a majority is more important. This amendment brings up the issue of fair and effective representation. The amendment is closer on population ranges but it doesn't meet the fair and effective test. We are a citizen legislature. At the store, at church, at social events is where we get the input from our constituents. Someone from Douglas doesn't get that in Torrington. The bill is a better version than the amendment. I think both the bill and the standing committee amendment will be held up in court. Vote in favor of a system which gives more effective representation, without those big districts."

Russell Zimmer of Goshen: "We shouldn't try to outguess the court. I was here 10 years ago and heard the same arguments."

Frank Prevedel of Sweetwater: "The argument is the size of the district vs. the size of the population. This amendment would reflect a truer picture of what the state is within the legislature itself."

Hank Coe of Park: "The combined county districts are a problem, like our hospital districts. You elect one person and then the two counties are in competition with each other. A legislator just can't represent two counties successfully."

Eddins: "Imagine trying to campaign in a district from Freedom, Wyoming to Wamsutter!"

Applegate: "We shouldn't decide on the basis of what's convenient for a particular legislator. This plan puts two people in these big districts. Look at the combined districts we have now. These are effective legislators. I hold them in high regard. Now people are saying "we can't do this." The

1983 decision has warned us that Niobrara will be taken out."

Scott: "Eddie Moore, who used to represent Converse-Niobrara, used to complain about the two counties having diametrically opposed positions on the issues. Three counties to represent would be worse. What have we gained by putting them together? It is better to split their districts rather than figure they'll each represent a part of their large district."

John Perry of Johnson: "What has been said is a matter of perception. The issue is equality of service that may be offered to a district by a legislator. I'm in this position. The issue isn't convenience. The more demographic blends we put in the more difficult we make it—not for the senators but for the constituents. We have to do what is right for our constituencies. We need to stick out our necks and take our chances. Both plans are commendable."

The amendment was defeated. Second Reading ended.

Next day the Senate convened at 9:00 am. After the prayer and before Journal Committee report was accepted, Senator Scott requested that his report of the "Reapportionment Committee" be inserted in the Journal. This was the statement-of-intent Braden requested of the Corporations Committee on February 13th. "Reapportionment Committee Report" was a misnomer.[298] Though presented to the Senators in their Chamber, Scott was making a preemptive move against the judiciary.

His "report" contained 29 paragraphs and approximately 3,350 words. First he acknowledged that the United States

---

[298] On February 19th there was no Reapportionment Committee to make a report. On February 11th, in Corporations Committee, Senator Scott placed before the Committee his wish to have a statement by the Committee on how county lines prevent gerrymandering. Kinnison observed that Scott had such a statement already written. Scott replied it was being kept up to date. The Committee did not see nor did they vote on his document. The *Reapportionment Committee Report* was Scott's work and was placed in the Journal as a routine part of the Journal Report, after Scott read it to the Senate.

Constitution prevails when there is a conflict between it and the Constitution of Wyoming.

Scott claimed that the legislature attempted to follow the "...general guidelines provided ... in *Reynolds v. Sims*"[299] with the objective of achieving "...fair and effective representation for all Wyoming citizens. The Committee has concluded that this objective can best be accomplished through the preservation of county boundaries...."

Without saying "rational state policy,"[300] he tried to establish Wyoming's justification for its overall population range exceeding 10%.

> Wyoming counties are accurate representations of divisions between social groups, economic interests and political communities.... The Committee has determined that a legislator cannot properly represent his constituents, nor can voters from a district exercise the ballot franchise intelligently when a legislative district is nothing more than a fragmented unit divorced from and indeed possibly in conflict with the various other political communities established by the state. Moreover, counties are vital and effective units of Wyoming local government....

After laboring for five more paragraphs justifying counties as election districts, Scott turned to deviation range.

> An obsession with numerical equality conflicts with the need for representation of all significant interests in a society including geographically isolated minorities. This is extraordinarily true in a state such as Wyoming with a vast land area and a small population. It is important to remember that legislators represent people not numbers.... [We] do not believe that fair and effective representation of Wyoming's urban and rural mountain and plains business and agricultural populations will be achieved through a formulation of exactly equal population districts as opposed to a county structured system....

---

[299] *Reynolds v. Sims* was handed down in 1964, 27 years before Scott wrote this report. He made no mention of case law developed during the intervening 27 years.

[300] *Reynolds v. Sims* at 579 states, "...the state will have the burden of showing ... more than 10 percent overall range is necessary to implement a 'rational state policy.'"

For 16 more paragraphs Scott continued these themes. Then he adamantly said,

> In Wyoming, exact equal population districting would not be the functional equivalent of fair and effective representation....

Then he stated—without citation:

> More modern views [hold] ... that the legislative representative acts for, or on behalf of the represented, and is accountable to the represented, but need not be a mirrored image of the electorate. The right to elect representatives is every citizen's portion of sovereign power.

Finally he concluded,

> This Committee believes the proposed reapportionment plan provides every Wyoming citizen a fair and effective portion of the state's sovereign power.

When the Senate got to Third Reading of HB 295, no more substantive amendments were proposed. The vote was called: 22 ayes, 6 noes, 2 excused.[301]

Senate Message No. 222, dated February 19, 1991, asked the House to concur with the changes made by the Senate on Engrossed HB 295. The vote occurred two days later: 43 ayes, 21 noes. Five Republicans switched their third reading votes: Dan Budd from aye to no, Eric Alden, Eli Bebout, Rory Cross and Bruce McMillan from no to aye.

The 21 Democrats continued to oppose HB 295. The 85.4% deviation range made equality among the several election districts impossible.

On the 35th day, February 25th, the Speaker and President signed Enrolled Act 81.[302] The Governor did not sign it.[303] Sullivan said that he "was not fully satisfied" the legal principle of one-man, one-vote was resolved. "The Republican majority is not likely to submit a substantially different plan without court direction."

---

[301]The Democrats voting "no" were James Applegate, Elizabeth Bird and Guy Cameron of Laramie County; Della Herbst of Sheridan; Lisa Kinney of Albany and Robert Reese of Sweetwater. John Perry, a Republican of Johnson-Campbell and Frank Prevedel a Democrat of Sweetwater, were excused.

[302] Senate/House 1991 Reapportionment, EA 81.

[303] The Governor's letter, was dated February 28th, the 38th and last day of the 1991 Session. See Appendix D.

He supported the county system and agreed the state's demographics make it unique. He was pleased Niobrara got its House seat but he wanted subdistricting, especially for Natrona and Laramie where voters faced a ballot with 18 names for 9 House seats. "Frankly, I do not believe a slate of candidates that large fosters appropriate representation or the ability to assess issues and responsibly select candidates."

Sullivan said the best way to expeditiously resolve the debate over reapportionment was to send it "...to a judicial determination as to its constitutionality and that will be my direction to the attorney general...."

The 1991 version of Reapportionment of the Wyoming Legislature was finished. Citizen Bern Hinckley's counsel was ignored—the integrity of the whole was compromised in the attempt to preserve the power base of some of its parts.

Fairness and equity in representation for everyone in Wyoming continued to be elusive. Governor Sullivan was right; the mind-set of the Republican majority was to make as few changes as possible.

On the last day before the legislators went home, Joe Meyer, the attorney general, was in Federal Court. He filed a complaint for declaratory judgment[304] in the United States District Court seeking review of HB 295, Enrolled Act 81.

"The Class Defendants" were legislators from Carbon, Fremont, Washakie, Laramie, Platte and Uinta because these counties were "...primarily affected by HB 295 under existing case law concerning the extent to which deviations from the one-man, one vote concept are permitted."[305] The legislators were:

Carbon —Senate: Robert Grieve
        —House: Fred Harrison Patrick O'Toole, Bill Vasey
Fremont—Senate: Robert Peck and John Vinich

---

[304] Ballentine's Law Dictionary: "A declaratory judgment is a judgment which declares conclusively the rights and duties, or the status of the parties but involves no executory or coercive relief.... An action for declaratory judgment is the appropriate remedy for the determination of a justiciable controversy where the plaintiff is in doubt as to his legal rights and wishes to avoid the hazard of taking steps in advance of the determination of such rights."

[305] From Meyer's letter to Bernard Phelan, one of the named defendants. All defendants got the same letter from Meyer. Copies of Phelan's letter were distributed to House Democrats.

—House:	Eli Bebout, Bruce McMillan, Scott J. Ratliff, Dennis Tippets, Harry B. Tipton
Washakie—House:	Ray Harrison
Laramie—Senate:	James Applegate, Harriet Byrd, Guy Cameron, and Gary Yordy,
—House:	Edith V. Garcia, Pat Hacker, Shirley Humphrey, April Brimmer-Kunz, Cynthia Lummis, Bernard Q. Phelan, Mary Kay Schwope, Don Sullivan and Carol Watson
Platte—Senate:	Jim Geringer, House: Eric M. Alden, Bob Grant
Uinta—Senate:	John Fanos,
—House:	Janice Bodine, Ron Micheli

Meyer listed reasons for his action in his February 28th letter to the Management Council:

1. To decide the issues expeditiously and economically;
2. To not leave the questions outstanding until someone decided to initiate litigation;
3. To exert state control over the forum, over the issues to be resolved, over the timeliness of resolving the issues; and
4. To cover the costs.

He wanted a three-judge federal panel[306] and one trip to the United States Supreme Court, outside legal assistance for his office, limitation of legal fees to the $250,000 in HB 295. He intended to keep reapportionment firmly under his control.

He executed a contract for outside legal services with Mark Braden, James R. Miller and Tom Evans of the Denver firm of Baker & Hostetler.[307] Meyer saw no conflict of interest for Braden between this new contract and the previous one as outside legal counsel for the Joint Corporations Committee. He justified his quick action as his "tactical decision to seek judicial relief via declaratory judgment ... before other suits were filed...."[308]

---

[306] A 3-judge panel is required in reapportionment cases according to Rule 28 in the Federal Rules of Civil Procedure, U.S. C.S. 1973 (b).

[307] The entire $250,000 was committed in the contract. Only Management Council saw the contract. In fact, the law firm was hired, not the men named in Meyer's February 28 letter.

[308] From Meyer's letter to the Management Council.

Meyer claimed that HB 295 was passed for the sound reasons in the Senate Committee Report[309] and was "in furtherance of and in compliance with" the 14th and 15th amendment to the United States Constitution and 42 U.S.C. & 1971, *et seq.*

He took as serious threats the statements of "members of the defendant class" to challenge HB 295. He anticipated the actions to be in "multiple state venues" with the potential result of "inconsistent decisions, undue expense" to the state and a boatload of work for the Attorney General.

Meyer stated the case for the State in 55 paragraphs. He got to the crux of the issue in paragraph 20.

> The actual reapportionment of legislators under the Act [HB 295] creates by some statistical measure a greater deviation between the numbers of inhabitants per legislative representative than has been permitted by the Supreme Court of the United States in prior cases in other states which do not have the unique characteristics and history of Wyoming.

The complaint listed all manner of evil and/or serious consequences if fundamental changes were made to Wyoming's political and legislative process.

The Wyoming election administration will become more complex. County Clerks and the Secretary of State will need considerable time prior to the next election to adjust to changes. The ballot tabulations and reporting will require changes. Precincts will have to be redrawn.

Substantial time will be needed to create new representative districts. The Legislature will need an extended period to develop alternative plans. Election officials need time to create different ballots and adapt to different administrative responsibilities.

The political process is clouded with uncertainty. Who will decide to seek office? What will be their constituency? Will the new constituency give sufficient political and financial support to those who seek office?[310] Will the county-based political parties be adversely affected?

---

[309] Meyer renamed the Reapportionment Committee Report inserted by Senator Scott in the Senate Journal on February 19th.

[310] In paragraph 41 Meyer used Teton and Sublette counties as examples. Teton County's tourism-based economy and homeowners seeking 2nd residences were clearly different from the sparsely pop-

Citizens need time to get used to a new system. An informed active electorate is required for successful democratic governance. Recasting the system shortly before an election erodes the electorate's ability to know the candidates. It is impossible to campaign for an office with an undetermined electorate—thus denying the fundamental right to cast a knowledgeable ballot. A truncated campaign gives the electorate candidates and a legislature they don't want.

If the Federal Court did not grant the relief requested in the complaint, there will be all manner of injuries to the State.

Large and inconsistent legal fee awards will be made in multi-county litigation.

There will be multiple and inconsistent determinations from multiple state courts about the validity of the Act.

There will be irreparable injury to the State's ability to administer elections, irreparable injury to the State's political party system.

The citizens will not know their legislators, or who can run from which district.

There will be impairment of the State's representative form of government as well as deprivation of citizen's rights under the 14th amendment.

Meyer's "prayer for relief" asked the Court to get to work right away and decide if the defendants' rights were violated under the 14th and 15th Amendments and the Voting Rights Act. He wanted preliminary and permanent injunctions to keep the defendants from filing in any court. And he asked for the granting of other legal and equitable relief "as may be deemed just and proper."

1991 SESSION ENDS AND TENSIONS BUILD

The day of Meyer's complaint was the last day of the session—a time of "hurry up and wait." When copies of his complaint were distributed, the Republicans were pleased that he acted promptly on their request to get into court fast.

Democrats were mystified: how could a complaint for declaratory judgment bring clarity to the legality of the 1991 reapportionment? How could Meyer defend the legislators—as

---

ulated, multi-use ranch-based economy of Sublette County. President Bill Clinton carried Teton County in 1992 and 1996.

the law required of him—at the same time that he sued them as plaintiff for the State? What did the Republicans fear—a resurgence of Democratic political power?

This action by Meyer was not the way to get to where he wanted to be, that is, plaintiff in control of the issues before a court. As attorney general Meyer had to defend the State, in this instance the Legislature. With the complaint he, in the name of the State, tried to be the plaintiff seeking to prevent Wyoming's "restless and fuss-making citizens" from going to Court again.

The retention of political power by the Republicans was the driving force behind this conundrum. All posturing, all the time spent in debate, all the rationale to justify a seat for Niobrara County, all 3,350 words of Senator Scott's Committee Report, all justifications for any deviation in the 80% range, all of Meyer's litany of impending injuries should HB 295 be found unconstitutional, were about the Republicans' fear of losing control and of losing power.

The 1991 session was over. With reluctance, the Republican leadership realized there was nothing more they could do. They were done. These holders of political power, these managers of actions, had to step aside and become spectators.

The next major players were the new batch of restless citizens, their counsel—and, again, three Federal Judges.

No one had long to wait. Two weeks after the legislators went home and before the wheels of justice in the Federal Rules of Civil Procedure got to Meyer's complaint, suit was filed in Federal District Court in Cheyenne: *Gorin v. Karpan.*

The *Gorin* suit was the only one to challenge the 1991 reapportionment. The Republicans' fears of suits in many state courts proved groundless. With this new filing, Attorney General Meyer quietly and quickly withdrew his complaint.

Gorin got him out of the box of being counsel for the plaintiffs (the State) and counsel for the defendants (the legislators). Serious students of law thought the complaint fraught with legal pitfalls and black holes. The "grapevine in the court house" reported a disinclination to consider the complaint. *Gorin v. Karpan* provided excellent face-saving.

Then silence prevailed. For weeks there was no public discussion of reapportionment, as counsel for both sides prepared for their day in court.

18

Gorin v. Karpan

The "restless fuss-making citizens" were back in Court. Steven Freudenthal was counsel for the plaintiffs. Ford Bussart was counsel for the interveners. They laid the question of the constitutionality of HB 295, Enrolled Act 81, squarely before Federal Court in Cheyenne.

Freudenthal was a Legislator in the House from 1987 through 1990. He was a Democrat and an attorney with the Cheyenne law firm of Herschler, Freudenthal, Salzburg, Bonds & Rideout.[311] With him on the briefs were Hardy Tate of Sheridan, a Representative from 1985 to 1988, and William John Disney of Converse.

Ford Bussart had been a Representative (1977–78) and a Senator (1979–82). He was a Democrat with the Rock Springs firm of Greenhalgh, Bussart, West & Rosetti. With Bussart on the brief was Linda A. Botham of Green River.[312]

Freudenthal and Bussart were not in the legislature at the same time. Freudenthal and Tate did serve together during 1987–88. However, all three served with the Republicans who were in the leadership during the 1991 reapportionment. Their knowledge and familiarity with both the legislative process and the personalities of their opponents added spice and suspense. Three questions worried the Republicans:

1. How will these influential and very articulate former legislators frame the reapportionment issue?

---

[311] This was Attorney General Freudenthal who defended the State in 1981 in *Brown v. Thomson.*

[312] *Gorin v. Karpan* 775 F. Supp. 1430 (D. Wyo 1991).

237

2. Will they follow the recommendation of the Court in *Brown v. Thomson* and look at reapportionment in every district? Or
3. Will they limit their challenge to the huge deviation caused by Niobrara County's one seat?

This time, the lead "restless and fuss-making citizen" was Sarah Gorin, a graduate student in the Political Science Department at the University of Wyoming, who made HB 295, Enrolled Act 81, the topic of her Master's thesis.[313] She knew the case law for one-person, one-vote beginning with *Baker v. Carr* in 1963. Moreover, she knew Wyoming. She had an informed historical perspective on reapportionment.

She could count. She could read. She knew her vote in Albany carried less weight that the vote of family members in Park and Big Horn.

She explored the numerous—sometimes fallacious—old arguments used to justify the distribution of Senate and House seats. She looked at voting patterns, cost of campaigning and voter turnout. She cited facts and commented on how the legislative seats were distributed contrary to Wyoming's constitutional requirement of equal representation.

Joining Gorin as plaintiffs were citizens from the under-represented counties: Bern Hinckley of Albany, Chelsea Kesselheim of Fremont, John M. Faunce and Linda Kirkbride of Laramie County, Jesse Guidry of Natrona, Verna Crusch of Platte, Ernest A. Roybal of Sheridan, Wayne E. Morrow and Teri J. Royer of Uinta and Larry W. McGonigal of Washakie. Representative Chris Plant of Sweetwater was also a plaintiff.[314]

The plaintiffs directed Freudenthal to frame the issue broadly. They did not want to hear the Supreme Court justices say, as they did in 1981, that the issue before them was too narrow.

The defendants were again the State Canvassing Board led by Secretary of State Kathy Karpan, Governor Michael J. Sullivan, Auditor David Ferrari and Treasurer Stan Smith.

Counsel for the defendants were Attorney General Joseph B. Meyer and his senior assistant Clinton D. Beaver, outside counsel Mark Braden, Marc D. Flink and Thomas B. Evans of Baker & Hostetler of Denver.

---

[313] Gorin, op. cit.

[314] *Gorin v. Karpan*, 775 F. Supp. 1430 (D. Wyo. 1991).

Peter Maxfield of Albany, a Senator from 1993-1996, filed an *amicus curiae* brief for the Wyoming State Democratic Party.[315]

The case was heard September 3-6, 1991, before Circuit Judge Wade Brorby and Wyoming Federal District Judges Clarence A Brimmer and Alan B. Johnson. Defendants perceived these judges to be "friendly to Wyoming." Brorby was from Campbell. Brimmer had written for the State in 1971 and 1981. To him, Wyoming reapportionment was "same-old, same-old." Before Johnson came to the Federal Bench, he was a State District Judge in Laramie County.

The first lawyers to arrive in the courtroom were Freudenthal and Bussart.[316] They went to the plaintiff's table and emptied their boxes. Freudenthal unloaded his pockets of all jangling coins and keys—he wanted no distractions. The plaintiffs arrived and took their "observer" seats. The ambience surrounding the plaintiffs and their counsel reflected inner quietness and confidence. They appreciated and understood their roles in this historic confrontation in the dignified setting of the Federal Courtroom.

Nearly late, in trouped the lawyers for the defense. They caused somewhat of a stir deciding who sat where, what documents went where, what last minute whisper just had to be said. With them was Gordon Baker of California, who appeared before the Senate Corporations Committee, and was to testify.

This bunch of lawyers was also confident. Their predecessors had beaten-back the challenges in 1963, 1971, 1981. They exuded commanding confidence in anticipation of prevailing in 1991 as well. There was a modicum of arrogance in their demeanor. They were eager to "slay the dragon" again. There was respect for the justices before whom they were soon to stand. But historical precedent was on their side.

The stage was set. The bailiff announced the Judges. Freudenthal began his case knowing Wyoming's 102-year-old Constitution guaranteed equal legislative representation to all citizens.[317] Based on *Baker v. Carr,* he claimed equal

---

[315] Ibid.

[316] Matilda Hansen was a spectator in the Courtroom during opening arguments in *Gorin v. Karpan.*

[317] The actual archaic language in Article III, Section 3 "...They shall be apportioned among the said counties as nearly as may be according to the number of their inhabitants..."

representation was a *right* under the Fourteenth and Fifteenth Amendments to the United States Constitution.

He said that legislators, for years, had ignored constitutionally mandated equality in voter representation. He presented Gorin's research documenting regional interests consistently conspired to deny this equality. He claimed legislators acted in arbitrary and capricious ways. He sought to abolish the myth of the dominance of counties as the organizational base for Wyoming society.

> For the first time this contention was buttressed with evidence and testimony on the importance of political subdivisions other than counties. The evidence included listings of session laws enacted from 1983-1991 dealing with everything from water projects to community colleges to state government reorganization.[318]

He brought distinguished Wyoming history scholar T.A. Larson who stated, "The primary cultural and social units in Wyoming are the municipalities."

Freudenthal used Gorin's research to identify the evils of multi-member House districts with so many candidates on the ballot: Albany and Campbell with 8 candidates, Sweetwater with 10 candidates, Natrona with 16 candidates and Laramie County with 18 candidates. In these multi-member districts voter registration decreased, voter participation decreased and the costs of campaigning increased over single-member districts.[319]

The defendants did not challenge the Gorin research. They focused on the *de minimus* concept from 1981 for Niobrara County. They used Meyer's Declaratory Judgment Complaint and Senator Scott's 3,350-word Reapportionment Committee Report.

The defense raised the possibility of gerrymandering should county-based election districts be abolished. Gorin observed,

> This threatening invitation did not faze the plaintiffs, who already saw gerrymandering embedded in the county-based reapportionment. From the 1963, 1971, 1981 and 1991 … Plans for Wyoming, there emerges a consistent, institutionalized pattern of over-representa-

---

[318] From Gorin thesis, where she sites Plaintiffs' final Pretrial memorandum, Exhibit A. Plaintiffs Exhibits 5-14 *Gorin v. Karpan*.

[319] Gorin, *op. cit.*, Tables 1-19, Appendix.

tion of rural election districts and under-representation of high populated urban districts.[320]

The defense lawyers brought their own statistics; volumes of data on the changes in population of each Wyoming county, compared to every other county in the United States, and the differences between the 1980 and 1990 Federal Census. They identified the high mobility and small size of Wyoming's population, saying that it was unwise to rely too heavily on "snap-shot" census. "Why get too picky about population deviations when halfway through the decade the percentages will be way off anyway?"[321]

Gordon Baker testified a deviation of 500 or 1000 people would be completely unnoticed in his home state (California). The Wyoming judges were not impressed. They kept asking, either Baker or other defense counsel, "Why should we care if the absolute number of people affected by malapportionment in Wyoming will not be significant in California?"[322]

The defense counsel seemed fixated on people-counts. They brought spice to the proceedings by subpoenaing the regional director of the Census Bureau. Gorin described this encounter in her thesis.

> Upon taking the stand, the regional director declared his intention to answer only certain questions [upon the advise of counsel for the Census Bureau]. The three-judge panel thereupon threatened him with 30 days in the Laramie County jail for contempt of court. After some negotiations he agreed to answer all questions, but his first statement—that the Census Bureau would not recount Wyoming or revise its population figures for the state—put an end to his appearance.[323]

For Judge Brimmer the defense argument was "old hat"—concepts dusted off, reworded and expanded. His demeanor on the Bench showed weariness with verbosity as he listened to lengthy convoluted justification for county boundaries.[324] But

---

[320] Ibid., from Plaintiffs Final Pretrial Memorandum, 12-15.

[321] Ibid.

[322] Ibid.

[323] Ibid.

[324] Ed Risha clerked for Judge Brimmer in 1991. Risha recalled that when the defense attorney began his opening statement with, "Judge Brimmer, as you wrote in 1981…." the Judge interrupted saying, "A lot of case law has changed since then. There have been enough changes

Brimmer did his homework; he was a serious student of constitutional law. He understood and profoundly respected the opinions of the United States Supreme Court.

All of the intervenors were legislators and Democrats from counties where the citizen's votes carried the least weight. Except for Senator Harriet Elizabeth Byrd, they were all Representatives: Edith V. Garcia, Pat Hacker, Shirley Humphrey and Carol Watson of Laramie County; Fred Harrison, Pat O'Toole and Bill Vasey of Carbon; Scott Ratliff of Fremont.

Gorin identified two new points from Bussart: the need to retain flexibility for single-member, multi-member or floterial delegations and to identify the direct impact on leadership selections of the seniority gained by rural counties under the challenged system. This seniority had a disproportionate influence with the legislature itself.[325]

The plaintiff-interveners did not want the court to dictate just one mode for districting. Carol Watson liked floterial districts. Some wanted to keep the option for multi-members. Others wanted only single-member districts. Gorin said their reason for wanting flexibility was important because, "…changes in small absolute numbers of votes will dramatically change the outcome in Wyoming elections, this Court should permit _less_ deviation than Courts have at times permitted."[326]

It took three days to argue *Gorin v. Karpan*. Justices Brorby, Brimmer and Johnson did not hesitate to ask probing questions of both counsel and witnesses. They received thoughtful answers. Then the Justices retired: to read, to discuss and to write. Silence again descended on reapportionment of the Wyoming Legislature.

IN THE OPINION OF THE COURT – 1991

The decision came on October 15, 1991. It began with geography:

---

to make any statements made in 1981 not applicable to 1991." Risha's perception after that exchange was the case the defense was making was in serious trouble.

[325] Complaint in Intervention; Gorin, op. cit., footnote 30.

[326] Ibid.

Wyoming is a land of high altitudes and low multitudes.[327]   Straddling the continental divide, Wyoming's population typically congregates in small, hospitable towns…. Scattered among miles separating … towns and cities are ranchers and mineral extractors…

Then the opinion described square miles in counties large and small, populations large and small—and they get to the root of the problem before the Court, "The citizens of Wyoming's more populous counties have historically been under-represented and those citizens in Wyoming's less populous counties have been over-represented…the less populous counties have more than their fair share of legislative voting power."[328]

The facts: The legislature did reapportion in 1991 using the 1990 Federal Census. Each county got at least one senator and one representative. The ideal ratio for the House was 7,087:1 with the deviation range of 83%. "Voters in Niobrara County have 3.3 times the voting power in the House of Representatives as voters in Washakie County…[yet Niobrara] has one-third the population of Washakie."[329]   The Court concluded, "…representatives from counties containing 46% of the state population theoretically control 52 % of the House vote."

In the Senate the deviation range was 58%. Voters in Platte-Goshen had 1.82 times the voting power as voters in Uinta. The Court noted that alternative plans were discussed that had more equality for voters because of lower ranges of deviation. However, the legislature adopted Enrolled Act 81,

> …a plan which fails to achieve substantial voter equality among election districts…[even when the case law on political equality] … from the Declaration of Independence to Lincoln's Gettysburg Address, to the 15th, 17th and 19th Amendments can mean only one thing—one person, one vote."[330]

The Opinion talked about basic standards of equality, the equal protection clause in the 14th Amendment, good faith efforts by legislatures, the amount of permissible divergence from population equality, rational state interests, *de minimus* in *Brown v. Thomson*, dilution of the weight of individual votes, fair and

---

[327] From Milward Simpson, former Governor and Senator.

[328] *Gorin v. Karpan,* 755 F. Supp 1430 (D. Wyo 1991) at 1432 & 1433.

[329] Ibid. at 1434.

[330] Ibid. at 1435.

effective representation, invidious discrimination under the 14th Amendment, substantial equality and intolerable invasions of individual voting rights.

The Justices had questions: Were the percentages of deviation for the House and Senate large enough to be facially invalid? Yes. The population in Niobrara was not great enough to allow them one House seat.

> [T]he Wyoming 1991 Reapportionment Act is facially unconstitutional simply because the population inequality created by the Act exceeds tolerable equal protection limits.[331]

Did the evidence support a claim of being either unavoidable or legally justified? No.

> [G]ross percentage deviations among the populations of the legislative districts [are] intolerable and unjustified because they are avoidable. …the magnitude of intrusion [on citizen's voting rights] was overwhelming.[332]

The Court looked at the purpose clause and reviewed the testimony of Charles Scott and Mel ZumBrunnen in their quest to find why the legislature thought Enrolled Act 81 was constitutional. The Justices were swift in rejecting the old arguments justifying preserving county boundaries with a quote from *Reynolds* "…Legislators represent people, not trees or acres. Citizens, not history or economic interests, cast votes."[333]

Next came the issue of fair and effective representation and the overriding objective of substantial equality of population among the election districts. The Justices concluded,

> A plan with population inequalities greater than 10% must be justified by the state—supported by a rational state policy, not by attenuated arguments concerning possible census inaccuracies and population fluctuations. This court does not desire, nor are we in the position to grant, the legislature greater license to intrude upon this established principle.[334]

On gerrymandering the Wyoming judges said,

---

[331] Ibid. at 1440.

[332] Ibid.

[333] *Reynolds v. Sims* 377 U.S. at 562, 580.

[334] *Gorin v. Karpan* at 1443.

244

Defendants presented no evidence to demonstrate a reasonable likelihood that future Wyoming legislatures would act in bad faith to promote partisan interests over the State's best interest. Wyoming's ... lawmakers [are] of outstanding integrity. We are unwilling to assume the future holds otherwise.[335]

The defense asserted that the constitutionality in the 1991 Act of counties as election districts was based on the Federal Court's 1963, 1971 and 1981 rulings. Justices Brorby, Brimmer and Johnson responded,

This argument is completely without merit.... [The] decisions in *Schaefer v. Thomson* and *Brown v. Thomson* are neither authority for nor relevant to the question of validity of the 1991 Reapportionment Act ... because two wrongs do not make a right....[336]

On the use of rational state policy to justify regional representation, the Court said that

[The 1991 Plan]...best effectuates a system of regional representation ... [but the legislature] ... carried effectuation of this policy to an unconstitutional extreme ... [by allowing] factors other than population equality to emasculate the one-person, one-vote principle.[337]

On whether or not the legislature considered viable alternatives, the Judges listened carefully to Senator Scott,

The primary grounds for the legislature's rejection of those alternatives ... were geographical concerns, as well as the difficulties encountered when a constituent base is composed of competing and diverse interests.[338]

But the Judges did not buy Scott's argument—noting the differences between rural Pine Bluffs and urban Cheyenne.

There were acceptable alternatives, yet the legislature chose a plan with an "overwhelming magnitude of intrusion upon individual rights. The Judges were compelled to conclude the 1991 Plan was "constitutionally intolerable." After identifying the basic tenets the Court found:

---

[335] Ibid.

[336] Ibid.

[337] Ibid. at 1444.

[338] Ibid. and Opinion footnote #21.

1. The 1991 Plan constituted invidious discrimination and violated the 14th Amendment to the United States Constitution for representation in the House.
2. The 1991 Plan constituted invidious discrimination and violated the 14th Amendment to the United States Constitution for representation in the Senate.
3. Article III, Section 3 of Wyoming's Constitution was inconsistent with the one-person, one-vote principle. Consequently the Legislature may disregard this provision when reapportioning the Senate and House.
4. The judgment was final, subject to review.
5. The court retained jurisdiction.

THE REMEDY

The Court really did not want to apportion. The legislature was the best institution for this job because they had the ability to identify and to reconcile all the traditional state policies. But the Judges gave the legislators no clue what was an acceptable deviation range.

> We cannot predict what percentage of population deviation will be constitutionally permissible once the legislature has presented us with its best effort to achieve substantial voter equality.[339]

Justices Brorby, Brimmer and Johnson were not innocents. They tried to decrease the amount of wiggle-room Senator Scott and other Republicans might use to circumvent the Court by giving a list of guidelines.

1. Substantial population equality shall be the overriding objective.
2. No population deviation shall exceed 10% to assure that the vote of any one citizen is approximately equal in weight to that of every other citizen. If a deviation is over 10% the State has the burden to justify non population considerations.
3. There is an undefined upper limit beyond which the State cannot justify larger than 10% population deviations among election districts.
4. To achieve a higher than 10% range of population deviation the State has to demonstrate a rational state

---

[339] Ibid. at 1446.

policy supported by legitimate considerations. The Court said it was legitimate for the legislature to desire each county to have a representative. What the legislature *may not do*...is elevate that pursuit above the pursuit of substantial equality among individual voters. Reapportionment according to regional interests, if achieved at the expense of significant intrusion upon individual voting rights, is intolerable. Counties do not stand on equal constitutional ground with citizens at the ballot box. The Constitution commands that we not exalt groups of citizens by given them inordinate voting power.[340]

5. If we, the Court, have to reapportion we will use stricter standards than 10% population deviation.

6. And, if the Court were to reapportion they will create single-member districts. Multi-member districts per se are not unconstitutional, just draw them so as not to minimize or cancel out the voting strength of racial or political elements of the voting population.

The Court retained jurisdiction, set February 24, 1992 at 5:00 pm as the time when the new reapportionment plan had to be in their office. After that a hearing to consider the validity of the new plan was to be held. The plaintiffs and intervenors requested reasonable attorneys fees. The Court agreed to consider their request upon presentation of itemized statements subject to review by the defense.

THE "RESTLESS AND FUSS-MAKING CITIZENS" WIN

After decades of selectively using historical precedent that was contrary to federal case law, in 1991 the three Wyoming justices did not hesitate to rule against the entrenched power of Wyoming's Republicans from sparsely populated counties.

The defense counsel found themselves boxed in by the veracity of the arguments of plaintiffs' counsel—and by the reality that the Judges agreed with the plaintiffs.

In Court everything said was said under oath. Truth had to be spoken—unlike in legislative committee discussions or debate on the floor of the House or Senate. Court was not the place to

---

[340] Ibid. at 1446.

disguise disparate representations. There was no dissembling. There was no room for speciousness.

Freudenthal, Tate and Bussart proved, to the satisfaction of the Court, that invidious discrimination did exist in Wyoming in violation of the Equal Protection Clause of the 14th Amendment. These lawyers achieved for Wyoming what Casper attorney Mayne Miller achieved for the people of Tennessee 28 years earlier in *Baker v. Carr.*

Wyoming's century-long saga of skewed reapportionment putting regional interests above citizen's rights ended. Not only did citizens win in 1991, but they won for all previous plaintiffs—clear back to *Sullivan v. Schnitger* in 1908.

Regional interests, mineral extractive resource interests, were at the heart of the circumstances for the under-or over-representation between rural and urban counties. Clearly the dichotomy between the two centered on the diverse economic activities and life-styles of those living in urban settings versus the natural resource economy and simpler life-style of those living in rural Wyoming.

Mineral extractors were everywhere on the landscape except within city limits—usually. They paid royalties to landowners, mostly ranchers and their heirs. They established shared communities of interest with large- and small-town service suppliers, landed title-holders and on-site workers doing the actual extraction of the minerals.

Mineral extraction was the fourth economy to arrive in Wyoming. Fur trappers, soldiers and trail travelers preceded them. Gold miners set up the first mining district, the Lincoln on South Pass, in November 1865.[341]

The builders of the Union Pacific were eager to get to the coal at Hanna. Union Pacific remained a major player in mineral development due to the presence of coal, oil, gas and especially trona in their federal land grant of every-other-section of land 20 miles on each side of their right-of-way.

Since the State's earliest days mineral interests had lobbyists in the Capitol. The mineral interests elected "their legislators." Initially they were men. But by the 1980's beautiful young women lobbied the Senators.[342]

---

[341] T.A. Larson, *History of Wyoming.* University of Nebraska Press, 1965, p. 112.

[342] In 1991 there were 20 women in the House, too many for female lobbyists to have an impact. The House got men as mineral lobbyists.

Working with the men and women in agriculture—cattle and sheep, irrigated and dry acres—the mineral men elected governors too. For more than a century, each legislator and each governor was under the scrutiny of the mineral interests—before and after each election.

All the verbosity about county election districts was just double-speak by those trying to retain the power position of the mineral extractors. From gold in 1865 to the plethora of minerals in 1991, mineral or regional interests came before citizens' rights.

Then, on October 15th, 1991, the three Wyoming-friendly federal judges said *nothing* was more important than the right of Wyoming's citizens to equal representation in their legislature under the Equal Protection Clause of the Fourteenth Amendment. Any intrusion into any individual's voting rights was intolerable.

The Judges were not abolishing any small-town service-supplier or rancher, nor any royalty holder or lawyer landsman. They were not attacking the Union Pacific or any other extractive natural resource interests. The Judges just said: *People Come First.*

With the possibility that "the fox was guarding the chicken coup," the Joint Corporations Committee, now designated the Legislative Reapportionment Oversight Committee, had in their laps the responsibility to create a new reapportionment plan good enough to "pass muster" of the Federal Judges. Patti MacMillan and Charles Scott were again co-chairs.

A constitutional plan was a challenge. The legislators needed time, money, computer hardware and software, staff, public hearings and multiple plans from Democrats and Republicans.

Attorney General Meyer's $250,000 was committed in his contract with Braden and company. The Legislative Service Office had some of its $50,000 left but more money was needed. Rick Miller learned other states spent more than a year and millions of dollars to draw plans acceptable to the Court.

The years spent protecting counties as election districts turned out to be an expensive commitment. Protecting regional

---

However, there were only 3 women in the Senate. The mineral men assigned comely young women to the Senate, where they first got the Senator's attention—then they talked issues.

interests, not citizen's rights, was a costly undertaking for Wyoming's taxpayers.

19

Rick Miller's Challenge

Serious reapportionment began as soon as Richard Miller, Director of the Legislative Service Office, read the October 15, 1991 opinion in *Gorin v. Karpan*. The terse opinion indicated two things:

1. The Court wanted no more obtuse arguments justifying continued avoidance of the federal case law; and
2. They demanded the legislature make a good faith effort to achieve equal voting strength for all Wyoming citizens.

His bosses, the Management Council, would "have had his head" if he had done contingency planning prior to the opinion.[343] As the top person in the LSO, it was Miller's job to make sure the legislators had the wherewithal to generate a timely districting plan that met the standards of the United States Supreme Court.

From a CEO's perspective, Miller faced his worst nightmare. It was like "searching for needles in a haystack" because somehow from somewhere he had to pull together all the elements legislators needed to create a new constitutional reapportionment plan.[344]

---

[343] Interview with Rick Miller, April 9, 2001.

[344] The justices wrote in *Gorin v. Karpan* at 1443 that "redistricting versus reapportionment is a distinction without a difference under the equal protection clause ... [because] ... all citizens must be equally powerful at the ballot box." Hereafter, these terms will be used interchangeably.

The districting had to be done quickly, correctly—in completely unchartered Wyoming waters with an inexperienced crew. No words exist that can overstate the enormity of the task.

Miller needed five things: time, census blocks, money, staff and equipment.

Time—the ponderous process of law-making can be time consuming. Reapportionment was not easy. The opinion required the new plan to be delivered to the Federal Court by close of business on Monday, February 24, 1992.

That gave the legislators and staff 132 days. Not 132 working days but 132 consecutive days: work days, Halloween, Opening of Hunting Season, Thanksgiving, Christmas, the "down" week after Christmas, New Years. October 15th was the first of Miller's 132 days. By the time Miller got to the first of the 17 Saturdays and 17 Sundays, he had a "hold on the monster."

Census blocks—the smallest area for which the Census Bureau released data was where reapportionment began. Since *Baker v. Carr* the Census Bureau, as part of the 1970, 1980 and 1990 census, required the chief elections officer of each state, and the county clerks, to have a program to match census blocks to precincts to make voter districts (VTD's).

During those 30 years the county (and state) elections officers were required to write a plan that matched precinct lines to census block lines. In Wyoming, these details of the directive were ignored. Consequently, in October 1991 there were no correlations between census blocks and precincts lines. Except for inadvertent congruity Rick Miller declared, "The twain of which had never met."[345]

Money—no budget was available for redistricting. Because the majority party planned to defend the constitutionality of the 1991 Plan, funds were provided for lawsuits but not for map drawing. Other states spent hundreds of thousands, or millions, of dollars preparing plans on legislative districting. But Rick Miller had no money—only a court order to produce a constitutional plan.

Consultants on Redistricting—Miller had none. There was not enough time for an RFP (Request for Proposal) to be circulated to qualified vendors, should there happen to be someone out there somewhere interested in "doing" Wyoming. Some legislatures assigned redistricting to "special offices" or to

---

[345] Miller interview April 9, 2001.

252

redistricting commissions—but not Wyoming. Miller had to set up in-house districting.

Staffing—to "do" districting was not available within the Legislative Service Office. There the assignments were already made to budgets, audits, committees and bill drafting. Each person carried a heavier than usual load because Miller was on reapportionment. He told his staff,

> Unless there is a fire, don't come to me. I will answer
> no legislator's request. I will draft no bills. I will do
> nothing on State Budget matters. I will spend all my
> time on districting.

Equipment and office space—Rick Miller had to find it. Fortunately he was no novice to Cheyenne.

During 1987 and 1988 he was on Governor Mike Sullivan's staff. Prior to 1987, himself an LSO staffer, he worked with other state agency employees—notably the number crunchers at DAFC.[346]

He began by pirating from other agencies. His first staff choice was Steve Furtney. Prior to the 1990 census Governor Sullivan designated Furtney as Wyoming's Census Coordinator. He was administrator of the Division of Economic Analysis in DAFC. By no stretch of anyone's imagination was Economic Analysis kin to reapportioning. But Furtney had good analytical skills. He knew how to make computers spit out information for specific purposes.

The next to be pirated was Rick Memmel, an information technician for the Highway Department stationed in Furtney's division. Memmel was a geographic systems man.

Memmel led "Pirate" Miller to David Clabaugh, a Highway Department map-man with expertise to make maps large enough to manipulate the data of Wyoming's 97,548 square miles and 453,588 people. He also had a roller copier at his workstation in the I-25 Highway Department Complex.

Next Miller needed someone with specialized districting experience. The Revenue Department's sales/use tax collection/ distribution districts had a modicum of similarity to the districts Miller needed. Their "man with the know-how" to craft census blocks into precincts was Bryce Freeman. Miller wanted him.

---

[346] The executive branch's Department of Administration and Fiscal Control—later to be named the Department of Administration and Information.

But these four men were fulltime state employees in essential positions in their respective departments. However much "Pirate" Miller wanted them, he couldn't just snatch them away and sit them down at new desks in a new location.

Miller cemented his pirating of employees by going to the top. As a former Sullivan staffer, he had the credibility and enough moxie to march in and straight-talk his Governor.

> I need your help. We're talking about four men. I want them assigned to me so they will be mine—for as long as I need them. I will pay their salaries, their benefits and their overtime. I will provide the workstation. I ask you to request each department head to release them to me.[347]

Sullivan wrote the letters in support of the top legislative administrator's request that four of the Governor's department heads temporarily give away key staff for an unspecified amount of time. The department heads accepted the governor's demand and Miller got his men.

Having promised workstations, Miller had to find them. With Furtney's help they found pre-session space. It was three windowless hard-to-find rooms and hall on the third floor-east, at the back of the Emerson Building, with public accessibility only by elevator. During the 1992 session they moved to the vacated offices of LSO staffers temporarily assigned to desks in the House or Senate chambers.

Computers—access to adequate capability and capacity was a challenge even to "Pirate" Miller. Nothing was easy and portable then. Intergraph was a private company with whom Miller built a contractual public/private relationship.

They were geographic information people. He borrowed, begged and legally used their equipment and software capable of manipulating the data with the capacity to draw the maps he and his four men needed. Multiple licensing agreements were made with Intergraph.[348]

---

[347] From October 15, 1991 through March 31, 1992 Miller authorized payment of $100,526.39 for staff salaries, overtime and logistical support: Minutes of the Management Council for April 28, 1992. Staff received overtime. Miller got no overtime pay—only a Joint Senate and House resolution thanking him and from the Senate, a necktie from Janice Bodine's clothing store in Evanston.

[348] April 9, 2001 interview with Rick Miller. He kept some of the Intergraph capability for training the county clerks after the Court

When Furtney, Memmel and Freeman finished with computer map drawing, Miller had to get in his car and take the disks to David Clabaugh and his roller copier at the Highway Department at the Central Avenue Exit of I-25. This was the only place in Cheyenne able to print and to copy the large 32" by 24" maps.

Only legislators had access to Miller's reapportioning set-up. Each version of each plan had 6 pages: a statewide map for the House, a statewide map for the Senate, two town/city sheets for the House, two town/city sheets for the Senate.

Because the reapportioning was Court ordered, Miller went to the Management Council for the authority to access funds. On January 29, 1992, he told the Council that the "current allocation" for both the Joint Corporations and the Management Council "will be exceeded" because of additional meetings.[349] Also, before he could authorize payments from the $50,000 in HB 295 he needed the Council's approval. The Intergraph Corporation reached their contract maximum of $35,000. The $40,000 for interim work of the Joint Corporations Committee was spent. Salaries, benefits, overtime, equipment rentals and photocopy exceeded $157,778. Miller had "slack" in both his Central Duplicating budget and the Temporary Session Staff budget but he needed Management Council approval to make budget transfers.[350]

Many districting plans were drawn. Some legislators were satisfied with just learning the dynamics of combining precincts into contiguous clusters with population variations no greater than 10%.

---

approved the 1992 Plan. His pirated staff did not return to their departments until each clerk, separately, was given the data on the composition of that clerk's election districts as created by the legislature.

[349] Management Council Minutes for January 29, 1992.

[350] The Annual Reports of the Legislative Service Office for 1991 and 1992 contain numerous line items related to reapportionment.

The $100,526 in footnote 347 is included in the $157,778. Considerable effort was made to identify the expenditures on reapportionment by the Attorney General's office—including plaintiff's fees and expenses in *Gorin v. Karpan*. Other than the $250,000 in the Mark Braden contract, numbers were unavailable due to the accounting method used by the Auditor's Office during that biennium.

Other legislators drew complete plans using Miller's document that listed all the precincts in each county—its number, name and how many people lived there according to various combinations of census blocks.[351] Plan-drawing legislators received multiple 32" by 24" maps on which to indicate their precinct combinations for election districts.[352]

Federal case law required election districts to be compact, contiguous and share a community of interest. The first two criteria were manageable using data from Miller's documents. The community of interest criteria was unmanageable due to the lack of comprehensive consistent, definitive, dependable state-wide data.

The legislators who made multiple versions of their plans for House debate were Les Bowron, Eli Bebout, Matilda Hansen, April Brimmer-Kunz and Don Sullivan. The Senators with plans were Jim Applegate, Charlie Scott and Gary Yordy.[353] Yordy drew the most plans: 6. There were plans labeled Scott/Yordy melds.[354]

Before a plan was discussed, copies were distributed to all members as "home work" prior to full committee consideration. Thus, for each version of each plan Miller's staff prepared 84 32" by 24" sheets of paper or at least 1,344 maps. There were at least two versions of every legislator's plan(s).

In 1991 copying technology was not that good. The black delineating precinct lines too often were too faint to read. There was no "darkening" command on the Highway Department's roller copier to improve print clarity. Therefore, most maps needed to be retraced. Miller decided it made no sense for his computer-smart, census block-precinct enabling gurus to redraw

---

[351] Besides census blocks, census bureau ID numbers were used in the people-scarce parts of rural Wyoming. For instance 0001 Rural in northwest Carbon County covered 160 nearly empty square miles. A 100 square mile precinct in southeast Carbon County had 7 people.

[352] In many instances Miller and his men were able to match precincts and census blocks. However, they were not always successful.

[353] Lawyer Les Bowron of Natrona County was not on the Joint Corporations Committee. Patti MacMillan, House Corporations chair and co-chair of the Joint Committee, did not draw a plan. She perceived her role to be manager of districting and of the committee activities.

[354] A meld plan combined the work of two or more legislators where election districts were taken from different plans and melded together for varying combinations of precincts and/or districts.

the lines. His solution was to "conscript" his LSO audit division people to retrace the lines.

Lead auditor Barbara Rogers, with Joyce Hron and Gerry Hoppsmann, set aside their auditing work to spend countless hours at large tables using smelly black grease pens drawing in the faint or missing black lines on the white pieces of paper.[355]

Miller wanted it easy to make comparisons among the several plans so he ordered a system of overlays—printed on transparent Mylar. But the lines on the Mylar were as unsatisfactory as the lines on the paper. So, Barbara Rogers and her auditors, now bored almost beyond speech, worked day after day doing kindergarten-level tracing with smelly pens on stinky Mylar—another 672 maps! With so many maps, the exposure to the ink and Mylar made them ill. But no sick leave for this job. Miller's 132 days were dwindling. Readable maps were essential.

By October 31, 1991, when the Joint Corporations Committee met in Casper, Rick Miller and his men had their "ducks in a row." Plaintiffs, lobbyists and interested citizens were in attendance—some of whom testified—as reluctant legislators began yet another round of reapportioning. First to address the Committee was Rick Miller.

> We lost the case. We have to district within the 10% deviation range, or else have *very good* reasons to justify a larger range. We have to forget about county boundaries. We have a lot of work to do. We have to show a "good faith effort." We have to seriously consider all alternatives. We have to get our new, 1992 legislative districting law down the street to the Federal Building no later than close of business on Monday, February 24, 1992. We have to be cognizant of relevant federal case law.[356]

He was direct. He was concise. He did not mince words. All the 1990-1991 work to reapportion the legislature was "down the drain."

He was gracious, but with intensity and success he stated there was to be no wiggle-room or dissembling in this reapportionment—no more espousing of "regional interests" or

---

[355] Interview with Barbara Rogers, April 18, 2001.

[356] From notes and materials of Matilda Hansen, a member of this Joint Corporations Committee. She attended all meetings.

"rational state policy." The Court had spoken: only citizens can have representation.

Reasonable Republicans, like John DeWitt of Park, Tom Kinnison of Sheridan and Carol Jo Vlastos of Natrona, were saddened about losing in Court but they were philosophical and willing to get to work.

The mineral lobbyists were anxious—but comforted—because three of their people were on this Committee: Eli Bebout of Fremont,[357] Bruce Hinchey of Natrona and Laramie County's April Brimmer-Kunz with mineral interests in Carbon County.

The "fire-brands" were "chomping at the bit." The Court succeeded in thwarting Charlie Scott's attempt to write new federal case law defining "regional interests" and "rational state policy." Laramie County's Doctor of Law and Doctor of Medicine, Gary Yordy, saw his "states' rights" proclivities tromped on by the good Wyoming justices.

Democrats Della Herbst of Sheridan, Jim Applegate, Don Sullivan of Laramie County and Matilda Hansen of Albany were thinking, "We told you so." They were pleased those three Wyoming judges brought Wyoming, though kicking and screaming, into compliance with the rulings of the United States Supreme Court. Finally, the people will achieve equal voting strength guaranteed by the Fourteenth Amendment and equal representation mandated by the Wyoming Constitution.

Each committee member made a significant time commitment to draw and to read plans—homework done on their own time. For committee meetings they were paid $75 per diem and $60 per day salary plus 34 cents a mile.

Drawing election districts (VTD's) according to the new rules was a major challenge. The Joint Corporations Committee set the size of the House at 60 seats, the Senate at 30 seats. Each House district had to have 7,560 people, each Senate district 15,120 people. The allowable 10% deviation range applied collectively to all House districts as well as to all Senate districts.

Now a taskmaster, Miller laid out the ground rules. He gave specific directions for accessing the computer-crammed Emerson Building office. Each committee member was invited to create as many plans as each wished and then to set up appointments

---

[357] In October of 1991 Eli Bebout was still a registered Democrat. He often voted with, and usually worked closely with, the Republican leadership. He was—always would be—a minerals man. After the 1994 session, he switched political parties.

258

with Furtney, Memmel and Freeman for finalization and distribution of each plan.

Because the Census Bureau and the County Clerks did not agree on the bedrock data for reapportionment—VTD's or voting districts—Miller and his men faced the same dilemma as the 1905 and 1915 State Census Enumerators.

The dilemma was finding people in Wyoming's open spaces. In 1905 and 1915 county assessors were sent to count people and economic activities. In 1991 Miller and his men counted people for representation in their legislature.

The reason the dilemma was so acute in 1991 was because, since 1864, county clerks indiscriminatingly drew precinct lines wherever in those open spaces they choose. Polling places were "handy" to clusters of people—with many living far from their neighbors.

Thus the precinct political boundaries in non-urban areas were casual at best—too often non-existent. Creative license was used by the headcounters in 1905 and 1915. The 1991 headcounters also used creative license to draw the VTD's.

An example of this creativity was Wardwell Water precinct 8-3 in Natrona, comprising most of the area immediately north and east of Casper. In it no one lived in 134 census blocks,[358] six blocks had one person each, four blocks had 2 people each. The remaining 46 census blocks contained 1090 people—most of whom were in the outskirts of Casper.

In Fremont, too, there were challenges. The precinct containing the Lander Training School had 206 people. First Miller's men looked east and south hoping to find more people in precinct 21-1, Reclamation. This was Sand Draw country, then along the Beaver Rim to Separation Flats and the Ferris Mountains—and they found 4 people at a ranch headquarters. Not enough people, so after looking at more and more empty census blocks they finally got to Jeffrey City 94 road miles from the Lander Training School. But those 251 people (plus Atlantic City's 48) were needed in the west Albany (Rock River), north Carbon (Medicine Bow, McFadden, Shirley Basin, Hanna, Leo, west Rawlins) and east Sweetwater County House/Senate district.

---

[358] The usual census block contained about 70 people—give or take a few.

Drawers of plans and Miller's men ignored natural features whether mountain ranges or deserts, lakes or reservoirs to keep all election districts within the allowable 10% range of deviation.

For the first time in the state's history the legislature and the Court dictated to the clerks the specific boundaries of *each* precinct in each county—right down to the nitty-gritty detail of which house on which block on which side of the street went into which VTD.

Secretary of State and Chief Elections Officer Kathy Karpan and Rick Miller perceived among the county clerks there was a lack of attention or inclination, a lack of knowledge or understanding about all substantive elements in *Gorin v. Karpan.* Therefore, before Christmas 1991 Karpan called the clerks to a session in Casper, with Miller as "the program."

Near the beginning of the meeting, Mary Ann Collins, the County Clerk and chief elections officer of Natrona asked, "Why is this important to us?" Her question astounded Karpan and Miller because they assumed the county clerks knew and understood the integral connection between census blocks, precincts, legislative reapportionment and the Courts. Karpan's meeting became a fast-paced teach-in. With Miller now in the role of teacher, he proceeded to explain how the familiar world of Wyoming elections turned upside down. Miller began with, "The Federal Court, not you, will have the final authority over where your precinct lines are drawn."

By meeting's end the county clerks understood districting. They recognized the significance of Karpan and Miller's help. Henceforth, they followed the tortured course of numerous plans through the House and Senate. When HB 117 got to the Governor, they quickly told him exactly what they thought of it.

Soon after the October 15th opinion, Republican leaders looked at Wyoming's minority population. The Census Bureau said Hispanics accounted for 4.8% of the state's population.[359] They were dispersed in varying size clusters in every county. Even in Cheyenne, Hispanics lived "all over town" thereby not qualifying for their own VTD.

Because Shoshone and Arapaho on the Wind River Reservation dominated clusters of small communities in Fremont, Wyoming may have had exposure to the Voting Rights

---

[359] Rounded up to the nearest whole number, 5%, Hispanics qualified for one delegate at the 1996 Democratic National Convention in Chicago.

260

Act. At the request of Republican leaders, a voter analysis was done of the precincts where, during the 1980's, Native Americans were the predominant voters.

The analysis showed that during that decade the reservation precincts provided the margin of victory for 4 of 5 Fremont House members. Thus the "will of the majority" had not been frustrated;[360] in fact it prevailed. Therefore, they concluded, the Voting Rights Act did not apply.

After many plans were distributed to committee members and to the public, the Joint Corporations Committee met in Casper on December 9, in Cheyenne on January 7 and 8, held a hearing in Buffalo on January 20th and a hearing in Casper on January 27th.

The Budget Session was to begin on Monday, February 17th—just 7 days before the Governor-approved plan had to be down the street in the Federal Building. The Management Council requested a Special Session—to begin Monday, February 10th.

But before the Management Council agreed to a Special Session, they considered doing districting during the Budget Session with "mirror" bills[361] considered at the same time in each chamber. This was Fred Harrison's motion with Ron Micheli's second. Because mirror bills gave conference committees enormous power, mirror-districting bills provided considerable latitude for mischief in drawing district lines. This idea was defeated with only Harrison, Micheli and Eli Bebout voting aye.

Prior to this January 29th Management Council meeting, Miller and his men foresaw a potential logistics nightmare serious enough to doom districting in 1992.

[E]ven with computers, developing new plans and amendments was very time consuming. It will be physically impossible for us to analyze a new plan and

---

[360] Frustration of the will of a minority group was the major criteria to ascertain potential application of the Voting Rights Act. The "majority" in Fremont County in the 1980's was of BOTH Native American and non-Native American voters. The Republican's interpretation for the 1992 Plan bordered on the nonsequitur. It certainly wasn't fair to the Native Americans.

[361] Mirror bills work for appropriations where the issue is specified amounts of money. Conference committees accept one version or another, or they split the difference.

prepare it as an amendment if it is submitted when the Session is under way.[362]

Deimer True moved and Bebout seconded the motion directing Speaker Cross as chair of Management Council to write each legislator, "...any new plan or major amendment submitted to the Legislative Service Office after 5:00 pm on Thursday, February 6 will not be processed in time for the Special Session."

Then Management Council asked for a change in the Joint Rules: "...no reapportionment amendment will be considered unless it is submitted to the Legislative Service Office[363] by 4:00 pm on the day before debate."

Thus was catastrophe averted.

Rick Miller, Steve Furtney, Rick Memmel, David Clabaugh, Bryce Freeman and the 14 members of the Joint Corporations Committee spent 117 of the 132 days in preliminary work on Wyoming's first foray into districting.

The calendar moved to February 10th. Roll was called for the Special Session. It was time to listen to the Governor.

---

[362] January 29, 1992 Minutes of the Management Council.

[363] Here Legislative Service Office means Miller and his men.

20

Reapportionment 1992
Attempt # 2

Dramatic undercurrents of partisanship swirled through the Chambers as Governor Sullivan welcomed the Republican-controlled legislature to the Special Session. With their Opinion, Justices Brorby, Brimmer and Johnson tossed into oblivion Senator Charlie Scott's dream of writing new federal case law. It was 29 years since *Baker v. Carr.* "One-person, one-vote" was the law.

The Republicans lost when HB 295, Enrolled Act 81, was declared unconstitutional. Many in the Majority Party decided the Court "sided with the Democrats." These legislators thought the three Wyoming jurists were "on their side"—their "ace in the hole" in maintaining Niobrara County's continued flagrant flaunting of federal case law. But these jurists took very seriously their responsibility and were not about to subscribe to the political posturing of Wyoming's mineral-interest controlled rural Republicans.

Some legislators were almost ill because the 1991 Opinion went against them—battering their hold on political power. They closed ranks against the "hated-feds" and against the criteria stipulated by the Judges. To show their high umbrage they looked for ways to circumvent the guidelines. They intended to draw election districts according to their own interpretation of the Opinion.

The partisanship of the Republicans was matched by the partisanship of the Democrats. Of the 12 plaintiffs in *Gorin v. Karpan,* 10 were Democrats. The lawyers for the plaintiffs were

Democrats. The governor was a Democrat. Even *Karpan* in *Gorin v.* Karpan, the lead defendant and Secretary of State Kathy Karpan, was a Democrat.

In practical terms the Court ruled for the plaintiffs—for the Democrats. The Democrats felt vindicated. Many Democrats thought or whispered, and likely their body language expressed, "We told you so."

Single-member districts were clearly doable as shown by the carefully crafted plans of Democrats Applegate, Hansen and Sullivan. They demonstrated to the Court that reasonable, understandable, compact, contiguous, and community-of-interest one-person one-vote equal representation was feasible for the large and small settlements—whether urban or rural—scattered throughout the open spaces of Wyoming.

The Democrats were proud of their tenacity to stay on task, the consistency and quality of their work. They were pleased with the power of their strategy of "standing firm" in the face of ridicule for "going against" Wyoming tradition. With small smiles of satisfaction on their faces, they looked forward with eagerness to the Special Session.

However much as the deeply resentful Republicans feared a political power shift, the compelling reality of the new court order was upon them mandating a signable bill acceptable to the three Wyoming jurists in accordance with the Equal Protection Clause of the Fourteenth Amendment to the United States Constitution. All 102 years of ignoring Wyoming's constitutional mandate for equal representation came to a screeching halt on February 10th.

Undaunted, the Governor walked into the charged atmosphere of the House Chambers were 94 legislators awaited him. He waded into this political quagmire.

> Your arrival in Cheyenne has been as somber an entrance as any I have observed since becoming Governor. The usual good humor has been replaced with a dark foreboding....[364]
>
> Our responsibility this session is ... to put aside partisan politics and the pressures of special interest groups and make those decisions that are in the best interests of all the people of Wyoming.

---

[364] Governor's Message to The Budget Session of the 51st Wyoming Legislature, Governor Mike Sullivan, February 10, 1992.

My experience as a lawyer and as Governor compel me to take very seriously the Opinion issued by the federal court. I think it also wise to remember that this is not some impersonal set of judges in some distant city. These are three distinguished citizens of Wyoming who know, love and for many years have served this state. But they also understand the law and are sworn to uphold it. If this body fails to develop legislative districts which give each Wyoming citizen an effective and representative voice in the election of its members … [the Court will draw the districts].

Sullivan pledged not to intervene as the bill progressed through the system unless "…the unpleasant undertones of partisanship … seriously threaten … a fair result for the voters…."

In many different ways, the Governor warned against incumbent protection. He wanted no deviation greater than allowed by the court. He wanted implementation of community of interest as well as compactness and contiguity in election districts. He requested that the legislators pay close attention to the Remedies beginning on page 38 of the Opinion. On single-member districts Sullivan said,

Whether you like single-member districts or not, the Court will clearly impose their own single-member district boundaries if we fail to develop our own plan consistent with the Court's guidance…. While single-member districts bring the greatest change to our system, they … offer the fairest means of meeting the one-man, one-vote test.

The Governor concluded his message. He and the other top officials were escorted from the House Chamber. The Senators returned to their Chamber. The House adjourned for lunch, with notice to reconvene at 1:00 pm.

It was a thoughtful group of people who scattered to their favorite luncheon haunts. Governor Sullivan had advised against protecting incumbents. The members of the Capitol Club[365] were

---

[365] This is an organization of registered, professional lobbyists who lobby the Wyoming Legislature. The Club's mission is to maintain the Wyoming Legislative Message Center, to promote among its membership the highest standards of responsible, professional lobbying in order to affect timely and beneficial public policy for the state of Wyoming its business and citizens. Source: membership directory of

not particularly concerned about retaining specific persons in the legislature; they were concerned about protecting their power base. From 1951 through 1999 men from the central region controlled the Senate for 32 years and men from the northern region controlled it for 14 years. The exceptions were J.W. Myers of Uinta in 1975–76 and Bob Grieve of Carbon in 1997–98.

During the same 50 years the House was in the control of men (and two women) from the central region for 35 years and the northern region for 8 years. Three southern-region men were Speaker: Jay R. House of Carbon, in 1959–60, Bob Burnett of Albany in 1981–82 and Bill McIlvain of Laramie County in 1989–90. The Democrats controlled the speakership for 4 of those 50 years.

With the Court mandate of equal representation, the voting strength advantage of smaller counties was likely to vanish, along with the advantage of preferential consideration of legislation. So, with misgivings, a modicum of fear and an underlying realization that control might slip away, the Republicans settled into their seats to "get on with this unpleasant task." Democrats whose plans had failed up to now, year after year, felt vindicated by the Court. They were eager to see what "legislative sausage" these 94 citizen-legislators produced.

Speaker Cross gaveled the session to order. It was time for First Reading of House Bill 177. The Reading Clerk, Barbara Johnston, read the title. The Speaker referred the bill directly to Committee of the Whole.[366] John Hines of Campbell took the chair:

> "The Committee of the Whole will please come to order."
> "The first bill for our consideration is House Bill 117."
> "The Reading Clerk will read the bill. [She reads.]"

1991. When districting was accomplished in 1992 Carolyn Passeneau of the Wyoming Woolgrowers Association became a legislator (in 1993), followed by Peter Illoway of Coastal Chem Inc. and Steven Youngbauer of AMAX Coal.

[366] Article III, Section 23 of the Wyoming Constitution, "No bill shall be considered or become a law unless referred to a committee...." As HB 117 was printed and on everyone's desk, referral to Committee of the Whole met the constitutional requirement.

"You have heard the reading of the bill. What is your pleasure?"[367]

Corporations chair Patti MacMillian at the back north microphone responded, "When the Committee of the Whole rises to report I move it do so with a recommendation that House Bill 117 Do Pass. There are no Standing Committee amendments. I will explain the bill."[368] The bill included:

1. The TIGER and GIS systems—topologically integrated geographic encoding and referencing database and Intergraph Geographic Information System. Both were the basic tools needed to create voter districts based on the 1990 census;
2. The requirement that all senators run in November 1992 with two classes of senators—a 2-year term class and a 4-year term class;
3. The criteria used to create districts;[369]
4. The residency requirement for candidates for 1992 and for outlying years;
5. The clean-up[370] language requested by the Secretary of State and the county clerks;
6. The new process for filling vacancies caused by death, illness or resignation;
7. The repealer for sections no longer applicable;
8. The 1992 version of the purpose clause, this time logistical directions for the 1992 election;
9. The effective date for the November 1992 election and the effective date for the balance of the bill;
10. A Senate of 30 seats in 26 districts;
11. A House of 62 seats in 33 districts; and

---

[367] From the Wyoming Manual of Legislative Procedures, Wyoming State Legislature, 1991. For the second time in just a few minutes the reading clerk read the title.

[368] MacMillan stood at that podium during all debate on HB 117: Committee of the Whole, Second Reading, Third Reading and the Motion to Concur with Senate Changes. For her these days were especially long and exhausting. The version she explained was House Bill 117, 92LSO-0401.01.

[369] County boundaries were to be maintained wherever possible.

[370] This term, sometimes called housekeeping, is used by legislators to indicate provisions needed to retain consistency in language and those elements needed to make the law operable.

12. The Senate deviation range is 9.775%. The House deviation range is 9.997%.

Rick Miller knew he and his men were guaranteed to receive requests for floor amendments. In order to preserve the integrity of the document, late in 1991 he filed with the Secretary of State a listing by name and numbers of all the precincts in the state.

In HB117 precincts for Senate districts were identified as "See Attachment A and B" and precincts for the House districts as "See Attachment C and D." Split precincts, those with people in more than one House or Senate district, were identified with (S) after the population number. Thus no tinkering was done to the body of the bill. All amendments were made to the Attachments.

There was a packet of attachments for each plan: pages and pages of columns showing Legislative District, County, Voter District and Population. "Voter Districts" were the county clerks' precincts.

Each precinct was identified by a combination of numbers and by name. Some names recalled Wyoming History: Fort Sanders, Fort Washakie and Fort Bridger. Others were more mundane such as Rock Springs precincts #1 through #12 and Gillette's precincts #1 through #17.

The names in Park required knowledge of median directions. There was Cody Center Inside, West Inside, West East South Inside, North South Outside. The Powell precincts also used inside, outside, north, south, east, west designations.

Geographic names were abundant: Little Missouri in Crook, Muddy Gap in Carbon, Hat Creek in Niobrara, Hawk Springs in Goshen, Lost Springs in Converse, Soda Creek in Weston, Paradise Valley in Natrona, Ten Sleep in Washakie and Prairie Dog in Sheridan.

Ranch brands were used: Jay Em in Goshen, Kay Cee in Johnson, Hat Six in Natrona. There even was Wapiti in Park and Beaver in Converse.

Each legislator faced the problem of making sense of the attachments and becoming familiar with the precincts. They had to think spatially. They needed readable maps. But Miller could not inundate 80 legislators with the paper blizzard he inflicted on the 14 Joint Corporations Committee members.

The technical capacity did not exist to project maps of the various plans on a large screen. So Miller's staff again traced lines on larger pieces of paper with stiff backing. This time they identified unnested House and Senate districts with colored crayons to differentiate between election districts.

Miller had six maps on six easels placed in the scarce available space around the edges of the House, then later in the Senate. "We had them hanging on easels around the chambers and people could walk around and look at them."[371]

There were two statewide maps—one each for House and Senate districts; two maps containing the precincts in Jackson, Worland, Cody, Kemmerer, Lander, Riverton, Casper, Evanston, Green River and Rock Springs—one each for House and Senate district; and two maps containing precincts in Powell, Sheridan, Buffalo, Gillette, Glenrock, Douglas, Wheatland, Torrington, Rawlins, Laramie and Cheyenne—one each for House and Senate districts.

Each new House and Senate district got a number. But in HB 117 assignment of the numbers reflected skewed order, limited logic and rejection of geography. Since *Baker v. Carr* "numbering tricks" were part of the lexicon of mischief used in other states to express "high umbrage by opponents of one-person, one-vote." It was one of the ploys of Joint Corporations co-chair Senator Scott when he inserted this mischief into the final version of the attachments in HB 117.

The bill was replete with value judgments. MacMillan acknowledged most of the Senate and House districts were not nested. However, her district in Albany and three others came "close" to being nested. Albany had two senate districts—each with one seat and four countywide House districts. Except Rock River was in Carbon's Senate #11.

Coal-rich Campbell County, home turf of Dick Wallis, chairman of the Appropriations Committee, also had two senate districts with one seat each and four at-large House seats.[372]

Natrona, home to Senate Chairman Charlie Scott, had two seats in each of two senate districts with four at-large seats in

[371] Interview with Rick Miller, April 9, 2001.

[372] To protect themselves from more taxes or more stringent environmental standards, the minerals men, especially those with connections to the coalmines in Campbell, were determined to keep control of their destinies in the hands of their legislators. In 1992 Kelly Mader and Dick Wallis co-chaired the Joint Appropriations, John Hines sat on Revenue, and Mike Enzi sat on education where huge pressures were building to allocate more money to K-12.

each senate district—except for Lysite, which was in with Fremont precincts.

However, MacMillan, Wallis and Scott had the political power to retain at-large House seats confined within their respective counties. Their county clerks faced minimal changes to their usual election practices.

Most of the senate districts were convoluted, unnested, districts similar to Senate #1 shown in Table 39.

TABLE 39
Unnested Senate District 1 in the Original HB 117

Senate Seats	Counties in Senate District	Precincts	Senate Precincts in which House Districts	Number of Seats in this House District
1	Converse	Lost Springs Walker Creek	House 6	2
	Crook	All precincts	House 5	1
	Niobrara	All precincts	House 13	1
	Weston	Weston Rural Newcastle East, North & South	House 13	

Unnested Senate and House seats in Original HB 117 troubled the clerks in Uinta, Sweetwater, Lincoln, Sublette and Teton—the old Idaho/Utah Territories that made Wyoming "square."

Senate District 14 (one seat) included portions of House Districts 17, 18, 23 and 25.

Senate District 16 included portions of House Districts 11, 19 and 23.

House District 11 was in Senate Districts 14, 17 and 19.

House District 16 was in Senate District 17.

House District 17 was in Senate District 12.

House District 18 was in Senate Districts 14 and 15.

House District 19 was in Senate Districts 15 and 16.

House District 23 was in Senate Districts 12, 14, 16, 17.

House District 25 was in Senate District 14.

The challenge for the county clerks was attributable, not to the necessity of election districts crossing county lines, but to the reality of House districts in multiple Senate districts and Senate districts in multiple House districts.

The first Committee of the Whole amendment was Matilda Hansen's fully nested, single-member, 30-Senate, 60-House plan. She said,

> The message from the Federal Court is very clear. Single-member districts meet the standard established by the Court to attain the <u>highest</u> standard of fairness with <u>one-person, one-vote</u>. I can not stand before you, and the people of Wyoming to support any "sorta-fair" plan...."

Her range of deviation in House was 9.232% and for the Senate was 9.417%. She used only population numbers and the three criteria of compactness, contiguity and community of interest. On power shifting due to districting she said, "...it is very likely to bring more wage earners into the legislature and fewer wage payers...." She declared her plan was fair and reflected legitimate state interests. Debate was minimal. Her plan failed on a voice vote.

Mark Harris and Pat Hacker brought Senator Applegate's version of a nested, single-member, 30-Senate, 60-House plan. It too failed on a voice vote.

Don Sullivan had a nested, single-member, 30-Senate, 60-House plan. It, too, failed.[373]

Then the tinkering began on Original HB 117:

Clarene Law tried to rearrange precincts in and surrounding Jackson in Teton. The amendment failed.

Fremont legislators Harry Tipton, Eli Bebout, Bruce McMillan, Dennis Tippets and Carbon's Fred Harrison tried to rearrange precincts in Fremont. They failed.

Bruce Hinchey, a minerals-man from Natrona, made changes in the House districts in Natrona and Campbell. His amendment passed.

Lauris Tysdall tried to make a single House district of House #1 and #2 with 2 at-large seats. He failed.

Carroll Miller successfully rearranged precincts in Senate districts 18 and 20 in Park, Big Horn, Hot Springs and Washakie.

Clarene Law tried again to make changes focusing on Teton—this time to create floterial districts. Her amendment failed.

---

[373] Hansen, Harris, Hacker, Sullivan and Applegate were Democrats from Albany, Sweetwater and Laramie.

John DeWitt tried to rearrange Carroll Miller's rear-rangements in Senate Districts 18 and 20. He failed.

Gene Call successfully moved the LaBarge precinct in the old Utah/Idaho territory from House 11 to House 23.

Bruce Hinchey, John DeWitt and April Brimmer-Kunz's amendment turned the senate into single-member districts by adding four districts and removing one senate seat from each of the four multi-member districts. This amendment passed.

Minerals-man Representative Eli Bebout shifted 79 census blocks in the wide-open spaces of the Red Desert and Wind River Mountains to change the Senate district for 249 people—216 lived in one community. It passed.

That day HB 117 was the only item of business. The House was in session until nearly 5:00 pm. There was no social event.

Second Reading was February 11th —with 14 days until February 24th. After the opening exercises at 10:00 am, the House spent the entire day on reapportionment with huge blocks of time spent by the Republicans in their closed caucus—debating the bill.

The Republicans went to caucus, returned to work, then back to caucus, then back to work. The Democrats hung around and waited, and waited. Before the House adjourned near 5:00 pm three amendments were withdrawn: Law #6, Law-Hinchey #9 and Hines-Wallis-Shippy #10. Debate on these amendments was done behind closed doors—in the Republican caucus.

On the Floor the only Republican to present a single-member 60-seat House plan was Les Bowron. A lawyer well read in federal case law on redistricting, his deviation range was 9.933%. He requested the ayes and noes. Don Sullivan provided the second: 13 ayes, 51 noes with eight Democrats and four Republicans joining Bowron to vote "aye."

Mark Harris and Pat Hacker again presented the Applegate Plan and called for the ayes and noes. Mary Kay Schwope provided the second. The vote was 20 ayes and 44 noes. All the Democrats except Eli Bebout and Pat O'Toole voted "aye."

Matilda Hansen wanted a recorded vote on her plan. She presented it and called for the ayes and noes. Keith Goodenough provided the second. The vote was 16 ayes and 48 noes. All the aye votes came from Democrats. Besides Bebout and O'Toole voting with the Republicans, this time so did Bill Bensel, Dick Honaker, Jim Perkins and Bill Vasey.

No one expected any of these three plans—Bowron, Applegate or Hansen—to receive a majority vote. The purpose for recorded votes was to document the vote of each legislator and to establish clear legislative intent that viable, constitutional, compact and contiguous plans were presented for consideration.

A lot of time was spent on Mel ZumBrunnen's[374] amendment for weighted votes; the relationship expressed in numerical form of the value of a vote in the House or Senate to the number of people living in a specific county.

This was the 1992 version of Niobrara lobbying. This concept fundamentally changed the counting of votes in the House or Senate. Niobrara's plan was for a 30-seat Senate and a 60-seat House. It was built according to Wyoming's traditional apportioning method but based on the 1990 Federal Census. Long ballots in the populous counties remained.

Once a candidate was elected and voting in the House or Senate, the way fairness and equal representation was achieved was to assign a "weight" of greater-than or less-than-one for each vote cast. Then that weighted number was multiplied by the number of representatives in each county to reflect the number of people living in each county. The values in Table 40, from the Digest of the House Journal, show the weight of the votes for each legislator from each county.

In weighted voting, the value or weight of the vote of the House member from scarcely populated Niobrara was .33 and of a House member from populous Laramie County was .98. The weightiest vote was 1.49 for the House member from Teton. The divisors used by ZumBrunnen and his Niobrara lobbyists were 20,750 for the Senate and 7,500 for the House, with a statewide population of 453.588.

The debate was long and all-over-the-map because each legislator, whether speaking for or against the concept, focused on just one element. It was like the ancient story of people describing an elephant—each interpreting the part they thought they understood. Quietly circulating among the Democrats was the phrase, "weighted votes are good for us."

---

[374] ZumBrunnen of Niobrara, a rancher-civil engineer and consultant, chaired the House Minerals, Business and Economic Development Committee in 1992.

TABLE 40
Weighted Votes

County	Number of Senators	Weight of Each Vote	Number of House Members	Weight of each Vote
Laramie	4	0.88	10	0.98
Natrona	3	0.98	8	1.02
Sweetwater	2	0.94	5	1.04
Fremont	2	0.94	4	1.12
Albany	1	1.48	4	1.03
Campbell	1	1.42	4	0.98
Sheridan	1	1.14	3	1.05
Park	1	1.12	3	1.03
Uinta	1	0.90	2	1.25
Carbon	1	0.80	2	1.11
Lincoln	1	0.61	2	0.84
Goshen	1	0.60	2	0.82
Teton	1	0.54	1	1.49
Converse	1	0.54	1	1.48
Big Horn	1	0.51	1	1.40
Washakie	1	0.40	1	1.12
Platte	1	0.39	1	1.09
Weston	1	0.31	1	0.87
Johnson	1	0.30	1	0.82
Crook	1	0.26	1	0.95
Sublette	1	0.23	1	0.65
Hot Springs	1	0.23	1	0.64
Niobrara	1	0.12	1	0.33
Total	30	22.12	60	60.8

Apportioning by weighted votes kept at least one senator and one representative in each county. Despite the specific direction given by the Court, counties continued as election districts. But weighted votes made moot all challenges based on deviation range. ZumBrunnen requested a roll call with Lauris Tysdale providing the second. The vote was 26 ayes and 38 noes. ZumBrunnen found 14 Democrats and 12 Republicans to vote with him.[375]

---

[375] Voting with ZumBrunnen were Democrats Sheila Arnold, Eli Bebout, Bill Bensel, Sam Blackwell, Edith Garcia, Keith Goodenough,

Under a weighted voting plan, as shown in Table 41, the balance of regional power followed the state's population.

TABLE 41
Regional Power Using Weighted Voting

	Southern Region	Central Region	Northern Region
Voting Power in Senate	9.57 43%	6.63 30%	5.92 27%
Voting Power in House	26.57 44%	19.14 31%	15.09 25%
Statewide Population 1990	44%	29%	27%

Next Don Sullivan wanted a roll call vote on his plan. Matilda Hansen provided the second. The vote was 13 ayes (all Democrats) and 51 noes.

The three Fremont Republicans—B. McMillan, Tipton and Tippets—and Democrats Eli Bebout and Carbon's Fred Harrison had a 64-seat House plan with no accompanying Senate plan. The only good idea in it was Fort Washakie, Arapahoe, Ethete and Crowheart precincts were together, thus assuring a House seat for residents on the Wind River Reservation.

This was one of the most complicated apportioning plans since the unnested Council and House seats of Territorial Wyoming. Their plan had five variables: single county with multiple seats, multiple counties with multiple seats, multiple counties with two seats, multiple counties with one seat and one county with one seat.[376]

Of the plans drawn in 1992 it was the hardest to understand. The challenge was to know which district was where, combined with whom, with how many seats. With no roll call, members forthwith dispatched it to oblivion.

Chamberlain, Bob Grant, Jim Hageman, Bruce McMillan, David Shippy, Marlene Simons, Bill Tibbs, Dennis Tippets, Harry Tipton, and Lauris Tysdal.

[376] For these combinations of counties and numbers of seats see, for example, Table 1.

Clarene Law successfully tinkered and moved four people in Teton's Airport precinct to join their neighbors in District 16 instead of being in the House district with Sublette and Lincoln.

Third Reading was just 13 days before February 24th. Again, the only business was HB 117. The Republicans continued their previous day's caucus/work pattern. The Democrats waited— and waited. They had their picture taken and waited some more while the real debate on the bill was done in the Republican caucus. The Democrats had no third reading amendments.

The Republicans continued their tinkering. Minerals-man Bruce Hinchey moved people around in the House districts in Casper's satellite towns and eastern rural Natrona. There was no call for the ayes and noes. Hinchey also moved people around in the House districts in the Big Horn Basin, in central Wyoming and in Cheyenne. There was no call for the ayes and noes. Both amendments passed.

Mel ZumBrunnen and Lauris Tysdale tried to move people in Niobrara and Weston. They failed.

The Republican caucus and these three amendments used up the time before lunch. During lunch someone checked the arithmetic on Hinchey's earlier amendment on the Casper satellite precincts.

When the House reconvened, Hinchey—with Patti MacMillan as co-sponsor to reassure the Republicans this was "only housekeeping,"—moved his "cleaned-up" arithmetic. Sam Blackwell called for the ayes and noes. Don Sullivan provided the second. The vote: 27 ayes, 36 noes. The Republican caucus split on this vote—but so did the Democrats.

Clarene Law did not agree with Gene Call's rearrangement in the Lincoln-Sublette-Teton House districts. She called for the ayes and noes. Les Bowron provided the second. The vote was 19 ayes and 44 noes.

Because Mel ZumBrunnen needed just a few more votes to pass weighted votes, he was back with a third reading amendment. He cajoled Democrats to support him. He called for the ayes and noes. Eli Bebout provided the second. The vote was 30 ayes and 34 noes. He picked up seven Democrats: Pat Hacker, Fred Harrison, Dick Honaker, Jim Perkins, Bernard Phelan, Scott Ratliff and Louise Ryckman. But he lost three Republicans: Dan Budd, Jim Hageman and David Shippy.

Then ZumBrunnen changed the value of the weights of votes. He requested the ayes and noes. Sam Blackwell provided the second. The vote: 28 ayes and 36 noes. This time he got

Dan Budd back and added Eric Alden. But he lost Douglas Chamberlain, Scott Ratliff, Marlene Simons and Harry Tipton.

The voting patterns on weighted votes showed ambivalence. At one time or another, 34 House members supported weighted voting. But 20 House members consistently voted "aye," 30 consistently voted "no" and 14 kept switching their votes—seven Republicans and seven Democrats. Always, there was vote slippage.

Then the "Delete The Enacting Clause" amendment was debated—which opened the entire bill to full debate. The final vote was 37 ayes and 27 noes. It was a party-line vote. All the Republicans voted aye except Les Bowron, Dan Budd, Bruce McMillan, Bill Tibbs, Dennis Tippets and Mel ZumBrunnen. All the Democrats voted no except Sheila Arnold.

The House adjourned about 5:30 pm. The evening's social events at the Hitching Post Inn included a fundraiser of the Committee for a Democratic Legislature and the Independent Telephone Companies' reception.

SENATE ACTION

HB 117 arrived in the Senate Thursday, February 13th—12 days before the new plan was due down Capitol Street in Federal Court. President Deimer True sent it immediately to Committee of the Whole, chaired by John Perry of Johnson-Campbell.

The first amendment was the Applegate Plan—the same one presented to the House by Pat Hacker and Mark Harris. It was rejected by a voice vote.

Then Charlie Scott presented "Scott F Senate Plan and Voting District Split Report." It failed by a voice vote. However, he instructed LSO to prepare his plan as a bill. It became Senate File 49.

John Fanos successfully tinkered with the three-senate districts in Sweetwater, Uinta, Lincoln and Sublette. More comprehensive, this covered the turf in the Call amendment and "rearranged the furniture" in the southern end of the old Utah/Idaho Territory.

An amendment by Charlie Scott kept multi-member senate districts in Laramie, Albany, Campbell, Fremont, Natrona[377] and Johnson-Sheridan. He changed 16 districts to 8. The remaining

---

[377] There were 4 senators in Natrona and 4 senators in Laramie County.

14 senate districts stayed single member. The amendment failed on a voice vote because senators did not like the mix of multi- and single-member districts in their Chamber.

Gary Yordy successfully reshuffled districts in southeast Wyoming to assure no Senate or House districts spilled out of Laramie into either Platte or Goshen. This involved the communities of Meridan, Albin, Horse Creek and Little Bear.

Bob LaLonde picked up Clarene Law's "cause" and twice tried to address the concerns of Teton residents. He, too, failed both times.

Gary Yordy was again reshuffling—this time in the Big Horn Basin. He succeeded.

Second Reading was the next day, 11 days before February 24th. HB 117 consumed the day.

Jim Applegate wanted a recorded senate vote on his plan.[378] The vote: 6 ayes, 23 noes, 1 excused. Only Democrats voted "aye." Jerry Dixon was excused the entire day. There are no recorded votes for him on HB 117.

Liz Byrd wanted to rearrange precincts in her county. She asked for the ayes and noes. The vote was 10 ayes, 19 noes, 1 excused. All the Democrats voted "aye."

Again the precincts in districts in the Big Horn Basin were changed—this time by Alan Howard. His amendment passed on a voice vote.

Bob Peck tried his hand at reshuffling precincts in Laramie County. His amendment failed on a voice vote.

Some Republicans with a wry sense of humor wanted to make HB 117 a valentine for Governor Sullivan and finish the bill on February 14th. To compress the time, they suspended the rules to vote on Third Reading the same day the bill was in Second Reading. The vote on the motion to suspend the rules was 28 ayes, 1 no and 1 excused. The no vote was from Jim Geringer. The Senate went to Third Reading and seven more amendments.

Liz Byrd tried again to rearrange the precincts in her County. Her amendment failed on a voice vote.

Bob LaLonde either got the right combinations of districts or he "jawboned" his compatriots. He got enough votes for his latest version of the shuffle of Teton precincts. There was no roll call.

---

[378] Seconds on the request for recorded vote were not required in the Senate.

The problem of two-year and four-year senate terms still bothered Gary Yordy. The "Herbst wash," first encountered in 1991 in HB 295, was still a knotty issue. He used his previous simple solution: two classes of senators identified by the even number or odd-number of their district. The Secretary of State was directed to pull a paper marked "even" or "odd" from a hat. His amendment passed on a voice vote.

Jim Applegate did some rearranging of his single-member districts and presented Plan B. It, too, failed on a voice vote.

Gary Yordy was deeply into reshuffling districts—this time focusing on the multi-member districts in Albany, Campbell, Fremont, Natrona and Sheridan. Lisa Kinney called for the ayes and noes. The vote was 22 ayes, 7 noes and 1 excused. Della Herbst was the only Democrat to vote "no." The Republicans voting "no" were Hank Coe, Bob Grieve, Tom Kinnison, Bob Peck, Charlie Scott and Deimer True. Kinnison and Herbst were both from Sheridan. They did not like Yordy's shuffle.

Having fixed the north end of the old Utah/Idaho Territory districts, Bob LaLonde zeroed in on John Fanos' reshuffling in the southern end. Fanos called for the ayes and noes. The vote was 14 ayes, 15 noes and 1 excused. All the Democrats joined Fanos to vote "no." The Republicans voting "no" were Boyd Eddins, Bob Grieve, Mike Healy, Bob Peck and Russ Zimmer.

Charlie Scott wanted to reshuffle the precincts in Senate districts 1, 2 and 3 in Crook, Weston, Niobrara, Platte and Goshen. His amendment failed on a voice vote.

The "delete the enacting clause" amendment was moved. When the Senate voted there were 20 ayes, 9 noes and 1 excused. Democrats Jim Applegate, Liz Byrd, Guy Cameron, Della Herbst, Lisa Kinney, Carl Maldonado and Bob Reese voted "no"—as did Republicans Jim Geringer and Charlie Scott.

While the Senate worked on HB 117, the House spent most of the day on the introduction of non-budget bills before recessing until 7:00 pm. At 7:00, immediately after the Speaker gaveled the session to order, Majority Leader Douglas Chamberlain called yet another Republican caucus. It was going to be a late night.

Meanwhile, the Democrats gathered in front of the chief clerk's desk to discuss the changes made by the Senate. They settled down to wait some more—and then some more.

The county clerks were carefully following HB 117 through the House and Senate, thankful for the December 1991 "school on districting" by Secretary of State Kathy Karpan and LSO Director and chief legislative districtor Rick Miller.

In their opinion this was an awful bill. Its worst sin was no nesting of the districts. They loudly proclaimed the job of running elections was now a nightmare. Every county clerk had to fashion election machinery with every other clerk who had voters in their overlapping and intertwined House and Senate districts. To the clerks HB 117 was such a mess that by comparison, the convoluted Council and House districts of the Territorial Government were not as great a challenge.

The Republicans, having finished discussing the bill, returned from caucus. Floor Manager Patti MacMillan made the motion "To Concur" with the Senate.[379]

The concerns of the county clerks were presented and supported. The mix of single-member and multi-member House districts was decried.

The supporters of the bill said all districts were within the Court's 10% deviation range: the House at 9.970% and the Senate at 9.886%. They were compact and contiguous. The size of each chamber was within constitutional limits.

Supporters said there was time to make sure all census blocks, precincts and districts properly matched. There was time for the governor to have his three days to sign the bill. There was time to get the new law to Federal Court before February 24th.

Watching which legislators were in their seats, who was whispering to whom and who was waiting to talk was Ernie Mecca, Governor Sullivan's Administrative Assistant. Though off-limits to the public and to lobbyists, the House Rules allowed him, as one of the Governor's staff, to be in the walkway "Behind the Glass" and in the Coffee Room while the House was in session. A former minerals-man skilled in strategy, he was there this night.

The debate went on and on—though the outcome was never in doubt. There wasn't enough time, nor did anyone want six members of conference committee(s)—three from the House and three from the Senate—to mess around with more reshuffling of precincts and then expect the House and Senate to accept changes on a simple up-or-down vote.

Les Bowron grew weary of the talk-talking. He called for the Previous Question. John Rankine, Bill Vasey and Sam Dunnuck

---

[379] The description of what actually passed is in the next chapter.

provided the seconds. Roll was called on the motion "to concur." The vote: 35 ayes, 27 noes and 2 excused (Bob Grant and Bill Rohrbach). All the Democrats except Sheila Arnold voted "no." Republicans Dan Budd, Bruce McMillan, Bill Tibbs, Dennis Tippets, Harry Tipton and Mel ZumBrunnen also voted "no."

Majority Leader Douglas Chamberlain adjourned the House until 9:30 am Saturday, February 15th. The Senate also convened on Saturday. Introduction of non-budget bills continued in each chamber while the LSO prepared Enrolled Act 1 for signatures.

On Saturday at 11:00 am Speaker Cross signed Enrolled Act 1. The House adjourned for the weekend. Then the Act was taken to the Senate, where Deimer True signed it. The Senate adjourned for the weekend.

The Republicans happily left their respective chambers, pleased with their work. They looked forward to the rest of the 1992 Budget Session.

House Democrats quietly, thoughtfully, left the Chamber. Some of them knew the Governor was out of town. Reapportionment was now in the Governor's hands: to be signed, to become law without his signature or to be vetoed. Which was it to be?

21

Democrats Exercise Political Power

While Herb Pownall continued to call the roll on the concurrence vote on HB 117, Matilda Hansen went in search of Ernie Mecca. She found him in the deserted Coffee Room, pensively looking out the window onto the north Herschler plaza. She told him,

> The Governor has to call a caucus of the Democrats— at the Residence. We have to share with him our insights, our understandings of what this bill does and does not do. He needs to hear our perceptions of just how big a monster this is. We must do this soon. It needs to be a Democratic caucus that is not advertised.[380]

The clock was ticking. It was late evening. Mecca agreed with her—based on his weeklong astute observations of the torturous path of HB 117. A visit with House Democrats was an important aid as Sullivan pondered what he was to do with this version of Court-ordered reapportioning. It was Democratic strategy time.

---

[380] For most of Matilda Hansen's 20 years in the legislature the Democratic caucus was closed. That changed during Mike Sullivan's tenure as Governor because some Democrats wanted to make a big fuss about the Republicans closed caucuses. As it was impossible to strategize significant political moves in a public setting Mike said to the Democrats, "So when you want to consult in private you are going to make me call the meeting and take the heat?" The answer was "yes."

As Valentine's Day, February 14th, came to a close, so was the Republicans' control on reapportioning. Clearly, they used their political power to foist impossible election districts onto the electors of the state. Just as clearly, the Democrats held the political power once the Enrolled Act was signed by the Speaker and the President.

Mecca knew the Governor was out of town and wouldn't be back until early Sunday afternoon. Hansen and Mecca anticipated the Enrolled Act would be on the Governor's desk before 5:00 pm Saturday. It was. The only realistic time for a caucus was 4:00 pm Sunday—an hour after the Governor's scheduled return.

Constitutionally the Governor had three days, Sunday's excepted, to make up his mind. Actually, the time was much shorter if he vetoed the act. A veto meant the legislature had to start over with a new bill but the "due date" in Federal Court remained February 24th.

Saturday Mecca talked with the Governor. The caucus was a "go." With no fanfare, word quietly passed from Democrat to Democrat, "Be at the Governor's Residence at 4:00 pm on Sunday."[381]

Sunday morning Matilda Hansen did laundry at the Hitching Post. The Midwives Association hosted a brunch. The Joint Appropriations Committee held "budget school" at 2:30 pm for anyone wishing to learn more about the proposed budget and the budget process.

Many House members spent a few hours at their desks, doing homework, correspondence and "jawing" in quiet conversation. One by one the Democrats left. Near 4:00 pm Hansen left. A Republican asked, "Are you guys meeting with the Governor?" She didn't answer. By then most, if not all, Republicans knew of the caucus.

By 4:00 pm the weather was overcast with a biting, cold, penetrating wind. The guards at the gate waved the Democrats in. No parking attendants were needed. Everyone knew where they were going. After the first arrivals, no staff answered the front door. The Democrats just opened it and walked in.

The 23 needlepoint "county" chairs lined the dining room. A chair for the Governor was at the east end of the circle facing

---

[381] Senators were welcome and Liz Byrd attended. This was a House caucus and therefore mandatory for House Democrats.

the fireplace. The Governor walked in with his yellow legal pad and pen in his hand. The legislators sat down.[382]

Mike Sullivan simply said, "Tell me about it." As he took copious notes, each House Democrat told him about the bill. They described the unnested House and Senate districts. They underscored the opinions of the county clerks who faced a monumental election in November if Enrolled Act 1 became law. They detailed the expected rampant voter confusion.

They interpreted the meaning of "numbering tricks" and "stacking and fracturing."[383] They portrayed the unfairness of some candidates standing for election in multi-member districts and some in single-member districts.

The House Democrats agreed that the most egregious element in Enrolled Act 1 was the single-member/multi-member mix for the House. One person represented some citizens while 2 or 3 or 4 persons represented other citizens. Fairness was achieved in the deviation ranges—but at the expense of the hodge-podge of the many "agendas" that pushed true equal representation out the door.

The sharing of questions, insights, perceptions, facts, fears and frustrations lasted until the sun set. Then one politically savvy Democrat, with understanding of Wyoming's constitution said,

> We know the Constitution prohibits you [Sullivan] from threatening a veto or directly discussing a veto. However, the Constitution is silent about what we, as legislators, can commit to you if you decide to veto Enrolled Act 1.

The legislators discussed this proposal in detail, followed by the obvious question, "If the Governor vetoes Enrolled Act 1, will you vote to sustain the veto?" Caucus Chairman Louise Ryckman and Minority Whip Mary Kay Schwope polled each person. The answer was, "Yes."

Sheila Arnold, the only Democrat to vote "yes" on the final votes, explained her switch,

> I served with Governor Herschler who frequently used his veto pen. I vote my own position even if it is in opposition to a caucus position or contrary to the way

---

[382] Quotes are from Hansen's notes.

[383] See Glossary for "Numbering tricks" and "Stacking and fracturing."

most Democrats are voting—until there is a veto. Then I always sustain my Governor's veto.[384]

While the polling was being done Governor Sullivan continued to take notes. Then the caucus adjourned. With subdued voices, fully cognizant of the power they potentially held, the Democrats left the Governor's Residence.

The evening's social event was the dinner hosted by the Associated Contractors of Wyoming at the Hitching Post Inn. The atmosphere between the Democrats and the Republicans was somewhat strained. However, they were speaking to one another.

Late Sunday the Republicans were not worried. Typically, the Democrats had not held firm on a caucus position. Sheila Arnold consistently voted "aye" on HB 117. The mineral-interest lobbyists were primed to "have a little talk" with the Governor to remind him not to veto Enrolled Act 1.

Monday morning was the beginning of the 125th of the 132 days given the legislature to "get reapportioning right." It began as a usual day. House Democrats met at 7:00 am with the Governor's staff in his Conference Room. Lawyer Fred Harrison began with, "Will he veto it?" Staff answered, "We don't know yet." The strategy for other matters was discussed. Then Harrison, Hansen, Schwope and Ryckman drifted on to their Standing Committee meetings.

The House reconvened at 10:00 am. It was a usual day of bill introduction, except for the undercurrent: "Will he sign it or will he veto it?"

Minority Leader Fred Harrison was agitated. He made frequent trips to the Governor's office—just to check! By late morning he told Assistant Minority Leader Matilda Hansen he was afraid the Governor will sign it. "What can we do?" Her reply, "The matter is out of our hands. It is now the Governor's call. Be patient Fred!"

By lunchtime there was no Message From The Governor. After lunch Standing Committee Reports were read. More bills were introduced. At 2:30 pm Majority Leader Doug Chamberlain adjourned the day's session and called a Republican Caucus in Room 302. The agenda was to present,

---

[384] Sheila Arnold served from 1977 through 1992. Initially, she was appointed to complete Dennis Stickley's term when he resigned. Hansen sat across the aisle from Arnold. The two Albany County legislators often discussed vetoes.

discuss, cajole, coerce and establish the Republican strategy on the remaining issues of the Session.

The Speaker recognized Louise Ryckman, "The Democrats will caucus in the LSO library." Tension was high among the Democrats because no Message From The Governor was on the Front Desk. The question was, "What to do?"

The Democrats drifted to the LSO library. About the time Whip Mary Kay Schwope finished counting heads, Scott Farris[385] came down the short hallway off the Rotunda waving a fistful of papers. Once inside he distributed one sheet to each Democrat, "Here it is. He vetoed it."

The veto was met with relief—and with appreciation—for everyone recognized the Governor's courage. Every one knew the next major move was theirs. There was speculation about the Republicans response. Farris said, "We won't have long to wait. I'm on my way down to the Chief Clerk's desk in the House to deliver this Message." But his announcement was met with a chorus, "We are adjourned for the day. There is no one there to receive it."

It was nearly 4:00 pm. His face reflecting his consternation, Farris asked, "But what am I do with this? You have it. The Republicans need to have it too." With laughter in their voices a chorus of Democrats replied, "Go across the hall. Knock on their door. Give it to them just as you have given it to us." This was very "heady" advice because no one interrupts the Republican Caucus.

The House Democrats were sending Farris to "beard the lions in their den." For moral support, a gaggle of Democrats ushered Farris to the other side of the Rotunda. He knocked on the door.

Inside, the Republicans were "having at it"[386] as they wrestled with issues and strategy—then the knock came. Silence engulfed the room. Someone near the door opened it. There stood Scott Farris, papers in hand. With no words he shoved them at the door opener and fled, flanked by his gleeful Democratic escort.

Inside soon the message was read aloud. Dismay flooded through the room. Dread descended on Patti MacMillan because

---

[385] He was Intergovernmental Affairs Coordinator for the Governor.
[386] This account comes from a Republican in response to the author's question, "What happened when Farris knocked on the door?"

she knew they had to do reapportioning all over again and time was getting very, very short. But the Republicans thought they were still in control—this time with a veto override.

There wasn't much point for either the Democrats or the Republicans to continue to caucus. Once the Republicans emerged from Room 302, the Democrats curbed their exuberance. With somber demeanor everyone went to their afternoon Committees or other assignments.

Lobbyists were in the Capitol waiting for the caucuses to end and for the Standing Committee sessions to begin. Soon Mel ZumBrunnen called to order the Minerals, Business and Economic Development Committee—the committee of particular interest to the mineral-interest lobbyists.

Space was a premium in the LSO library. Nine legislators sat at the large oblong table. The committee secretary and her desk consumed space behind and to the left of the chairman. Extra chairs were everywhere—including one row jammed against the wall behind the legislators facing the door. There the crowding was so real, a lobbyist's legs filled the space between the chairs of two legislators.

Matilda Hansen faced the door. With her proximity to the lobbyists she heard their whispers. Something had happened they knew nothing about. They hated not knowing the "inside stuff." So she unobtrusively pulled her copy of the veto message from her Minerals Committee notebook, slide it to her right and down to the edge of the table. The lobbyist, whose knees were close enough to put her right elbow on, leaned slightly forward and read the Message From The Governor. Then from lobbyist to lobbyist the word swiftly spread, "The Governor vetoed it."

When the day's work was finished, the Standing Committees adjourned. The only levity in the Capitol halls that night was nervous laughter. Otherwise somberness prevailed. The social event was cocktails and dinner hosted by the Trial Lawyers. Democrats talked to Democrats. Republicans talked to Republicans. Lobbyists talked to both.

Tuesday morning began like all other Tuesday mornings. By 9:00 am the Republican leadership had their caucus whipped into shape to override the veto.[387] But they knew their search for a wayward Democrat was a search in vain. Speaker Cross gaveled the House To Order. Pledge, Prayer and Journal Report were done. It was time for "Messages From The Governor."

The full four pages of the message were read.[388] First he commented on the presence of innuendo and implications of adverse consequences to him or his programs, from both sides of the aisle, depending on which action he took. He claimed he wasn't influenced by the threats. He cautioned,

> [U]nder the best of circumstances … we can ill afford the issue of reapportionment and the contents of this message to color the decisions … made in other areas. Wyoming and its citizens cannot withstand a disagreement over the mini-drama of reapportionment to influence other decisions.…

First and foremost, he wanted single-member districts in the House as well as the Senate. The multi-member/single-member mix was likely to confuse voters, submerge minorities and have constituents far from their representative. He didn't like the single-member House districts in Crook, Weston, Niobrara and Hot Springs counties while the districts in Lincoln and Teton counties were multi-member districts.

He didn't like the "stacking and fracturing" of electors in Fremont County where the Democrats held an 18% voter registration advantage but the districts were so constructed to give the Republicans a 35% advantage. Likewise, the 2% Republican voter registration edge in Laramie County was maximized to give Republicans a 17% advantage.

He agreed with the reasons for the county clerks' opposition to unnested House and Senate districts. He was not convinced fairness was accomplished in avoiding incumbent protection.

He thought Enrolled Act 1 "…does not reflect clarity, consistency, rationality or fairness.… He was very specific about what he wanted: "…an acceptable single-member plan with nested districts.…"

---

[387] Six Republicans voted no on concurrence, two were absent. They committed to vote to overturn the veto.

[388] The complete text of the Governor's veto is in Appendix E.

He gave the legislators a lot of slack and face saving in his comments on the quality of their work. It was possible HB 117 was the best he was to get, but he was not convinced of this.

Majority Leader Chamberlain moved to override the veto. Debate ensued. All 22 Democrats voted "no." The Governor's veto was sustained.

Thus on February 18th 1992, the Democrats clearly held the political power necessary to turn back a bad piece of legislation. Yet the search continued. For Wyoming's electorate did not have fair representation under the Equal Protection Clause of the Fourteenth Amendment to the United States Constitution.

In Enrolled Act 1, the Republicans showed they did not have the political will to draw a good plan. The Democrats had the political will to draw good plans as shown in the work of Applegate, Hansen and Sullivan. They had the power to stop a bad plan but this was not the same as passing good legislation. The Republicans still had the power, and the responsibility, to produce an acceptable single-member plan with nested districts.

In a few significant ways Rick Miller and his staff where back at square one—where they were 126 days ago. They needed time and they needed a plan.

Only now time was of the essence. Because of the time needed for amendments and debate in each chamber and the time needed to prepare the documentation for the Court, Miller had to count time in terms of hours—not days.

Fortunately, someone had the foresight on Monday—as everyone waited for the Governor's decision—to move Charlie Scott's Senate File 49 onto the Senate's General File, then through Committee of the Whole with Lisa Kinney in the chair. But SF 49 was a combination of Scott's House F plan and Yordy's Senate G plan with unnested multi-member and single-member districts.

There was no time to craft a new single-member district plan. Miller knew Applegate, Hansen and Sullivan's plans were nested single-member districts. But these plans were unacceptable to the Republican leadership because Democrats produced them.

Fortune smiled again. Miller and his three men had a solution. Les Bowron's House-Only plan was nested single-member districts. [389] Of prime importance was that Bowron was a Republican.

---

[389] Bowron presented his plan in second reading: HB0117H21/F.

Though the logistics of preparing Attachments A, B, C, D was time consuming, the hard work of matching census blocks to precincts was already done. All that was needed now was to cluster 60 House districts into 30 Senate districts.

On Tuesday, with the veto a reality and the lunch break over, the Senate turned to Second Reading and consideration of SF 49. Jim Applegate had the first amendment—his plan A[390] with nested single-member districts. He asked for the ayes and noes. The vote: 6 ayes 24 noes. The Republicans expressed their dislike of a plan drawn by a Democrat.[391]

Applegate and Della Herbst proposed Hansen's nested single-member district plan[392]—and called for the ayes and noes. The vote: 7 ayes, 23 noes. Thumbs down on another plan by a Democrat.

Jim Applegate tried his Plan B,[393] and called for the ayes and noes. The vote: 8 ayes, 22 noes. Poof went another Democratic plan.

The 4th amendment was Gary Yordy's—the resurrected and adjusted Bowron plan.[394] Yordy called for the ayes and noes. The vote: 27 ayes, 3 noes. The noes were from Democrats Byrd and Fanos, Republican Russ Zimmer.

Yordy was still working on the "Herbst wash" problem of the rotation of 2-year and 4-year terms for the senators. This time he first designated two classes of districts: those with even numbers and those with odd numbers. Then he used his previous simple solution of the Secretary of State drawing one of two pieces of paper out of a hat: one marked even, the other marked odd. On a voice vote the amendment was adopted.

The Republican leadership was in a hurry. So the Senate voted to suspend the rules and proceed to Third Reading. But there was a technical problem so they voted to expunge the

---

[390] Originally distributed as HB0117S21/FE on February 14th.

[391] The 6 Democrats voting with Applegate were Byrd, Cameron, Herbst, Kinney and Reese.

[392] Originally distributed as HB0117/HW1. Aye votes: Applegate, Byrd Cameron, Fanos, Herbst, Kinney and Prevedel.

[393] Originally distributed as HB0117/H7 and HB0117SW1/FE. Aye votes: Applegate, Byrd, Cameron, Fanos, Herbst, Kinney, Prevedel, Reese. The Democrats wanted on the record that well-conceived plans were presented for consideration on both HB 117 and SF 4.

[394] Originally presented as HB0117/H21.

record, then suspend the rules. These three votes required two thirds. Each time the vote was unanimous.

In Third Reading Liz Byrd tried to move precincts in Carbon and Sweetwater counties. She targeted the 662 people in west Rawlins and the 234 people near Muddy Gap, Seminoe Dam, Leo and Shirley Basin. She also sought to "fix" 785 people in Rock Springs and the 313 people in the Fort Bridger precinct. She called for the ayes and noes. The vote: 9 ayes and 21 noes. This time Vinich joined with the other Democrats.

The final Third Reading vote was: 24 ayes and 6 noes. Democrats Byrd, Fanos, Maldonado, Prevedel and Vinich voted "no." Republican Russ Zimmer voted "no."

On Tuesday the House stayed in session, waiting for the Senate to finish with SF 49. The Speaker announced SF 49. The Reading Clerk read the title. The Speaker immediately referred it to Committee of the Whole. John Marton chaired Committee of the Whole. There were no amendments. SF 49 moved to Second Reading, scheduled for the next day.

The evening's social events were a reception hosted by Coastal Corporation and a dinner hosted by the Defense Lawyers, both at the Hitching Post Inn. By evening tempers and hostility had only marginally cooled. The Democrats talked with Democrats. The Republicans talked with Republicans. The lobbyists talked with both.

Wednesday it was the 127th day. Standing Committees met on their usual morning schedules. The Pledge, Prayer and Journal Report were done. Then it became a very unusual day.

Doug Chamberlain called the Republicans to caucus. Again, the Democrats stood around and waited and waited. For most of the morning the Republicans were in caucus.

One amendment was considered in the afternoon. Eli Bebout was the sponsor.[395] He said he had a very simple solution. Just take the senate districts in Enrolled Act 1, give each two at-large House seats to make nested Senate and House districts—thereby meeting one of the Governor's criteria.

This was close to an "in-your-face" proposal. Only nesting was included. The concerns of the county clerks were excluded. Matilda Hansen asked for ayes/noes. Edith Garcia provided the second. The vote: 17 ayes, 46 noes, 1 excused. Bill Rohrbach was absent all day February 19th.

---

[395] SF0049H22/.

Many of the afternoon hours were consumed in the Republican caucus. The Democrats did not need to caucus. No longer were they in the driver's seat on reapportionment. Actually, Democratic caucuses were easier, less time consuming, because only 22 Democrats had opinions to express. In the Republican caucus there were 42 opinions.

Late in the afternoon, the House recessed for Standing Committee meetings. Corporations Committee members had only 45 minutes for supper before the House reconvened at 7:00 pm.

The evening's social calendar was the Union Pacific reception at the Hitching Post and the Realtors Association dinner at the Holiday Inn. Attendance by House members was poor for both events.

A RARE EVENING SESSION

Along with the earlier Bebout amendment, Dan Budd's evening amendment was also an "in-your-face" move. These two proposals, one from a minerals-man and the other from a rancher-recipient of mineral royalties, were blatant expressions of ill temper at the Governor's veto. It was the first manifestation of the "adverse consequences" Governor Sullivan referenced in his veto message.

Budd's amendment just inserted House attachments C and D from Enrolled Act 1 into SF 49 and deleted all House districts from SF 49.[396] Budd called for the ayes/noes. Patti MacMillan provided the second. The vote: 14 ayes, 49 noes and 1 excused.[397]

The third and last amendment considered on the 127th day was the House's old friend—weighted votes. This time Bruce Hinchey sponsored the amendment.

The reasons for and against the concept remained the same. But soon into the debate it became clear that weighted votes were discussed in the Republican caucus. Mineral-man Hinchey's sponsorship was another signal indicating potentially

---

[396] SF0049H23/.

[397] Those voting with Budd were Doug Chamberlain, John DeWitt, Sam Dunnuck, Bob Grant, Jim Hageman, Bruce McMillan, Carroll Miller, Pat O'Toole, Peg Shreve, Dennis Tippets, Harry Tipton, Clyde Wolfley and Rory Cross.

drastic changes were coming in the voting pattern. Despite implied support from the mineral community, three times "no" votes were recorded for Hinchey on weighted voting.

The Democrats never took a caucus position—only had casual conversations—on this issue. However, 13 Democrats had three recorded "aye" votes and four others voted "aye" twice. The long and torturous debate focused on shoring up and gaining Republican votes as well as keeping most of the 17 Democrats supporting weighted votes.

After much talking, Mel ZumBrunnen moved the previous question with John Rankine, Sylvia Gams and Scott Ratliff providing the seconds. The vote: 24 ayes, 29 noes, 1 excused. More minutes became hours as debate continued.

Long as this 127th day was getting to be, weighted voting was important. It truly did reflect the concentrated and scattered patterns of Wyoming's population. However, it played real havoc with the traditional clustering of political power in the northern region.

For legislation to pass in the Senate using weighted voting a numerical value majority of 7.83 of 15.64 was needed. The numerical value of the political power held by the southern region was 9.57—clearly enough to control all proposed legislation. Yes, weighted voting was good for Democrats.

Likewise, the House needed a numerical value majority of 30.41 of 60.8. The numerical value of the political power held by the southern region was 26.57—just 3.84 less than a majority. Few House members that night understood the potential of this power shift.

Finally, near 10:30 pm Keith Goodenough asked for the ayes and noes. Don Sullivan provided the second. Herb Pownall "Called The Roll." The vote: 30 ayes, 33 noes, 1 excused. Quickly the Capitol emptied as exhausted House members sought their beds.

As the Democrats sensed, the voting pattern did drastically change. In the three previous votes 28 Republicans consistently voted "no." Late that Wednesday night 16 of them switched to vote "aye." They were Janice Bodine, Barbara Cubin, John DeWitt, Sam Dunnuck, Sylvia Gams, Ray Harrison, Frank Hines, John Marton, Ron Micheli, Carroll Miller, Peg Shreve, Rick Tempest, Dick Wallis, Clyde Wolfley, Virginia Wright and Speaker Rory Cross.

Previously, 17 Democrats voted "aye." Late that Wednesday night all 17 switched their vote to "no." The 17 who switched were Sheila Arnold, Eli Bebout, Bill Bensel, Sam Blackwell, Edith Garcia, Keith Goodenough, Pat Hacker, Mark Harris, Fred Harrison, Shirley Humphrey, Chris Plant, Bernard Phelan, Louise Ryckman, Mary Kay Schwope, Don Sullivan, Bill Vasey and Carol Watson.

Mel ZumBrunnen of Niobrara County, the original sponsor of weighted votes and Lauris Tysdal, his Weston County neighbor—both with three recorded "aye" votes—switched to "no" on the final vote. Even amendment sponsor Bruce Hinchey continued his "no" votes on weighted voting.

In 1992 there was no precedent for weighted voting because there were no rulings from the United States Supreme Court. For years scholars of the law and of political science discussed weighted votes. Guesses on the likelihood of the high court's approval ranged from "nil" to "zip." Wyoming's taxpayers have the 1992 Democrats to thank for saving the state yet another court case and a finding of unconstitutionality of its reapportioning methodology.

On the 128th day of 132—once the Pledge, Prayer, Journal Committee Report, Messages from the Senate or the Governor and the Standing Committee Reports were finished—the House girded itself for yet another round of debate on reapportioning. It was time for Third Reading and Final Vote.

Park County legislators, Peg Shreve of Cody and John DeWitt of Powell, wanted precincts rearranged in their districts to guarantee two House seats within Cody.[398] Keith Goodenough asked for the ayes/noes. Chris Plant gave the second. The vote: 46 ayes, 17 noes, 1 excused.[399]

Marlene Simons of Crook and Lauris Tysdal of Weston County, both ranchers, conferred with Miller and his men and found his ranch was in her House district. An amendment was prepared involving many, many empty census blocks in order to move the three Tysdals from House District 1 to House District 2.[400] Keith Goodenough asked for the ayes/noes. Chris Plant gave the second. The vote: 43 ayes, 20 noes, 1 excused. Tysdal was one of six Republican "no" votes—thereby avoiding any appearance of a conflict of interest.

---

[398] SF0049H32/AE. This amendment entailed a massive amount of work because of the many census blocks with few to no people. Miller and his men re-split three voter districts.

[399] The excused was Bill Rohrbach, also of Cody.

[400] SF0049H33/AE.

Converse County Republican legislators Bill Tibbs and Rory Cross along with Goshen County's Jim Hageman—were aghast at the configuration of House District 5.[401] This district stretched from Douglas to Torrington. It included 5 southeast Converse precincts, 2 northern Platte precincts and 9 Goshen precincts—three of which were in Torrington.

The amendment sponsors knew the "lay of the land" in District 5. It was not a compact district nor was there community of interest between the agricultural workers in and around Torrington and the power plant/mine workers in Douglas. Tibbs, Cross and Hagemen wanted a more internally compatible and reasonable district. Bill Tibbs requested the ayes/noes. Les Bowron provided the second. The vote: 30 ayes, 33 noes, 1 excused.

Thus the monstrosity remained. The design of this district was intended to fracture the Democratic vote in Converse, Platte and Goshen counties to ensure the election of Republicans.[402]

The Bodine amendment was first-class tinkering intended to create a "safe" district for Speaker Pro Tem Ron Micheli.[403] The strategy was for Janice Bodine to sponsor the amendment putting him in her district. She accepted, even though it meant the end of her legislative career. In a Republican primary he was the stronger candidate.

To "protect Micheli," 313 people, including those on the Micheli ranch, in the Fort Bridger precinct in House District 18 were moved to House District 19. Prior to the switch Micheli's base, the Fort Bridger and Lyman precincts, had 54% of the population in House District 18.

Once the 313 Fort Bridger people were in the Mountain View precinct, Micheli's base was just 32% of the population in House District 19. The other communities in House District 19 were Rural-west Uinta, with 22% of the population, and Evanston North-East with 46% of the population.

Keith Goodenough asked for the ayes/noes. Sam Blackwell provided the second. The vote: 52 ayes, 11 noes, 1 excused.

---

[401] SF0049H34/FE.

[402] The elections of 1992 through 2000 show this fracturing of the Democratic vote succeeded magnificently. In fact, the splitting of Torrington and its immediate environs into 3 house districts has almost destroyed the Democratic Party in Goshen County.

[403] SF0049H36/AE.

Micheli was the only Republican to vote no—thus avoiding any appearance of a conflict of interest.

But Micheli may have understood those communities in Uinta County much better than the originators of the amendment. In 1992 he lost to Evanston Union Pacific Maintenance foreman Wayne Morrow. Micheli's base in House 19 was 32% and Morrow's base was 46%.

Joan Barron in her column in the May 20, 2001 *Casper Star-Tribune* asked Micheli about the outcome of the Bodine amendment.

> There was an attempt to switch districts around in Bridger Valley "to give me some strength"… Bodine thought she was helping him… "As it turned out it actually hurt me worse than it helped me."

But the Bodine amendment contained a "sleeper." Most of the debate focused on Micheli and Uinta County. However, 882 people were moved between House District 15 and House District 16 in Rawlins precincts 1-1 and 2-1. Tinkering was predictable between these districts because the land area they encompassed was huge—from Rock River in Albany County, north to the Jeffrey City and Atlantic City communities in Fremont County, all across Carbon County then west deep into Rock Springs in Sweetwater County.

Democrats sponsored the last amendment: Eli Bebout of Fremont, Pat O'Toole of Carbon, Dick Honaker of Sweetwater and Jim Perkins of Sheridan. It fractured the Democratic vote in Fremont County. Why the Democrats agreed to cosponsor this amendment can only be explained as "loyalty to their mutual friendship." It certainly wasn't done to benefit Democrats. Or, was Bebout leading them down the primrose path? Only they know the answer.

Bebout "rearranged the deck chairs on the Titanic" to split the Wind River Reservation, thereby making safe Republican seats for himself, Harry Tipton, Bruce McMillan and another Republican. It eliminated Democrat Scott Ratliff's voter base. It also ended Dennis Tippets legislative career because he lived almost across the street from Bebout.

But this Bebout amendment was about more than Fremont County. It was also about House District 38, which was rural north, west and south Natrona County, with 14,586 people. He traded "out" Mills, Mountain View and Vista West Church and traded "in" Paradise Valley School, Paradise Valley Church and Oregon Trail School. The resulting configuration stretched the meaning of contiguity to include not only "neighbor" but also "connecting link." Because the Paradise Valley precincts contained 59% of the population in District 38, Oregon Trail School provided the needed link to rural Natrona County. This also was the amendment that gave Fremont County's Lysite precinct to Natrona County.[404]

Bill Tibbs called for the ayes/noes. Barbara Cubin gave the second. The vote: 43 ayes, 20 noes, 1 excused. The "no" votes were from 12 Republicans and eight Democrats.

Someone moved to delete the enacting clause to allow debate on all parts of the bill. Eventually, Herb Pownall called the roll on SF 49. The vote: 40 ayes, 23 noes, 1 excused. It was a non-partisan vote: 16 Republicans and 7 Democrats voted "no."[405] The House sent SF 49 to the Senate in a Message that asked the Senate "To Concur" on the House amendments.

Thursday evening's social calendar included the Coal Information Committee reception and the Developmental Disabilities reception, both at the Hitching Post Inn. Republicans talked to Republicans. Democrats talked to Democrats. The lobbyists talked to both. By then, even spouses carried the label "Republican" or "Democrat"—socialization, and the lack thereof, adjusted accordingly.

THE 129TH DAY OF 132

The Senate's motion was not to concur. The vote: 29 ayes. Gary Yordy voted "no." President True appointed Charlie Scott, Jim Applegate and Gary Yordy to the conference committee. Speaker Cross appointed Patti MacMillan, Bruce Hinchey and Eli Bebout.

Using the justification that time was "of the essence" and with the silent approval of legislators in both Chambers, the

---

[404] This heavily Republican precinct was crucial to Passeneaux's wins in her hotly contested races during the balance of the 1990's.

[405] House members voting "no" were Eric Alden, Eli Bebout Dan Budd, Doug Chamberlain, John DeWitt, Keith Goodenough, Bob Grant, Jim Hageman, Mark Harris, Dick Honaker, Bruce McMillan, Ron Micheli, Carroll Miller, Scott Ratliff, Louie Ryckman, Don Sullivan, Bill Tibbs, Dennis Tippets, Harry Tipton, Lauris Tysdal, Clyde Wolfley, Mel ZumBrunnen and Speaker Rory Cross.

President and Speaker declared this first conference committee a "free committee."[406]

But the real reason for a "free committee" was to fix a very serious error in House District 9 in Cheyenne in Laramie County. Miller's men found the absence of contiguity, or a connection, between Anderson School/Buffalo Ridge precincts and the Sunnyside Baptist precinct. Between them were Dildine School and Baggs School precincts. It was possible to carve many empty rural census blocks and one city street from the Dildine School precinct in House 10 to make a "connecting corridor." This artistry moved nine people and achieved contiguity. The conference committee made no other changes to SF 49.

Both Chambers approved the Conference Committee report. The Senate vote was 19 ayes, 11 noes. All the Democrats voted "no" plus Bob Grieve and Russ Zimmer.

The House vote was 47 ayes, 14 noes and 3 excused: April Brimmer-Kunz, John Rankine and Bill Rohrbach. Three Democrats and eight Republicans voted "no."[407]

SF 49 became Senate Enrolled Act 1.[408] Before lunch on the 129th day the President of the Senate signed Enrolled Act 1. Then the Senate adjourned.

Soon after 1:00 pm the Speaker of the House signed. Then the House adjourned at 1:15 pm. Before close of business that day the Governor signed it.

It was a good thing the legislature quit early that Friday. The hostility between Republicans and Democrats was "thick enough to cut with a knife." Many Republicans blamed the Democrats for all the time spent during the past week on reapportionment

---

[406] Joint Rules, 1992 Session #2-1(a) "...If the first conference committee report is not adopted, each committee appointed thereafter shall be a free conference committee as defined in Section 773 of *Mason's Manual of Legislative Procedure.*" Section 773 "...has authority to propose any amendments within the scope of the issue between the houses."

[407] The "no" votes were Sam Blackwell, Dan Budd, Doug Chamberlain, Keith Goodenough, Jim Hageman, Bruce McMillan, Ron Micheli, Chris Plant, Bill Tibbs, Dennis Tippets, Harry Tipton, Lauris Tysdal, Clyde Wolfley and Mel ZumBrunnen.

[408] The body of SEA 1 contained the necessary changes to the election code to reflect districting based on population instead of reapportioning based on land area. All 90 seats were vacant for the 1992 election.

instead of on the next biennium budget or their favorite issues and bills.

The pending social calendar included a Friday evening pasta party sponsored by the Wyoming Nurses Association, the annual Wyoming Education Association Dinner on Saturday, Sunday brunch hosted by the Lodging association and the evening dinner sponsored by the Energy Council. Republicans talked with Republicans. Democrats talked to Democrats. Spouses were equally selective with whom they visited. Lobbyists continued to talk with everyone.

While the Republican legislators licked their wounded pride and the Democrats awaited the next Court ruling, Rick Miller and his men began to "pull all-nighters."

Senate Enrolled Act 1 was due in the office of the Clerk of Court in the Federal Building by 5:00 pm, Monday, February 24—the 132nd day. Working with Senior Assistant Attorney General Clint Beaver, Rick Miller had to prepare the legal response to the Court's October 15th Opinion.

The data in Attachments A and B for the Senate and C and D for the House had to be checked for accuracy of the number of people in each of 57,000+ census blocks placed into precincts that became voting districts. A monumental challenge for the very weary "Miller-men" was the 36,000 census blocks with no people and the need to split precincts.

The massive amount of work in the very short time frame was stressful for the co-opted staff of the Legislative Service Office. Breaks were few. Food was fast. Backs, eyes and heads were tired. Exercise was non-existent. On and on they worked.

Monday morning the legislators returned to the Capitol and the Budget Session. Beaver, Miller and his men were not finished.

The House and Senate recessed for lunch. Beaver, Miller and his men were not finished.

Then, shortly after 4:00 pm Rick Miller and Clint Beaver, with all pertinent papers in their hands, walked the documents the three blocks down Capitol Avenue into the Federal Building to the desk of the Clerk of Court.

As they walked, they looked at their watches and said, "We still have time to get a soda." The Clerk of Court time-stamped their packet—" 4:19 pm February 24, 1992."

Rick Miller completed his 132-day reapportionment marathon with 41 minutes to spare.

22

The 51ˢᵗ Session Continues

Tempers did not cool. Wyoming's first foray into a legislature based on population rather than land area was now a "done deal"—29 years after *Baker v. Carr*. However, the Session wasn't over.

Each of the remaining 16 legislative working days began with the Call To Order, The Pledge To The Flag, The Prayer and The Journal Report. The Action Sheets announced Standing Committee meetings. It looked like business as usual.

But the interactions among the legislators were far from usual. Gone were the friendly conversations and the daily greetings of "Good Morning"—except between those of one's own political party, legislative staff or a lobbyist. Gone was the coffee room banter between Republicans and Democrats. Gone was much of the respect Democrats had for Republicans—and vice versa.

Disgruntled at their clear loss of political power, the Republicans held the Democrats responsible for forcing the court to rule unconstitutional their carefully justified plans. Many Republicans said the Democrats destroyed Wyoming's "place in the sun" as the only state where legislative representation was based on rational state policy, not on population.

Shunning was one way many—but not all—Republicans chose to express their displeasure. During the rest of the session Matilda Hansen decided to find out if she was being shunned. Daily, she greeted Janice Bodine with a cheery "Good Morning" as Bodine passed Hansen's desk on the way to her own desk— just two in front of Hansen's in the second row on the north side of the Chambers. Never, after the Governor's veto, did Bodine return Hansen's greeting or exchange other morning "pleasantries."

Republican Mel ZumBrunnen's response to the veto was statesmanlike and philosophical. True, his Niobrara County lost "their" senator and representative. But this was not such a bitter pill to swallow because every other small to medium sized county lost "their" senator and representative too.

Unless there was a special-event luncheon, the usual custom was to eat with those whose company one especially enjoyed.[409] However, after the veto the House members re-sorted themselves; Democrats ate with Democrats, Republicans ate with Republicans.

The exception came on March 16th, the day before the Session ended, when Democrat Louise Ryckman ate lunch with Republicans. She was on each of the three conference committees for SF 35, which dealt with funding Wyoming's public schools. One of the conference sessions was during lunch.

Because it was so unusual for a Democrat to eat with Republicans, the other 21 House Democrats compared notes. None of them had eaten, even one, informal lunch with a Republican since the Governor's veto.

The charged atmosphere in both Chambers was obvious to the lobbyists. The headline for the March/April/May edition of *Frontline Report* of the Wyoming Outdoor Council was: "Contentious Legislative Atmosphere."

THE REST OF SULLIVAN'S MESSAGE

There were other items on the legislative agenda in 1992 besides reapportionment. Governor Sullivan was promised "adverse consequences" if he vetoed the Republican Plan. His Message on February 10th listed his priorities—ripe plums for the plucking.

He tried to soothe legislator egos by talking about their ongoing commitments to education, infrastructure development for cities, towns and counties, water development, services to our citizens in need and environmental protection. He asserted the right of the state to control our destiny.

---

[409] The more formal planned "by prior invitation" luncheons were sponsored by lobbyists. The informal lunches were just casual clusters of people deciding, after the House adjourned for lunch, to eat together.

301

His list reflected the basic values of our community and showed our citizen's expectations the legislature will preserve and advance these values. He acknowledged the decline in revenues as well as the use of the financial reserves or "coffee cans" in recent years to balance the budget. He continued,

> The past few years have seen little, if any, growth in general government. But the combined effect of federal mandates without dollars, judicial directives and our own desire to maintain and advance ... [the ongoing commitments] ... have led to expanded general fund support for human services and education ... [that along with corrections] ... now account for nearly 80% of our expenditures.

The Governor gave the legislature four possible options:

1. Entirely cut specific services and programs;
2. Across the board cuts of 5, 10 or 15%;
3. Strip large amounts of funds from the remaining earmarked accounts...; and
4. Address the integrity of our tax base....

Then he went on:

> In closing, let me reiterate my belief that Wyoming is not, and need not become, the lowest common denominator of American public life.... We must avoid falling into ... the tyranny of limited expectations.... We must have faith in Wyoming and courage ... to maintain the values we have chosen and the courage to continue to move forward.

With a kind of prescience of what was to come he said,

> The personal, partisan and special interest potshots of the last few months have not gone unnoticed. Some have hit their mark. I have never suggested that my budget recommendations were perfect or without error. However, I have tried to understand the substance of the comments and not to respond in kind. My restraint wasn't based on virtue. Restraint springs from the practical realization that on this February day, we would all be gathered in this room to complete the difficult tasks of reapportionment and budget.
>
> We can all draw a line in the dirt, but that has not been the distinguishing characterization of Wyoming politics nor is it what we promised the voters when we sought our positions. These are difficult problems that can't be solved by slogan and clever catch phrases.

Little is gained by one group answering every question with the simplistic assertion of "no new taxes." While the other side responds to every question with the charge that "you are balancing the budget on the backs of the poor, the elderly and our children." We need to perform less for the media and more for our conscience and for the future of Wyoming.

The budget may be presented to you as numbers but it is a guide to the services our citizens have come to expect. Kicking the government can be great sport if we ignore the fact that government is the means by which we educate our children, aid the needy, build water projects and highways and provide a host of other services. Ultimately, it is the way we designate our values—those things we deem important.... Our problems are real; our challenges are difficult; our choices are unpleasant.[410]

The Governor knew whereof he spoke. There were other knotty issues besides reapportionment. They faced a new biennium budget with many of the financial reserves—the "coffee cans" of the boom years—empty.[411]

Many in the majority party disavowed the reality of Wyoming's structural deficiency problem. They sustained their no-tax pledge. They shouted about the scarcity of revenues (compared to the boom years). They denied the economic importance of public employee spending at Main Street's retail stores, appliance and car dealers. They didn't connect cuts in state spending with recession on Wyoming's Main Street communities.

They just "bumbled along," hoping for more $20 million windfalls from state inheritance taxes on the estates of Teton residents—who refused to die with predictable frequency.

Required by law to craft a new biennium budget, Governor Sullivan massaged $1 billion in General Fund requests into the

---

[410] From the Governor's address to the legislature in the House Chambers on February 10, 1992, beginning at 10:00 am.

[411] The Legislative Service Office prepared a document on *Revenue Enhancement Options* dated February 1992, with 27 possible ways to raise taxes and fees, 5 diversions from earmarked funds, 9 suggestions for possible legislation to raise revenue. Nothing significant was done by the 51st Legislature in 1992.

estimated revenue projection of $717 million.[412] But in February he was warned of "adverse consequences" to his budget proposal if he vetoed the reapportionment bill.

On the day of the veto the Senate made the first significant "hit" to his budget. Vice President Eddins struck $3,039,796; then Michael Burke eliminated 11 positions from SF3. This was just the beginning.

REPUBLICANS BEHIND CLOSED DOORS

The Republicans with an agenda realized they needed private time with their colleagues to arm-twist or otherwise gain support for the "adverse consequences" promised Governor Sullivan if he used his veto pen on February 17th.

On Monday March 2nd, after the Opening-Pledge-Prayer-Journal routine, the Republicans went off to caucus—for three hours. The Democrats caucused, too, but for less time. There were more caucuses during the noon hour on Wednesday, March 4th, followed by a two-hour caucus on Thursday, March 5.

On Monday, March 9th, the General File was still open. But it finally closed in both the House and Senate on Tuesday, March 10th. The House adjourned at 4:00 pm. The Mining Association Reception was the last social event of the Session.

On the 12th, one education and seven budget bills were in second and third readings. The 12th was a "very difficult day," as line item cuts were made to agency budgets.[413] The Governor sent a letter upstairs to Speaker Rory Cross with a copy to Minority Leader Fred Harrison, identifying the impact of

---

[412] In 1992 the estimates came from the Consensus Revenue Estimating Group co-chaired by Mary Byrnes of Research and Statistics of the Department of Administration and Fiscal Control and C. James Orr of the Legislative Service Office. The other members were Don Basko, Oil and Gas Commission; Clyde Gerrard, State Auditor's Office; Gary Glass, Wyoming Geological Survey office; Earl Kabeiseman, Department of Revenue and Taxation; William Morgan, Economics Department, University of Wyoming; Barry Nimmo, State Department of Education; and Glenn Shaffer, State Treasurer's Office.

[413] From Matilda Hansen's diary.

amendments cutting line items. Before the final vote Harrison wanted to read it from a podium. Speaker Cross said "no."[414]

Sam Blackwell and Matilda Hansen took Harrison to The Owl Inn for supper to calm him down. The House went back into session at 7:00 pm. The "tempers were hot."[415]

On Friday, March 13th, caucus time consumed three hours. Conference committees met. That afternoon the Speaker ordered a Mexican dinner brought to the House Coffee Room. The House worked through the dinner hour, continuing on into the early evening.

The House was in session all day on Saturday. There was "...lots of caucus time. We are not finished. We worked till 10:00 pm. Very, very tired."[416]

The Constitution prohibited Sunday sessions. But it was legal for Conference Committees to meet.

On Monday, March 16th, the Democrats caucused for an hour and a half—the Republicans for three hours. Some Enrolled Acts were signed that afternoon—then the Republicans went back into caucus.[417] The House worked until 10:30 pm.

The debate in the closed Republican caucuses was purported to be "strategy setting." But they were talking "substance"—why which significant cuts were to be made to which agencies.
If policy was the purview of the public, then those long hours of discussion belonged on the House Floor—not sequestered away from public hearing in a closed caucus.

One of the strategies from behind those closed doors was labeled "The Cubin Amendment," cutting 5% "across the board" from selected state agency budgets. Actually, she was one of six Republicans to "sign-on" a series of attempts to implement the "adverse consequences." The others were Speaker Pro Tem Ron Micheli, Majority Leader Doug Chamberlain, House

---

[414] See Appendix F for the letter Fred Harrison was forbidden to read aloud.

[415] Hansen diary.

[416] Ibid.

[417] Between caucuses it was "hurry up and wait" time. Conference committees reported—a vote was taken. When one Chamber rejected a conference report, the old committee was reappointed or a new committee was named. Adjournment was not possible until all budget bills and the public education funding bills were passed.

Appropriations Committee chair Dick Wallis, John Hines and Les Bowron.[418]

Cubin was the spokesperson not only for "adverse consequences", but for those who wanted to curb government, to cripple enforcement of environmental laws and regulations, to curtail audits on mineral production, to cut the welfare rolls, to deny funds for health and human services and to reduce the demand for tax revenue.

Usually the cuts were specific to the 100 and 200 series line-item appropriations to a specified program. These lines were salaries and benefits. Sometimes positions were eliminated. Some of the amendments said "Under GENERAL FUND decrease amount by...." These amounts varied from as low as $10,890 to $3,493,607.[419] The amendments sponsored by Cubin, Micheli, Chamberlain, Wallis, Bowron and Hines made 216 of these line-item decreases from SF 3, 5 and 7.[420]

The targeted agencies in SF 3 were the Departments of Audit and Commerce. In SF 5 it was Health and Social Services. In SF 7 it was Corrections.

Consistently resisting the knives of the "Cubin amendments" were five Republican women and two Republican men. Despite all the "hammering in caucus" they stood firm in their belief that these amendments were poor public practice. The seven were: Susan Anderson of Natrona, April Brimmer-Kunz and Cynthia Lummis of Larimer County, Patti MacMillan, Sam Dunnuck of Albany, Clarene Law of Teton and Dennis Tippets of Fremont.[421]

---

[418] Wallis and Hines were from mineral-rich Campbell County. Hines was on Revenue, Agriculture-Public Lands-Water Resources committees. Bowron of Natrona County was on Travel-Recreation-Wildlife and Labor-Health and Social Services committees.

[419] After the 1974 constitutional amendment created annual sessions, one of which was a budget session, the Joint Rules stipulated multiple budget bills. Therefore, the 1993-94 biennium budget was in House Bills 2, 4 and 6 and in Senate Files 3, 5, 7 and 9.

[420] SF0003H25/AE, SF0003H328/AE, SF0003H330/AE, SF0005H25/AE, SF0005H333/AE, SF0005H334/AE, SF0005S37A, SF0007S/31A, SF0007H36/AE, and SF0007H37/AE were the "chopper amendments" to the Senate Files. Similar cuts were made in the House Bills but they are not listed to avoid redundancy.

[421] In past years three other women "stood firm" in resisting the dictates of the Republican caucus. They were Margaret Brown (Carbon), Mary Odde (Fremont) and Nyla Murphy (Natrona).

Line item cuts were also made in the Senate. There the choppers were Vice President Boyd Eddins of Lincoln/Sublete, Majority Leader Jerry Dixon of Weston, Judiciary chair John Perry of Johnson-Campbell, Revenue chair Mike Healy of Hot Springs-Washakie, Corporations chair Charles Scott of Natrona, Labor and Federal Relations chair Alan Howard of Big Horn,[422] Michael Burke of Natrona, Mike Enzi of Johnson-Campbell, Terry Guice of Albany, and Tom Kinnison of Sheridan.[423]

Because the Senate did not concur with the House cuts, conference committees were appointed. By March 13th, President Deimer True and Speaker Rory Cross designated each conference committee an "open" committee. On that date all the budget bills were in conference. The Speaker appointed House Appropriations chair Dick Wallis as the lead House member to all six-conference committees.

Because other legislators also successfully sponsored budget cuts, the net result was massive differences between the House and Senate. This generated an "open season opportunity" against state-run programs and services. All the agencies were vulnerable to the cutting knives of the conferees.[424]

TARGETED AGENCIES

The "bean counters" were in the Department of Audit, searching out which taxpayers did or did not pay taxes to the State. Thus the Department of Audit was a prime target for "adverse consequences." The mineral lobbyists had "their man" Deimer True in the Senate President's chair. This agency was fully funded by the state. While 20% of the mineral companies reported 80% of the mineral production, the remaining 80% of the companies reported on 20% of the production.

---

[422] Healy and Howard also served on Education-Labor-Welfare committee. Perry and Enzi were from the combined senate district Campbell-Johnson.

[423] Michael Burke was on Judiciary, Mike Enzi was on Appropriations, Terry Guice was on Revenue and Tom Kinnison was on Corporations.

[424] An "open" conference committee meant it was possible to change any line in any bill. They were not limited to just the differences between the House and Senate. When a conference report was presented, no Floor amendments were allowed. The vote was "aye" or "no" on the main motion.

The 1992 edition of *Wyoming Oil and Gas—Facts and Figures* cited "...nearly 49% of the state's total taxable valuation" was in the oil and gas industry. Wyoming was 6th in the nation in taxable crude oil production with 94,588,884 barrels and 5th in natural gas production with 690,356,068 MCF.[425]

Coal and trona production were the other major players in Wyoming's mineral-dependent economy. Wyoming was, for the fourth consecutive year (in 1991), the nation's largest producer of coal with 194.2 million tons—a 5.4% increase over 1990. Most of it—85% of the state's total production—was low-sulfur coal mined in Campbell County.[426]

Property taxes assessed on all minerals in 1990 were $273,546,726. The property taxes on all property in the state for that year were $433,949,003.[427] Clearly, the mineral industry dominated the economy and provided the lion's share of the tax revenues.

In the 1980's State Auditor Jim Griffith found not all mineral production was reported to the Department of Revenue under the so-called "Honor System." There was little incentive to "pay up" because the state did not impose penalties or assess interest for non-payment of taxes. Consequently, there was every incentive for companies not to report accurately their production.

When caught under-reporting, the companies argued about the numbers while negotiating reductions. It was obvious to Jim Griffith, to many legislators of both parties and to Governors Herschler and Sullivan that the mineral companies needed state auditing.

By 1992, the mineral companies found the Department of Audit, under Director Roger W. Dewey and Minerals Audit Manager John F. Cram, too successful. With the "Cubin

---

[425] During 1991, 614 companies/operations produced this crude oil and 323 produced natural gas in 14,187 producing wells. There were 5 active refineries with capacity for 164,000 barrels of crude oil per day, and oil was transported by 44 companies through 15,000 miles of pipeline. Source: *Wyoming Oil and Gas: Facts and Figures*, 1992 edition written under the direction of Richard Robitaille, Executive Director and chief lobbyist for the Petroleum Association of Wyoming.

[426] Gary B. Glass, "The Geological Survey of Wyoming," *Wyoming Geo Notes* No. 22 (April 1989) and 26 (April 1990).

[427] *Wyoming Oil and Gas: Facts and Figures,* 1992 edition.

amendments" the time and opportunity had come to cut funding for the Department.

Because of the linkage of federal dollars to state dollars, $2,260,632 was cut from the Department of Family Services. These cuts meant social worker caseload in child abuse, injury and protection increased from 25 to 60 per worker. The economic assistance caseload increased from 150 to 225 per worker for services to the poor. Services for troubled youth placed by the courts in the state's three juvenile institutions were reduced by 10 positions.

The Public Assistance and Social Services cuts eliminated the Youth Alternatives program, reduced general assistance, cut state-funded daycare, and reduced local provider rates for day-care, foster care, group home placements.

The Department of Commerce took a $1,195,550 hit in museums, arts, state parks, tourism, economic development and administration.

The Department of Employment was sheltered from draconian cuts because of heavy Federal funding. However, the Women's Commission was reduced to one meeting per year. A pilot program to improve workers compensation was eliminated.

The $6,457,311 cuts in the Department of Health hit the state's program of medical assistance for prescription drugs for the working poor and retirees not eligible for Medicaid, Adult Home Care services, Developmentally Disabled programs, the Training School, county mental health centers and the State Hospital.[428]

During debate, when confronted with the reality of shortfalls if the "Cubin cuts" were made, the proponents of cutting answered, "The governor can use his "flex" authority to move funds from another agency to cover shortfalls." Not only was this answer a fallacy, but it was hypocritical because cuts were made to so many line items that no agency had extra money to be "flexed."

The Republican majority clearly used their political power to impose their political agenda.

---

[428] The data for the above comes from documents distributed to the legislators by the Governor from responses to his directive to the agencies, "What is the impact of the Cubin 5% cut?"

THE SESSION ENDS

Finally, at 9:10 am on Tuesday March 17 the work was done. The House was ready to listen to the Governor's Farewell to the 51st Legislature.

[T]hese remarks have been difficult to fashion because of the Conference Committee marathon.... First, my comments should not be taken personally. Wyoming's system of government has already been damaged as a working institution and in the eyes of the citizens by the all too frequent use of personalized remarks intended as expressions of policy frustration.

Second, I am not sure my comments apply equally to all members of this body. It has been clear for several weeks that a minority of this body, which constitutes the majority of the dominant party's caucus, has their own view of Wyoming's future. It appears they intended, from the outset, to impose this view on their own party, this body and the State. ... Most of you will return home and attempt to convince both yourselves and your constituents that you have had a productive session and they should be pleased with your work. ...

First, you have balanced the budget. Second, you remained true to the ... "no new taxes."... Third, you have done no irreparable harm to the State and if you did, you, or someone else, can repair it in January before it is really bad.

Wyoming faces a structural deficit problem ... that cannot be hidden by spending one-time funds, earmarked accounts, casting aside decisions ... made a short 12 months ago, or by closed caucuses or political rhetoric. [Everyone has] to understand why Wyoming has a budget problem which requires ... we seriously and openly evaluate the ... tax system, spending policies and the indefensible dependence ... on extractive industries for our tax revenues. [T]he across-the-board cuts simply mean that the same programs will be delivered at a lower level of service with few people. Again we ask state employees to do more with less while refusing to acknowledge their dedication and commitment to the people of this state. And you have left no reserves!! ...

310

[M]any of you increasingly became prisoners of your own rhetoric and of your philosophical fear or resolve to not discuss taxes. ... The interest groups, the elected officials, the voters and even the people who didn't bother to vote, all have contributed ... to the decisions reflected in the budget....

The saddest part of this session are the lost opportunities....

And to those of you planning to return, I will be here next year and so will the problems that remain unaddressed.

The legislators toted their boxes out of the Chambers. The lobbyists returned to their offices. The Governor looked at the Enrolled Acts and conferred with the men and women managing the agencies. His decisions were as follows:[429]

1. **HB 2** "Allowed the $101 million ... for elected officials and various state agencies *into* law *without signature*, but *vetoed* two footnotes restricting the Department of Administration and Information's Procurement Services Division."

2. **HB 4** "*Signed* the $32 million ... for various state agencies including the Departments of Agriculture, Environmental Quality and Transportation but *vetoed* two footnotes restricting authority of the Transportation Commission.

3. **HB 6** "Allowed a $245.6 million higher education funding act ... *into law without signature* because of unhappiness with a controversial "flexibility" clause allowing the Governor to transfer money from agency to agency..."[430]

4. **SF 3** "Allowed the $45 million ... for various state agencies including the Departments of Audit, Commerce and Employment *into law without signature* but specifically expressed unhappiness over the demise of the Arts Endowment Fund, reduced funding for the

---

[429] From the Governor's letters on the budget bills distributed by Rich Lindsey to all legislators on April 2, 1992, at the request of the Governor.

[430] The Governor's comment continues: "...he 'reluctantly' retains the flexibility authority to minimize the impact of across-the-board cuts but questions its advisability and will use it sparingly."

311

Economic and Community Development Division and local government assistance at the expense of local government infrastructure funds."

5. **SF 5** *"Vetoed* the appropriations for three institutions for the elderly ... legislature review those budgets "in a responsible and focused fashion" and restore $644,000 in cuts." He also *vetoed* the reduction in the Standard of Need to $539 pending a waiver. He signed the balance of the $291 million Health and Social Services budget.

6. **SF 7** *"Vetoed* $42 million...for the Department of Corrections ... [because the cuts] seriously under-funded the State Penitentiary and jeopardized public safety." The Women's Center at Lusk and Probation and Parole received fewer dollars in the 1993-1994 budget than was approved in the 1991-1992 budget.

7. **SF 9** He signed the capital construction bill.

Agencies not benefiting from a veto worked with the Governor's Budget Office and the Upstairs-Men at the LSO to figure out what was cut from their budgets. With his veto pen and the work done by Executive staff and the top agency people, Governor Sullivan exerted his executive power and political privilege. The clear use of political power was again in the hands of Democrats.

On April 1, 1992, Governor Sullivan sent a letter to President Diemer True and Speaker Rory Cross calling the 51st Legislature back into Special Session because of the cuts to corrections and the elderly institutions. He said,

I am certain this announcement will not be greeted with enthusiasm by you and many Members of the Legislature. Let me assure you I am no more anxious for you to return than you are....

Noting his vetoes covered a "relatively small portion" of the budget, he was not asking the full state budget to be reopened or for taxes to be raised.

I have expressed deep reservations about numerous legislative actions, but I am willing to work with my agency heads to deal with the hand dealt us.... [However] ... for reasons that are unfathomable to me the Legislature did reduce funding for the State institutions for the elderly and our correctional institutions.[431]

The legislators showed up on May 11, 1992 at 9:00 am. Instead of the traditional Message, the Governor sent a letter asking for $3 million for corrections and the elderly institutions.

The Joint Rules for budget sessions were used. The Senate voted on introduction of four files—all failed to get a two-thirds vote for full consideration. The House voted on introduction of 12 bills but only three received the two-thirds vote for consideration.[432] Only the budget bill passed both Chambers.

In three days the funding was restored to corrections and the elderly institutions; the tax rebate program for the elderly and handicapped, footnotes on the standard of need, and highway funds were redone. One position was restored to administer the tax rebate program. The session ended. The legislators went home.

THE JUDGMENT

Miller's "borrowed" men returned to their families and some very welcome sleep. Down the street in Federal Court Justices Brorby, Brimmer and Johnson began their scrutiny of the Beaver-Miller documents.

Besides the original plaintiffs, interveners and the *amicus curiae* brief for the Wyoming State Democratic party, Douglas Chamberlain filed a statement *pro se*.[433] Karen J. Budd of the Cheyenne law firm of Dray, Madison & Thomas filed an *amicus curiae* brief for her legislator/father Dan Budd of Sublette. The Justices heard the arguments. The Opinion was handed down on April 6.

The Court said that the Wyoming Reapportionment Act complied with the Equal Protection Clause of the Fourteenth Amendment because it met the *de minimis* rule with a relative

---

[431] The Governor's proclamation for a Special Session, Legislative Journal.

[432] These were Crimes and Offenses: Stalking; State revenues: fees and charges; and Uniform Unclaimed Property Act. Once the Governor called a special session, legislators could, without limit, propose other bills.

[433] "For himself."

population deviation of 9.602% for the Senate and 9.973% for the House.

Writing for the Court, Justice Brorby noted plaintiffs and intervenors conceded the state's assertion that the Act "is *prima facie* valid."[434]

> We ... conclude the 1992 Act has achieved the overriding constitutional objective of substantial equality of population among the various legislative districts—the vote of any citizen is approximately equal in weight to that of any other citizen in Wyoming ... we hold the act constitutional, deny any injunctive relief and relinquish jurisdiction....

But the Justices saw two problems likely to continue:

1. The stacking and splitting in some districts to weight votes in favor of particular parties, such as Senate districts 5 and 8 in Laramie County and 9 and 10 in Albany; and

2. The absence of "county/community integrity" in House districts 2, 3, 4 and 5 (northeast and east central Wyoming) House 20 and 22 (in Sublette) and District 16 (Albany, Carbon, Fremont and Sweetwater).

House Districts 2 through 5 in Crook, Weston, Converse, Niobrara, Goshen and Platte were the focus of the failed Tibbs-Cross-Hagemen Third Reading amendment.[435] Though the Court did not see the failed amendment, they essentially agreed with the three legislators. The absence of community of interest was "largely ignored in Goshen County."

The configuration of the south Sublette Republicans with the south Lincoln (Kemmerer) Democrats was yet another manifestation of the open spaces/clustering of people phenomena in the Old Utah-Idaho Territory.

The problems in District 16 came from the "sleeper" portion of the Bodine amendment.[436] Because District 16 encompassed so much territory, and because the Justices knew the area well, they asserted community of interest here too was "largely ignored."

Justice Brorby used his understanding of geography and the reapportionment boundaries to describe District 16:

---

[434] *Goris v. Karpan*, 788 F.Supp 1199 (D.Wyo. 1992) at 1201-3.

[435] SF0049H34/FE.

[436] SF0049H36/AE.

[I]t stretches from the northwest boundary of Albany County across the top of Carbon County, picks up a portion of the City of Rawlins, extends west to the outskirts of Rock Springs in Sweetwater County, drops down to the Wyoming-Colorado boundary with its westernmost boundary at Fontenelle Reservoir and its northern boundary beyond Atlantic and Jeffrey Cities in Fremont County.

Yet the Court adhered "to the view that legislative apportionment is primarily a political and legislative process ... we nevertheless empathize with the dissatisfied voters in the 'problem' areas."

The justices suspected that 11th hour gerrymandering prevented alternative plans that did a better job of reflecting "community of interest." Actually, gerrymandering wasn't the reason why a better plan did not reach the Court. The reason was that partisanship prevented a better plan—wholesale opposition to any plan drawn by a Democrat.

The Judges suspected possible gerrymandering. But they were unable to make a finding of gerrymandering without a record on which to litigate.

Neither the plaintiffs nor the intervenors made this claim because they needed the *results* of an election in order to show gerrymandering. As the next election was in November—still six months away—there was no case. A lawsuit cannot be based on what someone "thinks" may happen.

Justice Brorby concluded,

At present this court finds no evidence of constitutional infirmity. The political wisdom of the legislative action can only be judged by Wyoming citizens who now exercise substantially equal power at the ballot box.

Justice Johnson concurred with Justice Brorby's writing. But Justice Brimmer was unhappy. He had a few things to say. He did not want anyone to construe their concurrence as "even halfhearted approval" of the Act because the legislature "was mighty careless of justice, to say the least." He seared those legislators who supported the Bodine amendment saying it "created abuses and imbalances by the carload."

He objected to the fracturing of the largely Democratic Hispanic minority in South Torrington "by smothering them with Wheatland Republicans." He didn't like Rawlins city precinct

#3 placed where they were "outweighed by Sweetwater Democrats."[437]

He didn't like the voters living along the Sweetwater River in Fremont "kneaded in with" the Sweetwater County Democrats. He disapproved of splitting Sublette forcing half its Republican voters in with Kemmerer Democrats. "This smacks of political gerrymandering.... I hope that aroused voters will properly sear and baste those who drafted, promulgated and passed the Bodine Amendment; they richly deserve it."

A century spent focusing on fairness in Wyoming's legislature by restless and concerned citizens ended. They were vindicated.

From the selection of delegates to the constitutional convention on July 8, 1889 to the final opinion in *Gorin v. Karpan* on April 6, 1992, the configuration of election districts was delineated by the political borders of the counties—the amount of land encompassed by a geographical boundary with adjustments reflecting population.

The three Wyoming Federal Justices, acting under the guidance of the United States Supreme Court and the Equal Protection Clause of the Fourteenth Amendment, fundamentally changed this practice. The April 6th ruling established the principle that equal representation meant equal-sized clusters of people in as many election districts as there were seats in the Senate and House. In terms of constitutionality, the amount of land in an election district was moot.

Torturous was the path needed to achieve this result—one-person, one-vote—nearly 30 years after *Baker v. Carr*. After the historic ruling that Wyoming's time-tested, understood and comfortable way of selecting senators and representatives was unconstitutional, the Republicans controlling the legislature were incensed.

From October 15th 1991 to April 6th 1992, the Republican leadership had no intention to produce a "good plan" recognizing communities of interest as the third criteria for fashioning election districts. It was theoretically possible for Brorby, Brimmer and Johnson to find Senate Enrolled Act 1 unconstitutional because of the abridgment of community of interest. However, the Court chose not to make such a ruling.

---

[437] The Brimmer family home was in northwest Rawlins. Thus the Sweetwater Democrats outvoted his Republican family.

The Republican leadership essentially chose to focus only on the *required* not to exceed 10% deviation range, knowing this criterion overrode all others.

After 30 years of defiance and avoidance Wyoming Republicans *reluctantly* accepted the law of the land, which evolved from *Baker v. Carr*.[438]

---

[438] An observation by Kathy Karpan.

23

Aftermath

Many Republicans held the Democrats responsible for injecting the Court into reapportionment.

The Democrats lost three House seats in 1992, but in 1994 they lost big time.[439] The 1992 election brought 47 Republicans to the House and 20 to the Senate. After the Republicans drew the district lines, fewer Democrats have been elected, as shown in Table 42.

TABLE 42
Democrats after Districting

Year	Session	Democrats in Senate	Democrats in House
1991	51st Session	10	22
1993	52nd Session	10	19
1995	53rd Session	10	13
1997	54th Session	9	16
1999	55th Session	10	17
2001	56th Session	9	14

[439] Governor Sullivan failed to reach the United States Senate. Bob Schuster failed to get Wyoming's seat in the United States Congress. Kathy Karpan failed to win the Governor's office. Nick Deegan lost to Diane Ohman for Secretary of State, Matilda Hansen lost to Stan Smith for State Treasurer, Bill Vasey lost to Judy Catchpool for Superintendent of Public Instruction. No Democrat ran against Dave Ferrari for State Auditor.

"Stacking and fracturing" worked well in Goshen where the Democratic population was split between four House districts. Though educator and highly qualified candidate Harold Bovee tried to be elected, his Democratic base in and around Torrington was fractured. In fact, this fracturing took the guts out of the Goshen County Democratic Party.

Stacking and fracturing was done in Laramie County. Three House seats were stacked Democratic. Three were stacked Republican. Three were competitive though slanted Republican. One was stacked Republican but consistently elected a Democrat.[440]

The six House districts in Fremont fractured the voting base for the Shoshone and Arapaho. Washakie's Shoshone dominated the Wind River Reservation but enrolled tribal member Democrat Linda St. Clair was defeated in 1998.

The Republican "voices" that drew Rory Cross, Ken Gropp and Eli Bebout to switch parties, in 1995 began to "speak" to Democrat Ross Diercks of Niobrara. Diercks' response was a smile and a sparkle in his eyes.

One day when Speaker Pro Tem Peg Shreve was doing the talking, Diercks asked, "Why do you want me to switch? You have most of the House seats now." She replied, "We want it all."

In the 1992 election a voters' initiative brought term limits to Wyoming.[441] While term limits had no visible effect on who ran for office, it did affect the House seniority of succession through the leadership chairs.

Petroleum Association lobbyist Rick Robitaille "advanced his man,", Bruce Hinchey, onto the leadership succession by working to have him become Majority Leader in 1995 and Speaker in 1997.[442] When mineral-man Eli Bebout switched to the Republican Party, he too moved into the leadership succession to become Majority Leader in 1997 and Speaker in 1999.

---

[440] Mac McGraw was elected in 1996, 1998, 2000.

[441] Initially House members were limited to three terms or 6 years and the Senators to three terms or 12 years. Subsequently, by statute, the number of years for Senators and House members was made the same: 12 years.

[442] Hinchey had 6-1/2 years of legislative tenure. His wife was Robitaille's daughter.

With term limits providing the "underlying reason/excuse" for changing the leadership succession, the minerals-men and the Republican closed caucus changed the sequence to Speaker, Majority Leader, Speaker Pro Tem, Majority Whip.

During the middle of the 1990's the legislature (and the mineral-interest lobbyists) faced the reality of three competent Republican women succeeding into the leadership. They were realtor Patti MacMillan of Albany, educator Peg Shreve of Park and rancher Marlene Simons of Crook.[443] Actually, MacMillan and Shreve were already "in the leadership"—MacMillan as Speaker Pro Tem in 1993, Shreve as Majority Whip in 1995 and Speaker Pro Tem in 1997.

MacMillian as Speaker Pro Tem in the 52nd Legislature had her picture at the top of the composite portrait of the Legislators. By 1997 she was "off of the leadership track." She chose not to be on the ballot in 1998—thus ending her legislative career.

For the 53rd Legislature (1995) Peg Shreve was Speaker Pro Tem. After the Republican caucus shuffling for the 54th she was again Speaker Pro Tem. She chose not to be on the ballot in 2000—thus ending her legislative career.

Marlene Simons held a coveted House Appropriations Committee seat from 1993-2000. She was on House Rules Committee from 1989-2000. She never got on the leadership track. She chose not to be on the ballot in 2002—thus ending her legislative career.

These Republican women with experience and seniority clearly qualified, on their own merit, for the top leadership positions in Wyoming's legislature. Influential mineral-interest Equality State men deemed it expedient to deny them Majority Leader and Speaker status.

By the end of the century gender alone did not keep a legislator from leadership status. Republican men were denied leadership roles. Harry Tipton of Fremont was elected to the House in 1980. Charles Scott of Natrona was a House member who went to the Senate in 1982. Neither has moved along the leadership track in either Chamber.

---

[443] John Marton, a sheep man from Johnson, had the same length of seniority as the three women. He was Majority Leader in 1993 and Speaker in 1995.

Both independent thinkers, they did their own home work. But too often they voted "as they saw fit" rather than stay hitched to a political agenda.[444]

The mineral interest lobbyists exerted their political power in other places besides influencing the leadership succession. They also influenced the tax collection practices of the Department of Revenue. If retailers collecting sales taxes are remiss in sending in the tax, the penalty is a felony. If a company in the extractive resource mineral industry is remiss in paying taxes, there is no felony. But worse, from the perspective of public policy, has been the legislature's refusal (until the mid 1990's) to grant the Department of Revenue the authority to impose interest and penalties on the companies for failure to pay all taxes due.

LOOKING BACK

The best laws "happen" when Democrats and Republicans from the middle of their respective political philosophies work together to address the issues. During the last quarter of the 20th century the best Republican leadership came from moderates Salty (Harold) Hellbaum of Platte, Nels Smith of Crook, Warren Morton of Natrona, Bob Burnett of Albany and Pat Meenan of Natrona. Under their wise and understanding leadership excellent legislation was enacted in a good atmosphere.

During their tenure, support and opposition were "fluid," handled with grace and a modicum or a plenitude of humor—depending on the occasion. One day's most effective opponent on one piece of legislation became the next days best supporter on other legislation.

During those years it was possible for political opponents Republican James Mockler of Big Horn and Democrat Matilda Hansen of Albany, to meet at the water cooler and say: "We are on the same side on this bill (local improvement districts)." Then the reply with a smile: "One of us must be making a mistake!"

Debate in the House sometimes became heated. On one occasion the subject was water law. Soon, in consternation, a

---

[444] Though Scott was often the architect of political agendas and himself a rancher, he was not an obedient follower of the agriculture/mineral interest coalition plots.

321

legislator rose to decry the hot tempers, the near-shouting, the arm-waving vigor of a series of speakers. Another legislator, one with a cooler head and some historical perspective admonished, "Our exchanges are good ones, appropriate to this time and to this place. Our predecessors used guns at headgates or on the streets of our towns. We are using the law, here, in these Chambers." Tempers cooled.

Tensions in law making "come with the territory." Small courtesies, woven into the fabric of daily interactions, defuse tensions and become "traditions of the legislature." These courtesies "grease the wheels" of civility—thereby making the process work. Another integral component that makes the process work is "institutional memory."

The proper keepers of traditions and of institutional memory are the legislators. Because of short seniority caused by term limits, the legislative process is exposed to serious harm.

Joan Barron of the *Casper Star-Tribune*[445] interviewed Senator Tom Kinnison of Sheridan about term limits. In the interview Kinnison said, "I think term limits is destroying the Legislature. ... [W]ith Wyoming's part-time legislature it takes four to six years before a lawmaker is effective in the legislative process." (The legislator is gone in another six years.)

Deputy Attorney General Rowena Heckert stated,

> If the term limits law is enforced it will curtail the rights of voters to choose the people they prefer to represent them. Although the term limits law appears in the Election Code, it effectively amends the statement of qualifications in the Constitution for holding office for all state officers and legislators.[446]

With term limits, the "institutional memory" and knowledge of "legislative traditions" shifts to state agency personnel who implement the law and especially to the lobbyists who involve themselves in writing the law.

This shift enhances the power and influence of all lobbyists—particularly Wyoming's mineral interest lobbyists who are not answerable to the voters.

Who, then, clearly wields political power in Wyoming?

---

[445] April 2, 2002, editorial page.

[446] *Casper Star-Tribune*, Casper, Wyoming, April 2, 2002, p. 1.

APPENDIX A
Wyoming Counties

County	Who Created	When Created
Laramie Carter*	Dakota Territorial Legislature	1867
Albany Carbon Sweetwater	Dakota Territorial Legislature	1868
Uinta	Wyoming Territorial Assembly	1869
Crook Johnson	Wyoming Territorial Assembly	1875**
Fremont	Wyoming Territorial Assembly	1884
Sheridan Converse Natrona	Wyoming Territorial Assembly	1888
Weston	Wyoming Territorial Assembly	1890
Big Horn	Wyoming Legislature	1890
Park	Wyoming Legislature	1911
Goshen Platte Niobrara Hot Springs Washakie Lincoln	Wyoming Legislature	1913
Sublette Teton	Wyoming Legislature	1921

Sources: Marie H. Erwin, *Wyoming Historical Blue Book-A Legal and Political History of Wyoming*, 1868-1943. Bradford-Robinson Printing Company, Denver, Colorado, 1946. And Robert H. Brown, *Wyoming*. Westview Press, Colorado, 1980.

*Carter County was changed to Sweetwater in 1868.

**Robert Brown indicates Johnson and Crook were not "recognized" until the 1880's.

APPENDIX B
Joint Corporations Committee

1989-1990

SENATE:	HOUSE:
Charles Scott, Chairman (R)	Patti MacMillan, Chairman (R)
Bob Burnett – Albany (R)	Eli Bebout – Fremont (D)
Della Herbst – Sheridan (D)	John DeWitt – Park (R)
Carl Maldonado – Sweetwater (D)	Steve Freudenthal – Laramie (D)
Dan Sullivan – Natrona (R)	Carroll Miller – Big Horn (R)
	Jerry Parker – Uinta (R)
	Dorothy Perkins – Natrona (R)
	Don Sullivan – Laramie (D)
	Rick Tempest – Natrona (R)

1991-1992

SENATE:	HOUSE:
Charles Scott, Chairman (R)	Patti MacMillan, Chairman (R)
Jim Applegate – Laramie (D)	Eli Bebout – Fremont (D)
Della Herbst – Sheridan (D)	John DeWitt – Park (R)
Tom Kinnison – Sheridan (R)	Matilda Hansen – Albany (D)
Gary Yordy – Laramie (R)	Bruce Hinchey – Natrona (R)
	April Brimmer-Kunz – Laramie (R)
	Bruce McMillan – Fremont (R)
	Don Sullivan – Laramie (D)
	Carol Jo Vlastos – Natrona (R)

APPENDIX C
Bern Hinckley's Testimony

January 26, 1991

Testimony regarding HB 295 – Legislative Reapportionment

Dear Chairman MacMillan/Chairman Scott:

As I have watched and read the discussion on legislative reapportionment leading to HB 295, I have become increasingly disturbed by the implied attitude of the Legislature. It seems that instead of asking how the people of Wyoming can be best served through the reapportionment process, we have fallen prey to an "us against them" mentality and are asking, "What's the least we can do and still get away with it?" The concept of reapportionment is based on fairness and equity, principles I hope we in Wyoming cherish every bit as much as does the US Supreme Court, and fairness and equity should be our only goals.

Sure the folks of counties like Niobrara can present a heart-warming version of "fairness" as they see it. But there is a much larger constituency to consider—the people of Wyoming. And if we cannot accommodate the wishes of the 2500 people of Niobrara County without violating the fair and equitable representation of the 450,000 people of Wyoming, there should be no argument about which constituency should take priority.

This debate is not (or certainly should not be) about one county in eastern Wyoming; it is about the whole state. And instead of aspiring to some convoluted defense of the status quo, just because it is the status quo, I hope the Legislature would first ask the very serious question. "Is the present system fair to the people of Wyoming?" There's no reason to think that the county lines which have slowly evolved over the history of the state will automatically be the best we can do. Maybe they provide useful lines for legislative apportionment, and maybe they don't. Now is the time to ask the question.

We have heard many arguments offered to support the current representation of specific counties (Niobrara most notably), but our concern should be with all the counties. Let's see how these arguments hold up when applied beyond one group's individual self-interest:

1 - Do county lines divide the state into well-defined, homogenous communities? Not particularly. In Albany Co., folks in the northeast are far more closely associated with Wheatland than with Laramie. In Fremont Co., the tourist and timber economy of Dubois has little in common with the agricultural interests of Riverton. In Lincoln Co., Star Valley certainly contains a community easily separable from that of Kemmerer and LaBarge. Even in smaller counties with only one major city, it would be difficult to argue that the interests of the outlying small towns and ranching areas are well-reflected in the city population.

2 - Do county-based legislative districts ensure everyone ready access to their representative? No. Bairoil is 160 miles from the county seat in Green River. Shirley Basin is 100 miles from Rawlins. And this is not just a phenomenon of small, outpost towns. The well-defined "community" of Lovell, Cowley, and Byron in northern Big Horn County is no less removed from Greybull and Basin, than Lusk is from Douglas. Yes, it's great that the citizens of Niobrara Co. can run into their representative at the grocery store, but this argues more for small, single-member districts statewide than for special status for Niobrara.

3 - Does use of County lines save us from gerrymandering? No again. They simply lock in place any inequities (original or developed) which presently exist. County lines were drawn through the same political processes of special interests, compromise, and wheeling and dealing which prevail in any age. Given the vast changes in the economy and population distribution of Wyoming over the 67 years since the last county was created, it would be surprising if the present lines even preserved much of their original legislative intent. Today's Legislature may be no smarter than those of old, but you are obviously in far better position to evaluate the 1990 relevance of county lines than we their original drafters. Please do.

4 - Does inclusion of more than one population center in the same legislative district preclude the smaller from ever being represented? Obviously not. Using the present Legislature as an

326

example, 25% of the Representatives list addresses other than the dominant population center of their county. Big Horn Co. provides the current extreme – the immediate neighbors of Bighorn's two representatives (from Cowley and Shell) make up only 5% of the county. Clearly, the vision Wyoming voters is much broader than their own residence when deciding who can best represent them in the Legislature.

Finally, there's the question, "what's broke that needs fixed?" The answer, I believe, is basic fairness. While the voice of Niobrara (and Platte and Bighorn and Crook) County is increased by the present disproportionate levels of representation, the ability of Senators and Representatives from Sheridan, Laramie, Uinta, and Teton Counties to represent the views and aspirations of their constituents is significantly compromised. Niobrara County provides a specific and vocal constituency, but the much larger equity lies with the diffuse under-representation of a great many more people from many counties.

Despite the tangled search for a computational parameter which minimizes the differences in representation, it seems obvious that, at some level, these differences are significant. I can't point to a specific vote in which the under-representation of a portion of the state had disastrous results, but, as a geologist, I am a student of incremental processes. History is replete with examples of mighty edifices reduced to rubble, one sand grain at a time. In Wyoming government is "just a little skewed": by malapportionment, over time, serious injustice may result.

The mission of this Legislature, as always, should be to provide what's best for the people of the State of Wyoming. The specific interests of each component of the state must be taken into proportionate consideration, but reapportionment is a statewide issue. Let us not compromise the integrity of the whole in our attempts to preserve the status of a few parts. Although the present county lines may provide useful legislative districts in some cases, in others, it is clear that you can do much better.

Wyoming is the Equality State. Let statewide fairness and equality be your guides. Let's assert our "uniqueness" through responsible legislation. Rather than looking for the least you can get by with, strive to do the best you can for all the people of Wyoming.

(signed)

Bern Hinckley
Laramie

APPENDIX D
Sullivan 1991 'no signature'

February 28, 1991

The honorable W.A. "Rory" Cross
Speaker of the House
State Capitol
Cheyenne, Wy 82002

Dear Rory:

I am allowing **House Enrolled Act 81,** of the general session of the 51st Legislature, being **Original House bill No. 0295,** to become effective without my signature.

This bill deals with reapportionment of the Wyoming legislature based upon the 1990 census and has had significant discussion during this session. I am submitting it without my signature for the following reasons:

(a) There has been much debate in Wyoming about the guarantee of each citizen to proper representation in the Legislature and the application of the one-man one-vote principal (sic). We have earlier been in litigation regarding our current structure which barely escaped reversal. I am not fully satisfied that this legislation resolves some of the obvious legal concerns.

(b) I am satisfied, however, from experience, the discussions which I have had with legislators and debates which have taken place in the Legislature and committees that the Republican majority is not likely to submit a substantially different plan without court direction.

(c) While I support the county system and believe that our demographics, including our population, do make us unique and while I am pleased that the Legislature, given its choice to retain the allegiance to county boundaries, chose to give representation to Niobrara County, I would have favored some subdistricting, particularly in Natrona and Laramie Counties where our voters are required to face the unenviable task of selecting from 18 different candidates in the general elections. Frankly, I do not believe a slate of candidates that large fosters appropriate representation or the ability to assess issues and responsibility select candidates.

(d) It is my conclusion that the best way to resolve the debate surrounding this legislation in the most expeditious manner is to submit the same to a judicial determination as to its constitutionality and that will be my direction to the Attorney General.

In anticipation of the litigation that is sure to come, I have directed the Attorney General to immediately institute a court determination of the plan and will monitor carefully the progress of litigation and consult with the Attorney General and the Legislative Oversight Committee, depending on the outcome, as to the advisability of continuing litigation through the appeals process.

Respecfully,

(signed)

Mike Sullivan
Governor

MS:smp
Cc: Rick Miller, LSO
Kathy Karpan, Secretary of State
Deimer True, President of the Senate

APPENDIX E
Sullivan's Veto Of 1992 Districting

February 17, 1992

The Honorable W.A. "Rory" Cross
Speaker of the House
State Capitol
Cheyenne, Wy 82002

Dear Rory,

On Saturday I was presented with **Enrolled Act No. 1, Original House Bill 0117,** passed by the Fifty-First Legislature. This Act represents the best efforts of the collective legislative bodies to address deficiencies pointed out by the Federal Court in the redistricting plan passed last year and, presumably, the comments which I made one week ago. The Act is a significant step forward from the previous redistricting legislation (which may yet be damning this Act by faint praise).

Before I provide you with the substance of my view, however, I am moved to first comment on both innuendo and implications of adverse consequences to me or my programs which I am aware have emanated from both sides of the aisle depending on what action I take. I am not unaware of those discussions but let me assure you I am uninfluenced by them. This session, under the best of circumstances, will challenge each of us and we can ill afford the issue of reapportionment and the contents of this message to color the decisions which may be made in other areas. Wyoming and its citizens cannot withstand a disagreement over the mini-drama of reapportionment to influence other decisions which will surely impact the future direction of this State and the individual and collective well-being of its citizens.

I find, notwithstanding my respect for the progress which has been made and the work which has been done, that this legislation is deficient and accordingly advise you of my decision to veto this Act. I will endeavor below to relate the basis for my decision.

First, the underlying cardinal democratic principle which must always be foremost in our assessment is that of "one person, one vote." The people are entitled to be equally represented within allowable and responsible areas of deviation. I have consistently taken the position that this principle was best advanced by single-member district representation and it appears clear from the opinion of the Court based upon legal precedent that will be the result of a Court ordered plan. The legislature, for reasons and rationale that so far as I can determine have not been vocalized, has chosen single-member Senate districts and a mix of multi-member and single-member House districts. The result is that some voters in Wyoming (16 districts) will elect and be represented by one House member while others (23 districts) will vote for and be represented by two House members. While I do not find this would necessarily violate legal precedent I view it as basically unfair, inconsistent with what the Court would be required to do if there is no acceptable plan submitted and contrary to my personal, and often expressed, preference for the basic fairness of single-member districts.

Secondly, there are "practical" weaknesses inherent in multi-member districting schemes, as pointed out in the Court's opinion: "...voter confusion is more likely, legislative representatives are more remote from their constituents, and electoral minorities tend to be submerged while majorities are over-represented." *Gorin v. Karpan*, p 41. In the present case, there is the added practical and economic problem and voter confusion resulting from the failure to "nest" house districts within senate districts as reflected by the concerns expressed by the County Clerk's Association. The confusion which would only become apparent to the voter at the next election is not in my view in step with the circumstances of the times or the fact that this is a long-term, not short-term, endeavor.

Third, I have tried to state as clearly as possible my concern that the legislature avoid incumbent protectionism and political partisanship. While it is recognized that neither can be totally avoided given the personal and political nature of our system, I was hopeful that the plan submitted to me would be reasonably free of such influences. I am not satisfied, however, that it is. This may simply be due to the inherent nature of the multi-member proposal (and its over-representation of the majority), but I fear it goes deeper. Without attempting to outline in detail all of the inequities which can be identified in the plan (for there will always be areas for disagreement), let me outline those which I view as illustrative of partisanship, protectionism or inequality. Whether the person in my position were a

Republican or Democrat, I believe he or she would identify the same concerns.

a) Teton County – A portion of Teton County is placed with Lincoln County in a multi-member House district. Under any circumstances the numbers would place the Teton County residents at a disadvantage but the fact that the resulting district is multi-member multiplies the disadvantage and arguably disenfranchise these voters. Yet in other combinations of counties, i.e. Crook, Weston, Niobrara or Fremont, Hot Springs single-member districts are selected.

b) Fremont County – A county with a Republican voter registration which exceeds Democratic representation by approximately **18%**. In the house race, the multi-member district would pit four incumbent members (two Republicans, two Democrats) against each other for two seats. Notwithstanding the County registration differential, the district is constructed so as to provide an in district differential of **35%** weighted in favor of Republicans.

c) Laramie County – A county with a slight **2%** registration favorable to Republicans. The plan has placed five incumbents in one two-member district. The district has, however, a weighted Republican advantage of approximately **17%**.

These examples are not intended to be exclusive but only illustrative of apparent inconsistencies.

Incumbent protection, Democrat or Republican, should not be the motivating factor. It is not the intention of these examples to suggest Democratic incumbents were not protected in other instances but to say that while the <u>Court's</u> overriding objective "must be substantial equality of population among districts," and that appears to be accomplished in this plan, the role of Governor must be to assure fairness and that there is no overreaching in the legislative process. In this plan, I am not convinced that fairness was accomplished.

This decision is intended to reflect my evaluation of the work product of the legislature and not the motives of individual legislators. I am convinced that the vast majority of the legislative membership wish to serve the interests of the people of Wyoming as voters, not the precepts of any ideology. Given the inevitable compromises of the legislative process, this plan maybe the best which can be accomplished but I am not convinced it is. Be assured I am willing to work with the legislature to adopt an acceptable single-member plan with nested districts, which would only adopt multi-member districts where there is "a singular combination of factors" or "persuasive justification" that dictate that result, as would be the Court's charge, see pg. 41.

With all due respect for the work you have done and the progress you have made, the plan which you have presented to me does not reflect clarity, consistency, rationality or fairness. As a result, I do not believe it constitutes good public policy.

With best regards, I am

Very truly yours,

(signed)

Mike Sullivan
Governor

MS:smp
cc: Deimer True, President of the Senate
Rick Miller, LSO
Kathy Karpan, Secretary of State

APPENDIX F
Sullivan Letter Harrison Was Not
Allowed to Read to The House

March 11, 1992

The Honorable Rory Cross
Speaker of the House
State Capitol
Cheyenne, Wy 82002

Dear Mr. Speaker,

I know it is late in the day and you have much work to do, but I am compelled to advise you about what I see as a potentially very serious problem with the current budget debate taking place. I referred to the Cubin amendment on Monday as the "Michelangelo Virus" of the Legislature and have heard repeated assurances since that time that the process was being corrected. I am concerned that that is not the case and that given the late hour much damage could be done before it is recognized by the body.

Let me give you four examples relating to Senate File 5 and ask that someone carefully consider these actions before they get beyond redemption. I have not had the opportunity to review the other Bills for similar problems.

1) Health – page 5, line 8 – Health Care Financing is reduced $3.7 million from 100 and 200 series yet the General Fund eligible 100 and 200 series is only $1.7 million (and the 100-200 is only $3.5 million) and carries with it at least two and potentially three times as much federal money.

2) Health – page 5, line 9 – Developmental Disabilities. The reduction in 100 and 200 series is $1.6 million yet the eligible 100 and 200 series is only $606,000.

3) Health – page 5, line 11 – Aging. The reduction is $206,717, yet the eligible 100 and 200 series is $197,000.

4) Family Services – page 8, line 7. The reduction is $3.5 million in Public Assistance, which is more than twice the amount taken from the first Cubin amendment and

carries with it a corresponding loss of $1.7 million in federal funds.

I am also concerned by what I sense may have been a miscommunication to the body on the floor of the House, but will save that discussion for another day. If the Leadership would care to recess and discuss this further, I will be happy to visit with you.

I respectfully urge the House to consider the consequences of these actions before concluding the debate on these bills.

With best regards, I am

Very truly yours,

(signed)

Mike Sullivan
Governor

MS:smp
Cc: Doug Chamberlain
     Barbara Cubin
     Ron Micheli
     Fred Harrison

APPENDIX G
Legislators of the 51ˢᵗ Session

SOUTHERN REGION

Senate:	County	Party	Occupation
Jim Applegate	Laramie	D	Lawyer
Liz Byrd	Laramie	D	Retired Teacher
Guy Cameron	Laramie	D	Firefighter
John Fanos	Uinta	D	Ranch/Business
Bob Grieve	Carbon	R	Rancher
Terry Guice	Albany	R	Businessman (oil)
Lisa Kinney	Albany	D	Attorney
Carl Maldonado	Sweetwater	D	Maintenance/ Mechanic
Frank Prevedel	Sweetwater	D	Educator- Comm. College
Robert Reese	Sweetwater	D	Attorney
Gary Yordy	Laramie	R	Physician/ Attorncy

House:			
Eric Alden	Platte	R	Attorney
Sheila Arnold	Albany	D	Self-employed
Sam Blackwell	Sweetwater	D	Operator
Janice Bodine	Uinta	R	Owns Men's Clothing Store
D. Chamberlain	Goshen	R	Farm/Ranch/Realtor
Sam Dunnuck	Albany	R	Gov. Marketing
Edith Garcia	Laramie	D	Purchase/Rep/ Buyer
Bob Grant	Platte	R	Rancher
Patrick Hacker	Laramie	D	Attorney
Jim Hageman	Goshen	R	Rancher
Matilda Hansen	Albany	D	Administrator
Mark Harris	Sweetwater	D	Mine Electrician
Fred Harrison	Carbon	D	Attorney
Richard Honaker	Sweetwater	D	Attorney
S. Humphrey	Laramie	D	Nutritionist
A. BrimmerKunz	Laramie	R	Attorney
Cynthia Lummis	Laramie	R	Attorney/Rancher

Patti MacMillan	Albany	R	Realtor/Retailer
Ron Micheli	Uinta	R	Rancher
Patrick O'Toole	Carbon	D	Rancher
Bernard Phelan	Laramie	D	Attorney
Chris Plant	Sweetwater	D	Prof. Community College
Louise Ryckman	Sweetwater	D	Teacher
M.K.Schwope	Laramie	D	Homemaker
Don Sullivan	Laramie	D	Attorney
Bill Vasey	Carbon	D	Dir. Carbon Co Ad. Ed.
Carol Watson	Laramie	D	Court Reporter, Business

CENTRAL REGION

Senate:			
Michael Burke	Natrona	R	Attorney
Jerry Dixon	Crook/ Weston	R	Trucking
Frank Dusl	Fremont 1991	R	Businessman
Boyd Eddins	Lincoln	R	Rancher
Jim Geringer	Platte	R	Farmer
Charles Scott	Natrona	R	Cattle Rancher
Bob Peck	Fremont 1992		Newspaper Publisher
Deimer True	Natrona	R	Businessman
Jim Twiford	Converse	R	School Transportation
John Vinich	Fremont	D	Businessman
Russell Zimmer	Goshen/ Niobrara	R	Businessman
G. Zimmerman	Natrona	R	Retired Stockbroker

House:			
Susan Anderson	Natrona	R	Journalist/Writer
Eli Bebout	Fremont	D	VP Nucor Drilling
Les Bowron	Natrona	R	Attorney

Dan Budd	Sublette	D	Rancher
Gene Call	Lincoln	R	Contractor, Business
Rory Cross	Converse	R	Rancher
Barbara Cubin	Natrona	R	Housewife
K. Goodenough	Natrona	D	Forerster
Bruce Hinchey	Natrona	R	Environmental Eng.
B. McMillan	Fremont	R	Horticulturist
Dorothy Perkins	Natrona	R	Chamber of Comm. Director
Scott Ratliff	Fremont	D	Outreach Counselor
Rick Tempest	Natrona	R	Life Underwriter
Bill Tibbs	Converse	R	Insurance Agent
Dennis Tippets	Fremont	R	Real Estate Appraiser
Harry Tipton	Fremont	R	Physician
Lauris Tysdal	Weston	R	Rancher
Carol Jo Vlastos	Natrona	R	Ed. Nurse Consultant
Peter Wold	Natrona	R	Oil/Gas Explore/Prod.
Clyde Wolfley	Lincoln	R	Farmer and Rancher
M. ZumBrunnen	Niobrara	R	Rancher/Const. Eng.

NORTHERN REGION

Senate:			
Hank Coe	Park	R	Investment Exec.
Mike Enzi	Campbell 1992	R	Accountant
Michael Healy	Hot Springs/ Washakie	R	Rancher
Della Herbst	Sheridan	D	Homemaker
Allan Howard	Big Horn	R	Production Operator
Tom Kinnison	Sheridan	R	Businessman
Bob LaLonde	Sublette/Teton	R	Retired

Kelly Mader	Campbell 1991	R	Real Estate Broker
John Perry	Johnson/ Campbell	R	Attorney

House:			
Bill Bensel	Sheridan	D	Businessman
Mike Enzi	Campbell 1991	R	Accountant
John DeWitt	Park	R	Retired Educator
Sylvia Gams	Big Horn	R	Rancher
Ray Harrison	Washakie	R	Educator/Rancher
John Hines	Campbell	R	Rancher
Clarene Law	Teton	R	Inn Keeper
John Marton	Johnson	R	Rancher
Carroll Miller	Big Horn	R	Dentist
Jim Perkins	Sheridan	D	Railroad Engineer
John Rankine	Hot Springs	R	Rancher
Bill Rohrbach	Park	R	Attorney
David Shippy	Campbell 1992	R	Rancher
Peg Shreve	Park	R	Teacher
Marlene Simons	Crook	R	Rancher/Outfitter
Dick Wallis	Campbell	R	Rancher/Contractor
Virginia Wright	Sheridan	R	School Principal

Source: *1992 Directory, Fifty-first Legislature*, U .S. West Communications

APPENDIX H
Leadership of Wyoming Legislature for the Reapportionment Years[447]

1st Session   1890 William R. Schnitger (R) Laramie Co.
President of Senate
Oliver P. Kellogg, (R) **Crook**
Speaker of House

2nd Session   1893 Frank W. Mondell (R) **Weston**
President of Senate
L.C. Tidball, (Populist) **Sheridan**
Speaker of House

6th Session   1901 Edward R. Stone (R) Laramie County
President of Senate
Jerome S. Atherly (R) Albany
Speaker of House

9th Session   1907 O.H. Brown (R) Uinta
President of Senate
Scott K. Snively (R) **Sheridan**
Speaker of House

11th Session   1911 Jacob M. Schwoob (R) **Big Horn**
President of Senate
L. R. Davis (R) **Crook**
Speaker of House

14th Session   1917 Joseph W. Todd (R) **Johnson**
President of Senate
W.K. Jones (R) Laramie, Platte,
Goshen Counties
Speaker of House

16th Session   1921 W.W. Daley (R) Carbon
President of Senate

---

[447] Northern-region counties are indicated in **bold** and Central-region counties in *italics*.

341

L.R. Ewat (R) **Park**
Speaker of House

22nd Session 1933 Roy H. Cameron, (R) **Crook**
President of Senate
William M. Jack (D) *Natrona*
Speaker of House

27th Session 1943 R. H. Nichols (R) *Natrona*
President of Senate
Richard J. Luman (R) *Sublette*
Speaker of House

32nd Session 1953 Floyd W. Bartling (R) *Converse*
President of Senate
David Foote, Sr. (R) *Natrona*
Speaker of House

36th Session 1961 Albert C. Harding (R) **Crook**
President of Senate
Joseph L. Budd (R) *Sublette*
Speaker of House

37th Session 1963 Charles G. Irwin (R) *Converse*
President of Senate
Rudolph Anselmi (D) Sweetwater
Senate Minority Leader
Marlin T. Kurtz (R) **Park**
Speaker of House
W.C. Lindmier (R) *Converse*
Speaker Pro Tem
William F. Swanton (R) *Natrona*
House Majority Leader
Edness K.Wilkins (D) *Natrona*
House Minority Leader

37th Special 1964 Earl Christensen (R) *Weston*
President of Senate
Harvey Johnston (R) **Sheridan**
Vice President of Senate
Andrew McMaster (R) *Niobrara*
Senate Majority Leader

Rudolph Anselmi (D) Sweetwater
Senate Minority Leader
House leadership for the Special Session in
1964 was the same as during the Regular
session.

38th Session   1965   Andrew McMaster (R) *Niobrara*
President of Senate
Dr. Pete Madsen (R) Sheridan
Vice President of Senate
Earl Christensen (R) **Weston**
Senate Majority Leader
Elmer D. Kinnaman (D) Carbon
Senate Minority Leader
Walter B. Phelan (D) Laramie County
Speaker of House
Edness K. Wilkins (D) *Natrona*
Speaker Pro Tem
Donald Hubbard (D) Albany
House Majority Leader
Ed Herschler (D) *Lincoln*
House Majority Whip
William F. Swanton (R) *Natrona*
House Minority Leader
Leon Keith (R) **Johnson**
Minority Whip

41st   Session 1971   Dr. Pete Madsen (R) **Sheridan**
President of Senate
Howard Flitner (R) **Big Horn**
Vice President of Senate
Dick Tobin (R) *Natrona*
Senate Majority Leader
Elmer D. Kinnaman (D) Carbon
Senate Minority Leader
Ward G. Myers (R) **Big Horn**
Speaker of House
C.H. "Cliff" Davis (R) **Campbell**
Speaker Pro Tem
William F. Craft (R) **Big Horn**
House Majority Leader

Harold Hellbaum (R) Platte
House Majority Whip
Arthur L. Buck (D) Laramie County
House Minority Leader
O.R. "Bud" Daily (D) Carbon
House Minority Whip

46th Session 1981 Donald R. Cundall (R) Goshen-Platte
President of Senate
Gerald E. Geis (R) **Hot Springs-Washakie**
Vice President of Senate
Edward D. Moore (R) *Converse-Niobrara*
Senate Majority Leader
D.R. "Dick" Sedar (D) *Natrona*
Senate Minority Leader
Steve Majhanovich (D) Sweetwater
Senate Minority Whip/Caucus Chair
Bob J. Burnett (R) Albany
Speaker of House
Russ Donley (R) *Natrona*
Speaker Pro Tem
Dean T. Prosser (R) Laramie County
House Majority Leader
Patrick H. Meenan (R) *Natrona*
House Majority Whip
Donald B. Scott (D) Goshen
House Minority Leader
John P. Vinich (D) *Fremont*
House Minority Whip
William C. Edwards (D) Laramie County
House Minority Caucus Chair

51st Session 1991 Deimer True (R) *Natrona*
President of Senate
Boyd L. Eddins (R) *Lincoln*
Vice President of Senate
Jerry B. Dixon (R) *Weston*
Senate Majority Leader
Frank Prevedel (D) Sweetwater
Senate Minority Leader

John Fanos (D) Uinta
Senate Minority Whip
W.A. "Rory" Cross (R) *Converse*
Speaker of House
Ron Micheli (R) Uinta
Speaker Pro Tem
Douglas W. Chamberlain (R) *Goshen*
House Majority Leader
John P. Marton (R) **Johnson**
House Majority Whip
Fred Harrison (D) Carbon
House Minority Leader
Matilda Hansen (D) Albany
Assistant Minority Leader
Mary Kay Schwope (D) Laramie Co.
House Minority Whip
Louise Ryckman (D) Sweetwater
House Minority Caucus Chair

GLOSSARY

Average Deviation: The sum of all deviations from a mathematical mean in absolute values, divided by the number of deviations.

Block Groups: A set of census blocks in a contiguous area.

BNA'S: Block Numbered Areas are aggregations of block groups. Example: BNA 9683 in Carbon County includes the northwest one-fourth of the county.

Census Block: The smallest area for which the Census Bureau releases data, about 70 people.

Census Tracks: Statistical areas averaging about 4,000 people.

Committee of the Whole: The first time a bill is given full consideration is when the entire Chamber resolves itself into committee status. When in Committee of the Whole, there is greater leeway on frequency of speaking to allow more debate and discussion than is allowed during 2nd, 3rd, and concurrence considerations.

Deviation Points: The total number of percentage points above and below the fixed value.

Deviation Range: The spread between the most under-represented county and the greatest over-epresented county usually expressed in percent. Example: Hot Springs County over-represented by +32.87% and Washakie County under-represented by –16.5% gives a deviation range of 49.39%.

Equal proportion: Based on population, this is the essence of "one-person, one-vote."

Feed Bill: The appropriation to run the Legislature.

Float District: Counties combined to achieve nearly equal population for the number of senators or representatives assigned to that district.

Floterial District: A technique to achieve equivalent representation by adding an at-large "floating" member, i.e., one member represents subdistrict A, another member represents subdistrict B and a third member represents both A and B as an at-large member. In the November 16, 1991 Minutes of the Joint Corporations Committee (p. 5), Mr. Braden notes that "Idaho rejected float districts because of perceived voter confusion with the way in which candidates had to file and run for office."

General File: the roster of bills from which the Majority Leader makes daily selections for consideration in Committee of the Whole.

HB and HJR: House Bill, identified with sequential numbers. HJR means House Joint Resolution, also with its own sequential numbers. All constitutional amendments starting in the House have to be HJR's.

LSO (Legislative Service Office): The administrative office of the legislature. It provides the staff and the research for all logistical and issue matters pertaining to the passage of legislation.

Major Fraction (or Portion) Thereof: Refers to rounding up of remainder fractions of .50 or above.

Maximum Deviation: See Deviation range.

Nesting: Nesting means two or more House districts are within a Senate district. The 1992 law put two House districts in each Senate district for 30 senators and 60 representatives.

Numbering Tricks: When VTD's are grouped into districts, identifying numbers are assigned to each district. Systematization suggests adjacent districts should be numbered consecutively. Example: Bowron used logical sequence in his Plan; however, before it was amended into SF 49, Scott, in a fit of anti-Democratic pique, had the LSO reorder them misleadingly. Laramie

347

County districts were renumbered 7 through 12 and 41 through 44.

Population Divisor: The mathematical mean calculated from dividing the total state population by the number of available legislative seats.

Sine Die: Means "without any time set for further consideration of legislation." This motion is made when a legislative body has finished its business and intends not to convene again.

SF and SJR: Senate File identified with sequential numbers. SJR means Senate Joint Resolution, also with sequential numbers. All constitutional amendments that begin in the senate are labeled SJR.

Stacking and Fracturing: Stacking is a majority party practice of packing minority party voters into designated districts to concentrate their votes. Fracturing is a majority party practice of dispersing minority party voters among many districts thus diluting their votes.

Tiger File: Tiger files are computerized maps showing latitude/longitude, rivers, railroads, roads, lakes, wetlands, military installations, nation-state-local parks, mountain peaks, town-city-county boundaries, reservations of Native Americans. Tiger files include precinct district boundaries and census tract boundaries.

VTD's: The matching of census blocks to precincts to make voter districts.

ACKNOWLEDGMENTS

June Boyle's "institutional memory" was very helpful in putting together this political history. Her 12 years in the Senate overlapped more than half of the author's years in the House. Boyle's 10 years in the House enriched the interpretation of the *Digest of the House and Senate* Journals. Her library of legislative papers and books were a "treasure trove."

Appreciation goes to the "front desk staff" at the Library of the College of Law, University of Wyoming, for their assistance in finding Federal and State case laws, the Session Laws of the territory and of the State. Their expertise was essential in finding the historical record. Thanks, too, to the reference staff at the Albany County Public Library.

Rick Miller, Director of the Legislative Service Office during the 1990's, was generous with his recollections of reapportionment work from 1989–92.

Joe Meyer shared his memories and perceptions of his tenure, both as one of the staff in the Legislative Service office, and as Attorney General under Governor Sullivan.

Win Hickey talked about the years her husband, Joe Hickey, was Governor. She shared his "philosophy for the state," thereby interpreting some of the history at the middle of the 20th century.

Vern Shelton's "institutional memory" of who was a lobbyist when, and for whom, was a "Who's Who of Wyoming."

Rich Lindsey and Kathy Karpan shared their insights on the history of Wyoming. Sara Gorin's thesis and Bern Hinckley's testimony defined the thinking of "citizens from the southern region" on reapportionment.

Rebecca Henderson gave welcome counsel on the "how to" of writing a book for publication. Thanks go to Robert Michener for his assistance with logistics and to Maria Krenz for her editing expertise.

Thanks also go to the many people who shared "snippets and gems" of information, as well as insights and perceptions for this *Slice of Wyoming History*.

And because of the commitment of Wyoming's citizen-legislators, there really is a story to tell about the *Clear Use of Power*.

INDEX

357